ADD▪ADHD✻
When Living *And* Learning Hurt

*Making Now Better,
So Later
Will Be Easier.*

And other social / emotional /
educational frustrations.

Thomas W. Scott
M.S., L.P.C.

outskirts
press

When Living and Learning Hurt
Making Now Better, So Later Will Be Easier
All Rights Reserved.
Copyright © 2022 Thomas W. Scott, M.S., L.P.C.
v3.0

The opinions expressed in this manuscript are solely the opinions of the author and do not represent the opinions or thoughts of the publisher. The author has represented and warranted full ownership and/or legal right to publish all the materials in this book.

This book may not be reproduced, transmitted, or stored in whole or in part by any means, including graphic, electronic, or mechanical without the express written consent of the publisher except in the case of brief quotations embodied in critical articles and reviews.

Outskirts Press, Inc.
http://www.outskirtspress.com

ISBN: 978-1-9772-1555-0

Cover Design © 2022 Frances Baszta. All rights reserved - used with permission.

Outskirts Press and the "OP" logo are trademarks belonging to Outskirts Press, Inc.

PRINTED IN THE UNITED STATES OF AMERICA

How This Book Should Be Read

This book is for anyone who's experienced or is experiencing social, emotional, relational, vocational, or academic frustrations. Learning to navigate life doesn't always come easily for any of us. Though the book is directed toward individuals with ADD and ADHD, I want to include a wide swath of individuals. So, whether or not you've even been diagnosed with ADD or ADHD, you will find parts of yourself within its criteria. We've all had ADD or ADHD moments.

I recommend you begin by reading whatever chapter addresses your circumstances. To some degree, each chapter can stand alone. However, you will find reoccurring facts and information throughout. After all, I'm ADHD.

Last Chapter First

When helping a kid or an adult ADHDer with a project or paper, I always ask, "What do you want this to look like when it's done? What would you like your audience to learn and understand? What would the last couple of paragraphs sound like?" This helps the ADHDer sense a direction and a finish line. Feeling "finished" being the operative sensation sought. So, I thought I'd offer you my last chapter first.

In conclusion, I hope I've been able to help you understand the intricate, sensitive, and vulnerable workings of the ADHDer's mind, body, heart, and spirit. I hope I've conveyed that our minds aren't just plopped on top of a body, lugged around like a rider on a horse. I hope you've understood that we possess a vast array of systems integrated into one big system.

I hope I've helped you realize that learning can and will take place if ADHDer's are understood from their points of view. And that nobody really needs a massive overhaul, but rather gentle inner corrections at extremely important junctures of their lives. And we all have the capacity to get better by changing the way we live inside and steering our minds instead of our minds steering us. And developing a language of comfort is essential from now until the time we poof.

I hope that I've imparted my beliefs about medication in a way that doesn't make you slam the book shut or send me nasty messages. But medication should be our last alternative. A little can both help and hurt, but when coupled with quality therapy, it has a better chance of being effective. A chemically engineered personality should never be the sole answer. Individuals find themselves quite pissed later on when they realize they've been choreographed, produced, and directed by a chemical. And that sometimes we have fun and sometimes we don't. Sometimes we feel peaceful and sometimes we don't. But we can sure learn how to make now better so later will be easier. I hope you enjoy these writings.

Table of Contents

Introduction i

CHAPTER 1   Being Diagnosed (Better Late than Never) ... 1

CHAPTER 2   Self-Regulation in Disarray and Executive Functioning 6

CHAPTER 3   Horizontal Identity 11

CHAPTER 4   Giving Jordan a Jump Start 18

CHAPTER 5   The Power of Pokémon 27

CHAPTER 6   ADHD and The Theatrical Performances: We All Can Get Better 32

CHAPTER 7   Tears: Completing the Past and Our Body's Instinctual Data 42

CHAPTER 8   Medication Beware 48

CHAPTER 9   When Sleep Isn't Restful 63

CHAPTER 10   The Magic Balloon 71

CHAPTER 11   The Dart Game That Isn't Fun 74

CHAPTER 12   Healing the Spirit 79

CHAPTER 13   The Best Time of the Week for 13 Straight Years 84

CHAPTER 14   The Limbic System and the Wonderful Prefrontal Cortex 101

CHAPTER 15   ADHD and Addiction 112

CHAPTER 16   Parenting Toward Peace of Mind 121

CHAPTER 17 What Matters Most: Friendships or Plankton?..140

CHAPTER 18 Intake Mechanisms................................150

CHAPTER 19 Output Mechanisms...............................164

CHAPTER 20 Estimating, Allocating, and Utilizing Time 174

CHAPTER 21 Thoughts Are Not Facts: Is It True? Is It Good? Is It Useful?............................188

CHAPTER 22 Learning How to Learn...........................192

CHAPTER 23 Being Okay with Being Okay: What the Mind Simulates 197

CHAPTER 24 Santayana...204

CHAPTER 25 Committing to Improvement.....................208

CHAPTER 26 I Wonder if Anybody Ever Told These People, "You'll Never Amount to Anything?"...214

CHAPTER 27 What Is It We're Paying Attention To?....218

CHAPTER 28 To Flow or Not to Flow, That is the Dilemma 236

CHAPTER 29 Memories and the Brain's Natural Negative Bias 252

CHAPTER 30 "Dad, ADHD Is Not a Disease"................263

Acknowledgments 266

Introduction

Dear Reader,

My name is Tom, and I was born carbonated, flavored with ADHD, dyslexia, and a heaping helping of family dysfunction. Following a workshop, I had led on families and parenting, my father would say, "If it weren't for our family's dysfunctions, you wouldn't be making a penny." I would then tell him the reason I was visiting was to load up on new material. My family never failed me.

Parents and society have a way of overestimating the permanence of a child's early impairments. Though there have been warnings, I've never seen a child's finger lodged permanently in their nose. The good news is, with time, patience, and repetitive compassionate help, the ADHDer can outgrow their impairments that genetics entice, and life's experiences have so generously fertilized.

And more good news: if you're ADHD, you'll always be ADHD, which isn't bad because being ADHD allows you to interpret and respond to the world from a very unique perspective. My ADHD has made for some very good days, chock-full of wonderment, excitement, and cherished memories. Unfortunately, there were also times when my bubbly effervescence led to painful struggles, poor judgment, impulsive behaviors, and frustrations with basic learning.

Swift accuracy, clear verbal exchanges, legible writing skills, adept recall, and recitation are all necessary to effectively ride the current of life's academic, social, and emotional waves. Visible shortcomings and consistent irregularities bring about shameful exposure that really hurts.

II

My brain didn't seem to be in sync with certain neurodevelopmental functions, such as sequences and spatial patterns. I was forever baffled by fractions. I don't know, but maybe my second-grade teacher, Miss Foster, felt the best way to help me learn was to strap a big piece of masking tape across my mouth and sit me in front of the class. Imagine the money a good hearty lawsuit like that could bring today. But not back in 1967. In those times, the parents were actually afraid of the teachers and the power they wielded over a child's ascent into the Ivy Leagues schools.

But with quality therapy and a never-ending basic belief in myself, I crawled out of the marsh, into the bog, staggered through the brush, and eventually reached some peaceful clearings. Therapy helped me like myself despite my unsolved problems. Therapy helped me preserve my endless source of enthusiasm and unbridled compassion. I'm naïve but street smart, skeptical but way too trusting. My heart bleeds empathy, and I can cry in a split second when seeing ads for dog and cat rescues. I am deeply moved by the struggle and spirit of others. I search for fun, am constantly curious, crave sensuality, and have an irreversible spiritual grounding.

Though I still need to be reminded to turn off lights, I've made big strides. My high school counselor told me at my post-high school planning session that I wasn't college material and I best learn to run a cash register. Since high school, I earned a B.S. in Psychology, Sociology and Corrections, got a Master of Science in Counseling Psychology and Education, and raised three wonderful children. I've been in private practice for 35 years. I've consulted in Germany, lectured in Ethiopia, and taught in Italy. Though I set my university school record in the mile, I've also had my leg in a cast for several months. I've soared spiritually to places that are sound and true and have been confined for a marijuana offense. So, you never really know.

My ADHD-ness permeated both my sleeping and waking hours. I've always tended to do things the hard way, never noticing that there is an easier way. Nevertheless, no matter what type of day awaited me, I knew I had to suit up for all of them.

We're all getting better, a little bit at a time, are we not? I mean the adults that I see in my office with ADHD are not coming in because they're still climbing on furniture. Nor are they making fart noises with their armpits during staff meetings. Unfortunately, they can still suck the air out of a room because they lack the ability to turn vision back on themselves in order to self-regulate. They lack the awareness to see their effect on others. But awareness can be learned in order to do moment-to-moment management. But most ADHDers both young and old have a visceral awareness when things aren't working. Unfortunately, the ADHDer mistakenly believes they must try harder to convince others of their goodness thus creating more issues and deeper separation.

Most ADHDers have never been accused of being discreet. Knowing when "not" to speak or think out loud is difficult for them. Being sensitive to the cues that scream, "Hey, pay attention, reel yourself in, there is something that's expected of you" is one of the greatest challenges for both young and old ADHDers. We are the accumulation of all our experiences up to this very moment.

Nothing slips our mind; it just gets lost in the museum of our implicit (beneath our awareness) memories. The innocent exposure of one's insecurities, neediness and vulnerability can lead to more rejection, especially if there's vivid evidence of incompetence. Taking emotional risks can be terrifying, especially if you're all yakked out on medication. Generalized anxiety and bouts with depression are prevalent among ADHDers. Loving yourself is the best medication possible.

Childhood is like practice offstage. Sadly, the curtain's being raised daily on ADHDers well before they are capable of performing. We all are handed a script, if I may, that we're expected to follow. ADHD kids have trouble comprehending their part, memorizing, and reciting their "lines" is very problematic; they'd much rather freelance. Poor rehearsals are cut short, and life's curtain waits for no one. Regrettably, such a trajectory does not usually follow the parents' or society's timetable.

We can teach an ADHDer to learn how to "cope ahead," so that everything doesn't seem to be a surprise. Intentionally learning how to shift, direct and redirect their attention feels not just good, but hopeful. Cultivating "hope-management" continually changes the way their brains fire, thus laying new neural circuitry. Consistently practicing exercises that heighten self-awareness creates these new neural pathways that lead to more productive thoughts, more manageable emotions, and acceptable behaviors. In other words, learning to steer their minds instead of their minds steering them helps the ADHDer establish a growth mindset.

In these chapters the reader will learn how ADHDers can gain jurisdiction over their attention controls, positively affecting their emotional, social, and academic life. Learning how to pay attention, then decipher the intake of sensory information as it enters into awareness, helps the ADHDer learn the appropriate thought, behavior, or emotion to express. This is vital for anyone's peace of mind and success.

I've spent 35 years as a psychotherapist/educational consultant in private practice with thousands of hours of individual therapy, group, seminars, and workshops. I have counseled many, many ADHD kids, along with their ADHD parents. We can strengthen the ADHDer's weaknesses by pursuing their strengths. You just can't pound away on their deficiencies demanding they be as we need them to be We can enhance and upgrade their self-image, but we should never take lightly their emotional, behavioral, and academic struggles.

I've been influenced by great thinkers, writers, colleagues, neuroscientists, family, friends, and pets. Their words and presence kept me afloat when the waters became violent and the undertow severe.

Academic breakthroughs, professional acclaim, career satisfaction, athletic success, and musical accomplishments didn't just happen. They've all been earned despite the challenges of being an ADHDer myself. Cathartic spiritual moments and deeply loving relationships are the sorbet that has followed some of my life's distasteful entrées. Like all of us, I've had joy-filled moments and have been deeply sliced with razor-sharp shame and humiliation. Failures from poor judgment were experienced. Lessons were eventually learned, even on the third or fourth try. Triumphs, frustrations, and fiascoes have all taken their turn. However, I've always been optimistic and have never doubted that "much good still lies ahead."

In this book, I suggest ways to help ADHD children by offering strategies and compassionate understanding that I wish had been offered to me early on. We will also explore experiences and observations from divergent perspectives: the struggling child, the angry teenager, the frustrated parent, and the baffled but resolute adult, which, for many of us, is still a work in progress.

In the 1946 book, *Zorba the Greek*, Zorba, in his boisterous and mysterious manner, told the young Greek intellectual who desperately wanted to escape his bookish existence, "In life, we get the full catastrophe." We can all agree that many things beyond our comprehension still lie ahead.

I have seen ADHD individuals display tremendous courage and fortitude when seeking solutions for their frustrations. All problems become smaller when you meet them head-on. I've never defined a problem as unsolvable. Now you might not get the results you want but learning to be "accepting" of that reality is solving in itself. All things are hard before they become easier.

This book is for parents, therapists, teachers and, of course, ADHD individuals who want to forgive the past, make sense of the moment, and move on in an exciting direction.

James Thurber advised us, "Let us not look back in anger, nor forward with fear, but around us in awareness." This book will help you do that.

CHAPTER 1

Being Diagnosed (Better Late than Never)

> *"I am my own comedy and tragedy."*
>
> ~ Ralph Waldo Emerson

One beautiful summer afternoon some years ago, my relatively new girlfriend, (1990), Betty, walked into the room as I was watching a Kansas City Royals baseball game. "Have you read this book?" she asked.

"What book?" I answered, not looking up.

"The one in my hand," she said. Not wanting to miss the next pitch, especially with runners in scoring position. She repeated, "Have you read the book, *Driven to Distraction?*"

"What's it about?" I asked, still glued to the tube. (Good lord, "the tube," that really shows your age).

"It's about adult attention deficit disorder."

That's funny, I thought. I had never noticed her having any significant issues with inattention or distraction.

"No sweetie, I haven't read it, but I do know quite a bit about ADD and ADHD in children. Damn it, you're helping the pitcher by swinging at that crap. That wasn't close to being called a strike." I leaned closer to the TV, urging on the batter.

Until that point, my professional career had focused on depleted self-esteem in distraught children, (many of whom were diagnosed as ADHD), healthy and productive parenting, relationship issues, sexual abuse, eating disorders, addiction, performance anxiety and divorced dads.

She handed me the book. The batter hit a wicked shot down the left-field line curving, curving, curving ... foul by just inches.

Betty went on to say, "You have some behaviors that are frustrating to me, and I know they're not intentional. Like when you say you're going to do something and it never gets started, or you start it and never finish it. I know you're not lazy, and I know you'd do anything for me. This book seemed to make sense and explained some things to me that might be helpful for you. You ought to read it."

So, she had been doing secret research on me. I suddenly felt like a specimen in a Petri dish. I was holding a book that she believed would help me make sense of me. How fricken sweet.

"I'm just trying to make sense of some things you do that are frustrating to me," she said. What was frustrating to me at that moment was not being able to score the runner from second when there were no outs.

Oh boy, here we go again, I thought. I've marched onto this battlefield before. I could smell the powder. I could hear the triggers being cocked. It's time to scatter, to hunker down, to assume a defensive posture, and man my artillery. Here come the scud missiles of criticism, disappointment raining down like bunker busters exposing evidence of my shortcomings and defects. I readied my defenses: the camouflage of indifference, a locked and loaded trigger-sensitive sarcastic wit, a stoic resistance. If none of that worked, I had fire grenades of blazing anger meant to destroy and defend my last semblance of dignity. These defenses would fortify me for the moment, providing me time to adjust, regroup, wrap, and conceal my wounds that were so easily inflicted by disapproval. Though nothing was inherently wrong with her delivery, her words felt like an invisible chemical agent, swift and toxic. My chronic defensiveness triggered me to age regress, misinterpreting Betty's intention, concern, and constructive guidance. What I heard, and most importantly felt, was criticism, disappointment, and disapproval in who I was as a human being. It felt more like character assassination than helpful guidance. And mind you now, I'm just holding the book. I felt angry, confused, and mistrustful. All she asked was, "Have you read this book?" suggesting it might be helpful.

Betty is truly one of the smartest humans I have ever known. She is generous and compassionate with razor-sharp analytical business acumen. She's a Sudoku genius, a five-star chef, a master gardener, an exquisite painter, an excellent mother, mate, grandmother, stepmother, daughter-in-law, sibling, interior designer, piano player, and financial wizard. Moreover, she's spiritually grounded, a top-notch negotiator, and one "hot package" if I do say so myself.

For the most part, Betty-thinking is rational, logical, and intuitively linear. Her inductive and deductive reasoning is exquisite. She accurately projects her thinking into the future and can recall retrospectively with precise accuracy. She systematically problem-solves and possesses fastidious spatial and sequential ordering. Her capacity to juggle and multitask is mind-boggling.

She understood that my inconsistent behavior, rapid thoughts, overflow of energy, spontaneity, and unique interpretations, as well as my missteps, were not intentional or calculated; they just were. They didn't stem from anger or depression. I wasn't manipulative or inconsiderate. What I was, was hypersensitive, and my mind was anything but lackadaisical.

I struggled with the ability to steer my attention. I was relatively rational until I wasn't. I was very intuitive, but not linear. My inductive and deductive reasoning skills were gummed up, and at times my projective thinking didn't venture much further than my nose. A porous memory hampered my retrospective abilities and spatial and sequential ordering. I was never pattern-driven.

There were and are things I'm quite good at, I guess. In 9th grade, my class voted me "Most Talented." Such an acknowledgment baffled my family. "Talented in what?" they asked. Well, I played the drums a little, but my father was an accomplished jazz drummer. I could draw a little, but my mother was an art major and exceptionally talented in numerous artistic mediums. I was a decent runner, but my brother, a year older, was a state champion and all-American in college. So, in comparison to mom, dad, and bro, I was just average in my own family.

To date, I've read *Driven to Distraction* many, many, times and have referenced it often in therapy sessions with patients and in my workshops. I came to realize the frustrations I experienced when attempting to learn weren't because I lacked effort, had a bad attitude or was just plain stupid. I have a brain glitch called ADHD that was fertilized by family dysfunction. I had attention deficit hyperactivity disorder. In the old days, it was called "minimal brain dysfunction." Whoa, wait a minute. I'd much rather have a few deficits than being viewed as "minimal."

I thought ADHD was really just a kid deal, but in 1994 when *Driven to Distraction* came out it showed how the symptoms flowed or stumbled into adulthood. Learning there was an actual name for the challenges I was continuing to experience as an adult, made me hungry for knowledge. I was already working with kids who were experiencing shame, pain, and humiliation, and now with this new personal self-awareness, I was able to figure out how to help myself. I had always known that if I could stop one kid from giving up and viewing themselves as inadequate, incapable, and stupid, it would all be worth it. But first I had to work on this big kid, me.

That little guy inside of me still needed comforting and compassion. For years, other people's external points of view shaped my internal makeup. So, I learned how to become a rather good actor, pretending "it wasn't that bad."

I became very accomplished, respected, and successful. I rose to heights not predicted, then fell from grace, only to rise again, stronger, and much more assured. I kept progressing professionally, but in some areas, I was frozen developmentally. Life provided me many opportunities to learn from my mistakes but learning about yourself against the backdrop of your fears and blunders is never easy for anyone. I have always said, "Never go to a therapist who doesn't go to a therapist," but more about that later. I can't take people places I've never been. Failure provides us the opportunity to begin again, and again, and again, but hopefully each time a bit more intelligently. I've never allowed failure to define and overtake me, because my desire to succeed has always been stronger. I have always believed that much good lies ahead.

CHAPTER 2

Self-Regulation in Disarray and Executive Functioning

*"What lies in our
power to do,
it lies in our
power not to do."*

~ Aristotle

I had what is called a disorder of self-regulation. However, I despise the word "disorder." Rather than disorder, I prefer to say that my self-regulatory capacity was in a "bit of disarray." Disarray sounds less permanent, less severe, though shambles, upheaval, and havoc would probably have been accurate also.

You often hear the term "executive functioning," tossed around when talking about the individual's emotional, social, behavioral, and academic frustrations. My take on executive functions is, that there's a board of directors, executives if I may, sitting around a big table in our heads making rapid-fire, "executive decisions." Often concerning what to do next. Obviously, it's important to have all of the participants on the same page, paying attention. But what if one member is ass end up in the chair, another spinning around, one gazing out the window, another getting up, getting a drink, going to the trash can, wadding up paper, another asleep and drooling, one doodling, etc. Then imagine the leader addressing his colleagues, saying, "Hey guys, let's pay attention, we got some important stuff coming our way at this very moment. We're expected to act upon immediately, come on guys, let's get it together." Well, you can imagine their reaction or lack of. They are expected to instantly shift into action.

Now shifting can take on many forms. But mainly it's a transition from one physical place to another, from a wandering mind to an attentive one, from frustration to resilience and curiosity, from a crappy mood to at least a neutral space, and from inaction to action. Our executive skills are to see to it that these transitions happen.

But in order to shift, you must be clearly aware of what's expected of you. In fact, you'll need to venture into your long-term memory and check whether or not you've "seen this request before." If the required action is recognizable, and you actually "remember" your strategy, and what you did, you must now take all your emotions out of the moment and shift into action. Shifting is a non-emotional act. And once you've shifted, it's advisable to forge ahead and not turn back, which means "staying present." So now, you're going in the right direction and you're feeling good about it. But that isn't all. You must remember what you just did, that worked, so you can replicate it. Maybe even in the next minute. Such shifting is a natural move for many, but for the ADHDer it's quite a struggle and a long evolution of thought and action.

The good news is that executive functioning skills can be learned and upgraded over time. But they differ greatly from individual to individual. You can see a lot of emotional hemorrhaging for the kids whose executive functions aren't functioning.

CHAPTER 2

Some examples of faulty functioning:

- Easily frustrated
- Trouble following directions
- Freak-outs
- Inflexible when offered suggestions or a different approach
- Distractions and not finishing work
- Focuses on the wrong, or insignificant detail
- Mixes up assignments and books
- Messy, disorganized backpack, desk, locker
- Panic and anxiety when routines change
- Won't abandon an ineffective plan
- Wants to involve themselves with kids who clearly don't want to engage
- Gets lost arranging things, thus not getting started
- Views life and their place in it as unfair
- Trouble finishing tests and quizzes on time
- Views constructive criticism and feedback as assaultive
- Impulsive and takes a lot of risks

I have also seen many kids outgrow these impairments.

The difference between a kid with ADHD and a kid with ADD lies in the "H." The "H" stands for hyperactive, not "hell-bound." ADHDers are carbonated and distracted, where the ADDer is more sedate, but still distracted and preoccupied with stimuli other than the material at hand.

Imagine both the ADHDer and ADDer are looking out a window. Both are clearly distracted, paying little attention to class instruction. The ADD kid might be lost in a blank stare, a thousand miles away, detached from the instructor but not physically percolating. Whereas with the ADHDer, it's an entirely different ball game. While staring out the same window, they could be fidgeting, squatting on their chair, or God forbid, standing on it. They could be vigilantly scanning the outer premises, imagining the "superstar" status that could be attained if they climbed out the window and onto the ledge, de-belting their trousers, wrapping the strap around the electrical wire and zip lining across the playground, escaping confinement. All the while, their classmates are lined up against the window staring in awe, then breaking into uproarious applause. Despite the daydream, the ADHDer still might be able to tell you what the teacher was talking about, where the ADDer had completely checked out.

ADD individuals are considered inattentive, typically slower, and more error-prone. When an experience hits their cortex, it leaves little impact on memory. The inattentive type is often overlooked and less likely to be labeled as "Oppositional Defiant" or "Conduct Disorder." The inattentive get all their work done, but produce a lot more errors, due to sluggish cognitive functioning. **<u>Stimulants don't work for the sluggish cognitive type</u>**. The ADD and ADHD child responds well to emotionally-based therapy, social skill awareness, and academic management training. However, the ADHD child struggles with performing and producing consistently. They have the skills but can't dial them up when needed the most. ADHDers have to pry their attention away from tantalizing distractions in order to actually pick up bits and pieces of what the teacher is saying. They catch more of the theme and less of the details.

As you'll read in a later chapter, during circle time in my Running, Relaxation, and Support Group someone would be sharing a heartfelt moment while one of their comrades would be spinning on his mat, contorting himself like a pretzel, making faces, attempting to lure anyone else into their seemingly bizarre sphere. I would turn to that ADHD kid and ask, "Did you hear one thing that Trent just said?" I was always amazed to hear them repeat verbatim the theme but be a bit sketchy on some of the details. The ADD kid who despite their lack of movement, would have no idea what Trent said. Nonetheless, a lack of self-regulation exists in both types. Due to a lack of self-awareness, self-regulation develops much later in ADHDers.

Sadly, people and parents freak out when developmental milestones aren't met in a predictable and timely manner. In some cases, we need to help the ADHDer jump start their development, but self-control "will" develop in this population, just probably not in the next twenty minutes or on your desired schedule. Self-control takes time to build, then install. We can help them develop the essential brake lining of the brain necessary to regulate impulsivity. We can teach them how to pump the brakes. Quality emotionally-based therapy emphasizes a mindful awareness. We can teach them to drill down into their bodies, or up, for that matter into their minds to tap the awareness of their awareness. Great gains can be made by simply heightening awareness. It takes time and patience, patience, and more time, to practice strengthening the type of awareness that enhances their ability to self-regulate.

We can help by softening and debunking the limitations the ADHDer learns to believe about themselves, due to their disarray. Limiting beliefs are part of human nature, but with ADHD, the beliefs are stronger and the antidote more elusive. There is no one "interior cure." When it comes to self-regulation, all of us must learn to succeed in the places we've failed. Admitting that you "don't know what to do" is a great starting point for learning how to do the next right thing.

CHAPTER 3

Horizontal Identity

> "*A man cannot be comfortable without his own approval.*"
>
> ~ Mark Twain

Andrew Solomon writes in his fascinating and meticulously researched book, *Far from the Tree: Parents, Children and the Search for Identity*, "In so far as children resemble us, they are our most precious admirers, and in so far as they differ, they can be our most vehement detractors."

Most children share at least some traits with their parents. Solomon refers to these traits as "vertical identities." These are the attributes and values passed down and shared across generations—not just through DNA but also from shared cultural norms and rituals, that bring about approval. Ethnicity, language, religion, and nationality help us form a significant basis for identity. These are "upward" trajectories.

ADHD kids have inherent traits that are familiar to their parents, as well as traits that are unfamiliar and often outlandish. Solomon referred to these as "horizontal identities." Instead of an upward trajectory that's assumed, expected and in some cases demanded, the ADHDer shoots off to the side, horizontally, much to the dismay of many. This developmental rerouting can be caused by brain anatomy and functioning, a gene or random mutation, prenatal influences, a head injury, or traumatic experiences. Simple beliefs, ideals, and interests that don't coincide with their parent's mindset, but are more a reflection of their own uniqueness, can lead to a rerouting.

Successful and devoted children usually result from having dedicated, connected, and content parents. However, as dedicated and content as you are, when raising an ADHD child, you find it to be part joy and part rebel combat. I've always loved the quote by Sam Butler, an iconoclastic Victorian-era English author, who wrote, "Parents are the last people on earth who should have children."

Every child needs unconditional love. They need warm, non-judging, mirroring eyes that directly reflect back to them the guarantee that they are loved for the very one they are. ADHD children learn about themselves from their parent's facial expressions and reactions to them. What is reflected back to them in their parents' eyes is often what the ADHDer comes to believe about themselves. Sadly, what I remember most is the reflection of exasperation in my mother's gaze as I relied on her to help me develop a sense of "I am-ness." Children value themselves to the degree they feel valued. Some very quality therapy helped me navigate through some very tough ADHD times that were filled with doubt and feelings of unworthiness.

When you're born, you're a "we" with your parents, before ever becoming "I." You are perfectly codependent. You are on the breast or the hip before you ever sense a differentiation. For healthy emotional development, it's crucial that we know and sense deeply that who we are matters and that our needs are being taken seriously. We need to believe that every part of us is lovable and acceptable, and we can count on our parents to fulfill our "dependency needs" well before we can speak a single word. These are healthy narcissistic needs. And we're dependent on our parents to meet them. If these needs are not met, then our sense of "I am-ness" is damaged. This damage creates insatiability that turbocharges children's instinctive neediness, leading to intense cravings for love, attention, affection, and most importantly, approval. Some say such neglect alone can cause ADHD. Slap on top of that a genetic predisposed wiring of the brain, and a heart the size of an elephant, then nothing ever seems to be enough.

For the deprived ADHD individual, the lack of attention, affection, and approval can take many forms, but shame is the most predominant. Shame fuels compulsivity, and when we are compulsive, we find ourselves constantly disappointed and unfulfilled. The compulsively driven ADHD individual searches constantly for the perfect mate, job, or philosophy that will fix everything and, in turn, validate and complete all aspects of their existence. Sadly, when the ADHDer doesn't get what they need, they give up or find other ways to attain it.

ADHDers are more prone to addiction than others. Many of us have good reasons to be mad and sad and so we reach for substances and/or material possessions to fill the holes in our souls. Such choices serve as pain-killing substitutes for legitimate suffering. This is where addiction begins. The ADHD individual learns to bring things from the outside to make the inside feel better, avoiding having to deal directly with genuine sorrow and anguish. Wouldn't it be great if we needed to use escape behaviors only once and then be free? Unfortunately, addictive solutions need to be repeated over and over. Substances and material goods don't have a very long shelf life in the brain and body. The ADHDer's inner loneliness and feelings of futility resurface rather quickly once the substance, activity or material new-ness wears off.

Even though we know that no two ADHD individuals are the same, it amazes me how pharmaceutical companies can claim that one pill fits all. Take this pill, and we can guarantee "vertical growth, and a sound identity." This is simply impossible. Every child's history and biology are distinct, and families must embrace and support the ADHD child's uniqueness. As Ralph Waldo Emerson wrote, "We all boil at different degrees."

The quality relationships within families are those in which each individual can be themselves—distinct and unique, and valued for the very one they are. Everyone wants to be strong and independent, but it's hard to do that alone. Ironically, becoming independent requires help and support. Healthy and balanced relationships transpire when each family member can assume a position uniquely their own. Steadiness and stability breed in an atmosphere of hope, trust, patience, honor, loyalty, flexibility, faith, humor, and fortitude. We feel abandoned when we are not loved for the very one we are.

Here are some suggestions to help minimize an ADHD child's feelings of futility when their horizontal proclivities don't match their parents, school, or society's blueprints.

* Be present physically. Parents provide activities but seldom participate in them. Children want to do things with us.
* Make direct eye contact. It helps them feel they are being understood and they matter.
* Model your emotions in a manner that you would like them to emulate. Kindness, patience, and softness are reassuring.

- Affirm their emotions. Don't discount or stifle them. Help them understand the origins of their feelings and let them decide if they are worth preserving. Teach them to ask themselves, "Do these thoughts serve my best interest?"
- Children have <u>developmental dependency needs.</u> This simply means they are dependent on you to get certain needs met. Each stage of growth has specific tasks. It's important that we know what those tasks are. And remember the ADHD child is 30 percent behind when it comes to emotional development. Don't depend on them to meet your needs or take care of your unfulfilling marriage or frustrating career choice.
- Be open. Don't carry around covert family secrets that the children can feel but can't make sense of until they are older. Sadly, they will take responsibility for your unhappiness.
- Admit your mistakes and shortcomings. When you are wrong, promptly acknowledge it.
- Model the ability to apologize, forgive and ask for forgiveness.
- A parent who acts shameless or guiltless puts everyone in a defensive posture, which can result in family members pitting one against the other.

Becoming a parent ushers us into a never-ending relationship with a stranger. The more different the child is from their parent, the greater the likelihood of negativity and conflict, especially if the parent is rigid and unfulfilled. There are moments when children don't seem to remotely resemble either parent. On the contrary, in times of conflict, the child might hear "You're just like your mother/father!" This never refers to the more appealing traits of that parent. Such an insult attempts to separate "your" genes from the behavior that's on full display. The reality is both parents' genes are put in a blender, and we pour out our kids. We're half our mom and half our dad.

Just because you love your ADHD child doesn't guarantee you always want to acknowledge in public that they are yours. Some believe that the first parts of our lives are ruined by our parents, and the second part is ruined by our children. It's also said that families are a lot like peanut brittle: mostly sweet, but with a few nuts. I say, learn to enjoy the whole ride. In life, we expand and contract. Keep expanding. An old farmer saying states, "If you're green you're growing, if you're ripe you're rotting." I still see myself as pretty green, even at the ripe age of 65.

Our children are astutely aware of how much fun we adults are not having. It's no wonder they don't want to grow up after witnessing some of their parents' follies. When a parent is not getting their needs met, the ADHD child's needs are magnified, making exhausting demands and inroads on their parents' little time and energy. On the other hand, over-involvement can stifle creative ingenuity where under-involvement prevents a child's talents from germinating.

A traumatic upbringing can delay, derail, and even extinguish talent. When the ADHD child experiences their parents' incessant need to fix them, they feel anxious, rarely enjoying a cleansing sigh or deep breath of contentment. When the ADHD child is handled with insensitivity and abruptness, demanding they, "Be as I need you to be, don't be as you are," they learn that their parents are incapable or unwilling to embrace their uniqueness. How can a child trust that their parents will be the ones to help them navigate the stresses of life when they seem to be freaking out over cabinet doors left open and socks on the floor?

CHAPTER 3

During parenting, we often have to feed the mouth that both snarls and bites, as well as kisses and holds, sometimes all within the same ten minutes. The right balance is difficult to strike, but when done properly, it will lift a child to the next level of curiosity and competency, but maybe not vertically.

CHAPTER 4

Giving Jordan a Jump Start

> *"We can't go back and splice and edit the past, but we can produce a much better now that makes for a more satisfying journey."*
>
> ~ Me

Before I took custody of my sons, I would get to see them the perfunctory "every other weekend," along with an overnight on Wednesday. Wednesday could never come quick enough. It was our favorite day of the week. It was a 45-minute drive to their mom and stepdad's home, and I never begrudged an inch of the excursion. Their elementary school was right across the street from their home. On Wednesdays when I'd get there early, I could watch them leave their school. When they spotted me waiting in the driveway, they would sprint across the lawns, jump into the car, and we'd dispense hugs and kisses. When arriving a little later, I would pull into the driveway and honk. The door would fling open and out they flew.

One day I pulled up, honked a couple of times, but no bodies emerged. After a minute or so I honked again. This time the door flew open and out charged their mother, my ex, who has since departed (RIP Janet). As she lurched toward the car, her face was pinched like a prune. Clutched in her hand was a crumpled-up piece of paper. Sadly, I had seen this play before. These theatrical, histrionic, rage-laced scenes had been seared in my mind with horror and trauma. I could only imagine what my boys were internalizing once again.

She came to my window, ranting about Jordan's ineptitude at managing himself and his responsibilities. "Jordan (who was in third grade) has a book report that's due tomorrow and he's known about it for a month. He's only read five pages."

At this point, it seemed safe to crack the window, but just an inch.

"What's the problem?" I asked softly.

She repeated, "Jordan has a book report due tomorrow! He has known about it for a month, and he has read only five pages. I talked to the teacher, and she extended the due date to Friday."

She shoved the paper through the small opening and heaved herself back into the house. A moment later my sons walked out heads down, in sort of a funeral march, and got in the car.

I recalled a lesson I had learned from my therapist, Dr. Morrison. He was so loving and kind. He knew better than to stuff me full of medicine. During one particular session, I was whining about having to prepare my taxes. I was on a roll, railing about the injustice of it all when he stopped me and said, "Tom, if you were the only one who had to undertake such a miserable responsibility that tax preparation certainly is, I would urge you to rebel, protest, demand an explanation. But since you aren't, and millions of other people face the same arduous assignment, I suggest you stop wasting our time with such blathering." He said, "Now look, everyone has to eat a spoonful of crap every day. No one wants to, but it's just part of being responsible. If you don't eat your one spoonful on Monday, then you are going to have to eat two spoonsful on Tuesday. And if you don't eat either of them on Wednesday, then you might end up having to eat a whole bowl on the weekend. Now, what's easier to get down, one spoonful of crap, or a whole bowl?"

"A spoonful," I answered.

He continued. "What that spoonful contains are things like getting places on time, paying bills, taking out the trash, moving the dishes from the sink to the dishwasher then to the cabinets, and washing, drying, folding, and putting away laundry. It's scooping the cat box, putting liners in the waste paper baskets, sweeping the floor, locking the doors, making sure the lights are out, removing the trash from your car, handing in assignments, going through the mail ... you get it?" He continued, "People who are responsible look at the spoonful, shut their eyes, open their mouths, insert and swallow. They then might shudder a bit, but it's over and done with and they now can pursue more pleasant endeavors. Get it?"

I did get it and have used that story many times with my sons and patients. I am much improved, and instead of wanting to take a headlong dive off a bridge or toss an uncooperative printer through the window, I've learned to manage the mundane and tolerate the intolerable.

As Jordan lumbered toward the car carrying his book, his older brother, TJ, jumped in first and said, "Mom freaked out again on Jordan. He didn't do his homework." When my little ADHDer, Jordan, pulled himself into the car, you could see dried tear tracks stained on his cheeks. An expression of complete defeat and demoralization hung on him like moss. He looked up at me and said, "Dad, I got to eat a bucketful." Dr. Morrison would have been proud. I told him not to worry, I would spoon-feed him the bucket. "You don't have to do it on your own. I'll help." He let out a big sigh of relief which helped him reset his nervous system. And the three of us drove down the road singing "Bungle in the Jungle" by Jethro Tull.

When we got home, TJ went outside, and I told Jordan that he could pick anywhere he wanted to sit, and I would help him with the reading. Rule #1, "You can't lie down." Rule # 2, "I will read two pages out loud, and you will read one. I will slide my finger under each word I read, and if I stop you have to finish the sentence, whether it's your page to read or not." This was to ensure that I was not reading only to the sheetrock.

This worked out fine and before dinner, we had knocked off some 75 pages. We were both exhausted and hungry. We knew we still hadn't reached the bottom of the bucket. Food consumed, kitchen cleaned, showers finalized and pajamas on, we sat on the couch and read another 30 pages until our resolve and fortitude had been depleted. I congratulated him on his perseverance and insisted that what he did wasn't easy. I told him I was proud of him, kissed him on the forehead, and he was asleep before I could remove my lips, with just five pages to go.

The next morning, we were up and out with a 45-minute drive ahead of us. We would often stop at Burger King for breakfast and listen to "NPR" or "The Mancow in the Morning" show. How they could choose "Mancow" over the plight of Kosovo, bank frauds, and political machinations was beyond me. Though I will say that Jordan recently called me mourning the loss of Cokie Roberts, the great journalist for NPR. He said he didn't recognize the name right off the bat, but when he heard her voice, he realized she had been with him, teaching and informing him for years.

 I took TJ to his school a bit early so Jordan and I could finish the final five pages. We went to a restaurant close to his school, sat in the booth, and ate waffle bites and syrup. We flew through the final five pages with 30 minutes to spare.

 Again, I told him how proud I was of him, and that his patience, discipline, and fortitude enabled him to eat a bucketful in less than 14 hours. You could see relief decorating his face.

 Next, I said, "Now let's get out a piece of paper and start the book report. We have plenty of time to get it done before school starts, and it's due today." He slumped down in the booth as if he just took a bullet. He started contorting himself like a pretzel saying, "Mom got an extension until Friday, and I don't know what to write." I'm sure he felt he had just ascended Mount Everest and before he could even relax or gloat on its peak, my request to start the report sent him tumbling, freefalling back down to the bottom. The pride that just moments before had painted his face, was now a dreadful traumatized glower.

 I didn't budge and repeated, "You're done with the book, the report is due today, now get out a piece of paper and let's get started. I'll cancel all my patients, and we'll sit here all day until it's done, you decide!" He disappeared under the table. You would have thought I had just run all his Pokémon cards through a shredder. I just sat there reading the newspaper as he remained submerged in a fitfully warped condition. I got up and went to the bathroom. Peeking back around the corner I could see the top of his head had resurfaced, his eyes peeking over the tabletop.

It's always amazing how quickly a child's antics will stop once you remove their audience.

When I returned, he was perched on the seat like an angry gargoyle. "We have about 30 minutes until school starts. Now let's get this done, so get out some paper and I'll happily help you. Oh, and by the way, you're welcome for all the help I've given you both last night and this morning."

He muttered, "Thank you," and reluctantly got out a piece of paper and a pencil. His lifeless head plopped down on the table next to the paper, his eyes inches away from where his writing was to proceed.

I let him lay there for a minute. He wasn't being defiant; he was low on brain energy and just didn't know where to start.

We need to understand the necessity of helping an ADHD child jump-start their cognitive processes and problem-solving machinery. I put my head down face-to-face with Jordan and asked, "Do you know how to start?" His eyes filled with tears, and he shook his head "no." I rubbed his back and asked, "What was the book about?"

"A horse," he replied.

He lay there motionless, eyes glazed with anxiety and mental fatigue.

"Write that," I said. "This book was about a horse."

Heroically he lifted his head and wrote, "This book is about a horse," then dropped his head back down.

Remember with ADHDers, if you don't know what to do first, second or third, where on earth do you begin?

Clearly, Jordan had no idea what to write. He knew what the book was about but had no inkling of how to format his thoughts in a proper sequence, to accurately convey the storyline. It was all swirling around in his head like fruit in a blender; nothing was tethered to anything.

I told him to hand me the paper and I'd show him something. I took his pencil and wrote down four topic sentences leaving three or four blank lines under each sentence.

- This book was about a horse.
- It lived on a farm in Virginia.
- It was a warhorse, and its owner took the two of them into battle.
- The man got shot.

I gave him back his pencil and showed him the direction that his brain needed to flow. All he needed was a scant outline to jump-start his thinking. These topic sentences helped Jordan locate, connect, and activate his long-term memory where this information was stored, though haphazardly. We located, then dislodged the input and moved the memory to output on paper. It was in there; he just didn't know where he put it or how to get it out.

He immediately filled in the story below each sentence.

- The book was about a horse named Thunder. He was three years old and would play with his two other brothers every morning.
- Thunder lived on a farm in Virginia. He ran in the fields and pastures. The farm was beautiful and had acres of fields where he pranced around with his brothers. The farmer had corn, potatoes, and wheat. He and the horses would pull the wagon into town on the weekends to sell vegetables.

- It was a warhorse, and his owner rode him into battle. Trouble broke out in the countryside nearby. The Civil War was starting to spread across the country. A group of neighbors gathered and rode off into battle.
- The man got shot. It was bad and scary. Thunder's owner was shot and slumped over asleep on Thunder. Thunder knew where the farm was and took him back to the house where the doctor fixed him. Thunder knew how to get back home without anyone showing him. Thunder saved his life. They treated Thunder like a hero after that.

He put down his pencil and looked at me sheepishly. "Good job, Jordan. You're done, and it's still Thursday." He buried his head in his arms trying to hide his smile. He felt both pride and embarrassment having spent so much time and energy freaking out. I put my arm around him and rubbed his shoulders recapping the events of the last 14 hours; his mom freaking out on him, him proclaiming that he had to eat a bucketful, the charge through the pages, both before and after dinner. This morning's struggle and freak-out and then victory. His face was still concealed though his ears were lapping up the praise like a kitten would cream.

We still had almost 15 minutes, so I said, "Now get out another piece of paper." His head shot up like lava out of a volcano. He gave me a prolonged stare of disbelief. Waiting for me to crack and concede that I was joking, which I wasn't. I said, "Now you have to copy it over onto another sheet." "But I thought we were done," Jordan proclaimed. "We are, but you can't hand this in, it has my handwriting all over it." Anyone not knowing the situation would have thought I had just hit him with a Taser gun. His body jumped and jolted as he slid under the table for another round of agony. This time I caught him before he hit the floor to drown in suffocating dread and defeat. I propped his ass up next to me and said, "We've got 15 minutes left, get rolling. I'm going to get us some mini cinnamon rolls." I retrieved a piece of paper from his bag and put the pencil on the paper and the original next to it. I purposely took my time as I monitored his progress peripherally. He fumbled around for a moment, gathered his composure, and dove right in. I meandered around a bit longer and returned with the delicacies. Without looking up he reached over and plucked a mini bun out of the cardboard boat and stuffed it in his mouth.

When he was done, which took all of eight minutes, he looked up at me as if nothing had happened and said, "We've got to go, or I'm going to be late," as he tucked the report neatly into his notebook then into his backpack like a rare, delicate cherished document. I don't recall if he remembered to hand it in, so he probably did, or I would have heard about it.

CHAPTER 5

The Power of Pokémon

> *"It is easy to tell the toiler, how best he can carry his pack, but no one can rate a burden's weight until it has been on his back."*
>
> ~ Ella Wheeler Wilcox

Laxity is a huge hindrance to attention and awareness. When the mechanisms of the ADHDer's mind begin to drag and they find themselves slogging through their work, their attention begins to dim like a weak flashlight battery. Once this downward slide begins and sloppy despairing slackness takes over, it takes a skilled diplomat, a mediator, if I may, to bring the ADHDer back to their senses, the desk, and the work at hand.

One of the more important pieces of advice I offer people who have trouble sleeping is to read something long and boring. Next thing you know a heavy cloud will descend upon you, and the publication will drop down upon your chest. To ensure that you fall asleep immediately, pick up the book or magazine and keep reading until the book drops again, and your eyes can't take it. Then hit the light.

Unfortunately, ADHDers have this same experience well before bedtime when placed in front of a pile of homework that's boring, tedious, and uninspiring. Before you know it, their posture begins to slump, their head droops, and their book and papers become their pillow.

I will never forget the time my youngest child, Jordan (my ADHDer) and I sat down to do his homework. Jordan is very loving, creative, and so compassionate, but his attention and energy controls would bottom out like a lowrider truck pounding over a speed bump. Sitting down and engaging his mind in miserable laborious homework, following a plentiful narcotizing meal was difficult for him to surmount. This was the 90s and one-sixth of my income was being spent on Ghostbusters and Ninja Turtle collectibles. But the most important life-sustaining and image-preserving staple I could provide for my little cherub at this time was an ample and ever-increasing supply of Pokémon Cards for his albums.

On this particular night, I stopped by the card shop and bought a couple of packs of Pokémon cards and deposited them in the breast pocket of my shirt. Following dinner, Jordan begrudgingly staggered toward the granite island in the kitchen, dragging his book bag as if it contained an anvil. With me on one side of the counter and him on the other, I feigned exuberance about our journey into his homework. He immediately saw through me like a cheap toupee. As he exhaustively pulled out the anvil—I mean materials—I asked what he needed to complete for tomorrow. Witnessing inheritability in action, from my genes to his, I audibly heard him express in an anemic and pallid tone, "I dunno." I snappishly replied, "Neither do I." We bumbled around for the next 20 minutes trying to establish what it was he was supposed to be working on. It was like trying to get a corpse to breakdance. Jordan began his work writing a sentence with his head flat on the counter and his eyes two inches away from the pencil's tip. This infuriated me, though I didn't freak out, but rather I pointed out that my day wasn't spent on a heated massage table. In fact, I reported to him step-by-step my arduous trek through the emotional lives of my patients, my stoic march through the grocery store, the mêlée with traffic, and my selfless dedication to my sons' nutritional needs. My sanctimonious self-regard did nothing to improve Jordan's demeanor. I should have at least given him credit for bringing his books home, which is often more than I did at his age.

The poor little guy was running on empty as I began idling higher and higher. Jordan didn't understand what to do or even where to start. Here I was demanding he tell me *specifically* what needed to be accomplished. Even if he knew what to do his ADHD would thwart his articulation of what his homework was. With a tender but clenched heart, I tried nicely to coerce him into compliance with a flowery but subtle verbal flogging. It was like I was trying to push pudding. It wasn't long before my frustration and Jordan's stuckness brought tears to his eyes. How did I expect him to know where to begin if he didn't know what to do first, second or third?

I backed off for a moment, running my fingers through my hair, exhausted and discouraged. I wasn't sure what to do next. But I wasn't going to give in. I didn't feel defeated and thought there must be a way to resuscitate his poor little soul. Trying to convince him that a "good feeling" of relief and competency would follow his efforts didn't seem to move the needle on his tank of inspiration. I asked myself, what would pull him, rather push him, to finish these assignments? What would be an incentive rather than a bribe? When I was a child, ice cream and cookies were a rare commodity in our home. The promise of a speck of sugar on my quivering tongue was enough to compel me to fulfill some directive. Over-compensating for my childhood deprivation, cookies, and other sugar-laden treats were always accessible to my kids, so edible delights had no pull whatsoever with Jordan.

Then I noticed the bulge in my breast pocket. Ah ha, Pokémon cards! As poor Jordan sat in a puddle of despondency and desolation, I leaned over the counter and said, "Jordan, look at me." He barely lifted his head, like an old hound dog on his last leg. With weary, tear-filled eyes we locked into one another. I reached into my pocket, gripping the Pokémon cards with my thumb and index finger. With my pinkie extended, I slowly pulled up the cards barely exposing the top portion of the packets. I said, "Jordan, you have to get this done, and I'm willing to help, but you've got to pull yourself up and get moving." I then opened my fingers and the cards disappeared into the depth of my pocket. Good Lord, you would have thought the circus had just opened in his soul. His whole countenance changed immediately, a military posture was assumed, and we delightfully maneuvered through the swampy thicket of thought and into a wide expansive meadow of productivity.

Watching this transformation from a shredded sense of self to a grounded and determined single-mindedness was quite astonishing. What relief Jordan experienced. He shifted his mindset from a debilitated self to a motivated self. He knew that with a sustained effort, his little Pokémon buddies, Charizard, Giratina, and Squirtle would be waiting to embrace him on completion of his long journey through the valley of despair, to the vast acreage of love, intrigue, and fantasy.

In troubling times, the Buddhist monks like to say, "No self, no problem." With the Pokémon cards looming in his future, Jordan stopped identifying himself as the problem and engaged with the task. The "poor me" mindset was cut out of the equation. His Pokémon buddies lured him out of himself.

I considered the cards an incentive, not a bribe and I marveled at how one of Jordan's selves gave way to another self. Initially, Jordan was unable to experience that moment of drudgery as temporary, rather than a thin manageable slice of time. With the awareness that Pokémon cards loomed in his immediate future, Jordan was able to pull himself out of the ditch and construct new neural pathways that weren't there before. These new pathways led him immediately to a better place.

Since our brain is forever changing, we can teach the ADHDer not to personalize the permanence of their frustrations, but to view the frustrated and stymied self as a fictional character whose complete story hasn't been written. Jordan learned that he was "not the problem," that he could incite and ignite his executive functioning skills, enabling him to shift into "git er done," mode. Jordan learned to view frustrations and inconsistencies as temporary rather than identifying with them. By depersonalizing the frustration, he could absorb himself in the process and not get lost in the emotional experience. Thank you, Pikachu.

CHAPTER 6

ADHD and The Theatrical Performances: We All Can Get Better

"Hope is the positive mode of awaiting the future."

~ Emil Brunner

ADHD takes center stage throughout the numerous theatrical performances in one's life. Let's describe some of those theaters. One is the <u>educational</u> stage. This is a tough stage with a very challenging script for the ADHDer to follow. You can only pack so much on your mind's stage before it becomes too full and stops the performance. When your mind's stage doesn't clear fast enough for the next troupe to come on, things get very congested. For many ADHD kids just listening and mentally metabolizing sequential instruction is overwhelming. If the teacher is going 15 mph and you can only go seven, then you get dragged along. The social spotlights are glaring. If you're not making it emotionally, socially, or academically, most everybody knows. Emotional pain and shame get entrenched in their neural circuitry, then written into the ADHDer's self-narrative or story.

Sadly, they don't just misinterpret incoming instruction, but often miss it altogether. ADHDers bounce back and forth between two polarities, overreacting and underreacting. Both are what you do when you don't know what to do. Sad, despairing, emotional plunges with droopy indifference is one extreme where the ADHDer believes, "no one can help me." The other extreme can be a frantic need to protect their vulnerability, spiraling into caustic self-righteous indignation stating, "I don't need any help." Both are defensive postures. The first might be an invitation, testing to see who would be willing to keep them from drowning. The other extreme is meant to push people away, protecting themselves from exposure and the futility they live with on what feels like a cellular level. These are just a few of the acts that play out when learning isn't working.

The <u>cognitive</u> stage features numerous thought distortions pertaining to the ADHDer's personal worth and potential. Productivity and understanding get derailed. When an ADHDer just plain doesn't understand, and remotely associated ideas never take root, poverty of interpretation and expression becomes a way of life. ADHDers get stuck in a loop, perseverating on, "what they aren't," rather than "what they could be." We can teach them how to shift into a productive, more constructive reality-based method of thinking and interpreting.

<u>Behavioral</u> performances are said to speak louder than words. Doing the wrong thing for the right reason is a classic ADHD misstep. The inability to consistently suppress their first impulse, then choose an appropriate response in order to merge with the moment is a continual struggle for most ADHDers. Parents and teachers get tired of listening to the ADHDer's words responding only to their behavior. Sadly, their words often indicate what they need that they're not getting, and what they're getting that they don't need.

A <u>spiritual</u> disconnect makes for a very frustrating recital. If you're disconnected from your unique instinctual self, despair and hopelessness abound. The relational aspect, where you're expected to connect with others in reciprocity and sustain a peaceful equilibrium is difficult if your spirit is in constant need of resuscitation. Unrealistic expectations from others demonstrate a lack of empathy. When an ADHDer constantly feels stretched they feel isolated in the deepest crevasse of their being.

Sadly, when the ADHDer is desperate to connect, anybody is better than nobody. Chess players don't hang around with hockey players. They seek out others on the same level of their dysfunctions; others who know the language. They connect with people who are not going to operate in their best interest. Blind devotion breeds unhealthy and often corrosive loyalties. ADHDers can have two or three new best friends within the course of a few months. Sadly, for some, it's simply because someone was nice to them. The intense desire to be connected leads to being used and manipulated, which for some is better than nothing. For some, this is worth tolerating in order to belong. Those types of relationships lack spirit-to-spirit connections. They usually end when the ADHDer is no longer a plus for the other party. Excruciating loneliness can set in.

The <u>family</u> playhouse, or melodrama, is where we receive most of our training, getting sucked into the family trance. It's quite normal to be influenced by the family's script but it's important to help the ADHDer ascertain if their part in this production was assigned, chosen, or imposed. Not all parts are bad. But if the family is the carriage and the members the horses, it's important to identify which horse is nipping at the other's hooves, dragging its ass, or completely pulling in the opposite direction. Unfortunately, unless people get help, these scripts become engrained, feel inescapable, and carried out throughout a lifetime. Some family members, for their own distorted reasons, won't let the ADHDer reinvent themselves outside their historical ADHD image. I've found in some families, that when one person gets better, someone else begins to get worse. ADHDers, because of their bumbling, are delightful objects of comparison if you need to feel better about yourself. Good therapy approaches the family as a growth unit. Uniqueness is recognized and flexibility is the norm.

What we do is not necessarily who we are. ADHDers have a strong desire to follow their dreams because matching other people's blueprints is extremely difficult. Hobbies, interests, and proclivities are incredibly important and need to be fertilized. One's overall well-being suffers daily when they default into a mindset, belief, job, or career where their strengths and uniqueness are neither noticed nor utilized. If you don't like your job, you better have a really nice life, but if you don't like your life, you better have a really interesting and stimulating career. If you have neither, it's a dreadful load to carry every day. Sadly, when ADHDers do find the job or career of their dreams, their emotional, cognitive, and behavioral impairments can make it short-lived. They are often better interviewees than they are employees. But not always. These impairments can range from mild to severe but when the ADHDer is provided the proper emotional support, comfort, and learned problem-solving strategies, an astute employer will recognize their long-term value.

There's specific teaching that needs to be taught at crucial junctures of development and points of performance. When the ADHDer feels understood and their feelings recognized, they can learn to dislodge themselves from fossilized thinking and move on. Getting better has much more to do with letting go, than holding on.

We must meet the ADHDer right where they are, on their map of development, not where we think they "should" be. Unfortunately, ADHD kids never seem to be where they're "supposed" to be—behaviorally, emotionally, or academically. Their attention bounces around like a ball in a pinball machine. The good news is we can teach the ADHDer to still their mind so they can intentionally steer their attention and relax their bodies.

Russell Barkley, a renowned author, expert, and rigorous researcher in the field of ADD and ADHD speaks of the 30 percent rule. The rule suggests that you can take 30 percent of a child's age and subtract it from where they are chronologically, and the sum is the developmental age where you'll find them emotionally. So, a ten-year-old might be in a ten-year-old body, but their emotional temperament and maturity level might be that of a six or seven-year-old. At age 16, when the ADHDer can drive, you're essentially handing the keys to someone who is emotionally 11 or 12. The same applies to an 18-year-old college freshman. Thirty percent of 18 is 12.6 years of age, so you're putting a developmentally 12–13-year-old kid on a college campus. It's no wonder ADHDers who are placed in college have a very low first-semester success rate. They have trouble handling frustration and managing themselves within time. I've witnessed this in group therapy over and over; a ten-year-old will relate far better with a seven-year-old than with an age-equivalent or older peer.

Some ADHD kids become surprisingly adroit at promptly ratcheting up their maturity level and taking on responsibility for their personal management when keys and the privilege of driving are dangled in front of them. It's amazing how quickly change can occur in order to take advantage of the newfound freedoms that driving provides. Conversely, some ADHD kids are frightened to get behind the wheel. In fact, there is a growing population of ADHDers that are just not interested in driving. To them, it's too much of a hassle. Deep down inside they're afraid they won't pass the test and have grave doubts about their capacity to see the whole picture. In a lot of cases, parents have convinced them (and sometimes rightly so) that society would be better protected if they would wait a few years. The inability to simply accomplish what is expected daily is hard enough without adding the attention to detail that driving demands. For some, just the thought creates tremendous anxiety.

With time, skillful instruction, and patient understanding, ADHD kids are quite capable of successfully converging their attention with their intention, regulating their emotions, and becoming quite accomplished. The good news is that all of us can get better at streamlining our efficiency no matter what age we are. Discovering how our brain works and the power we have over it, helps us monitor, then manage our thoughts, feelings, and behaviors. We begin to become acutely aware of their influences on one another. This is called self-regulation.

The brain regulates itself through a variety of biological mechanisms. Rick Hanson, the fascinating neuroscientist, and author of the wonderful books, *Buddha's Brain*, *Hardwiring Happiness,* and *Resilience,* refers to the mind as both a spotlight and vacuum cleaner. Whatever it is we focus our attention on is illuminated by the spotlight, then sucked right up into ourselves, and carried into our being-ness. So, it is important to know where we are casting our beam of attention. We then must ask ourselves, "Is it good for me and productive, or is it limiting and unhelpful?" Being able to cast our attention where we want it is obviously extremely important, but just as important is the ability to pull it away from what isn't helpful. This is a step along the way to getting better.

What we pay attention to creates and strengthens that particular neural circuitry. If we focus on hope, faith, and optimism, we create new pathways paved in that spirit leading us to better places. Equally, if we are rigid, pessimistic, and cynical, those pathways and circuitry are strengthened and entrenched, leading us to less than desirable emotional destinations. Learning to be hopeful can prune away old neural pathways that no longer serve our best interest. That right there is self-regulation.

To live with integrity, to have a strong moral compass and to do what's right relies heavily on self-regulation. For ADHD individuals, wisdom and stability come about when they learn to avoid their first impulse. That first impulse isn't always about gratification, but avoidance also. Impulse control is difficult for ADHD children because why stifle something that feels so natural. It's up to parents, teachers, and therapists to demonstrate more options, opportunities and the reward that comes from avoiding their first impulse. My dad used to tell me, "Tom, if it seems urgent then you should probably wait a bit." Sometimes just a few minutes can seem like an eternity for the ADHD mind. Managing these frustrations is a full-time job that requires a lot of overtime. Frustrating and destructive thought patterns and emotions that were learned can be unlearned with patience, time, and quality therapy. We all make mistakes, but ADHD kids often have a harder time learning from them. When they heighten their awareness and learn to correlate their thinking, feelings, and behaviors with both consequences and rewards, by avoiding their first impulse, that too is self-regulation.

An ADHD child who receives compassionate and patient treatment has a much better chance at outgrowing their impairments and tempering their impulses. Though they'll always remain ADHD, once unshackled, they can learn behaviors and adopt habits that work for them; simply put, they're learning to do it "their way."

The older the ADHDer gets, the more likely it is that they've learned through trial and error a manner of functioning and regulating that works best for them. As we have learned in the past couple of decades ADHD does persist into adulthood. Though the types of difficulties require more adult-like responsibilities, I don't see adult ADHDers because they've neglected to pay their utility bills. More often it's because they're besieged with relationship issues, lingering self-doubt, and inconsistencies in their behavioral and emotional flow. Usually, there is a load of baggage from the past still needing to be unloaded. Others are furious because they were regulated with medication throughout their formative years, losing access to their own instinctual data. A young woman once told me through tears, "How would you have liked to go through elementary, middle, and high school relating to everyone through chemicals? It wasn't relating, because "me" wasn't fully present."

There is a wonderful quote by Viktor E. Frankl, an Austrian neurologist, psychotherapist, Holocaust survivor, and author. He wrote in his much-respected book, *Man's Search for Meaning*, "Between stimulus and response there is a space, in that space lies our power to choose our response, in our response lies our growth and our freedom." This place between stimulus and response for ADHD kids is very small and short in duration. Subconscious thinking, fueled by implicit memories fills this space, creating the illusion that there's "no choice" on how to respond. The shameful experience that criticism produces quickly fills the space Frankl was referring to, leaving no other option than to silently simmer in painful exposure, revenge, and self-condemnation. When the ADHDer learns that they can design a space between stimulus and response that feels like a safe place, the duration of a peaceful moment gets extended. They can then learn to make intentional and mindful choices in that moment, in that space. This too is self-regulation.

Teaching an ADHD child early on that, "We create our own weather," provides for them the powerful incentive that "they themselves" can quiet the storms and calm the winds. Helping to nurture an attitude of peaceful confidence and persistent determination is imperative. Trumped-up behavior modification plans and being stuffed full of medication have proven to be much more effective with rats and monkeys than humans. Earning enough "My Little Pony" stickers in order to buy a privilege or gobbling down a narcotic in order to tether a state to its capital doesn't instill lasting understanding and self-discipline.

The three areas where ADHD causes the most havoc:

1) Parenting issues

2) Schooling, learning, and performance frustrations

3) Balanced and reciprocating friendships

Friendships tend to take priority over everything, but the first two constitute about 85 percent of childhood and adolescence. Sadly, success is often measured only when something is specifically visually accomplished.

Most of the difficulties I experienced growing up were from the first two categories, learning and parenting issues. I couldn't learn how to do well until I could figure out why I wasn't. No one showed me that. Over time, I had to learn that it's just as important to know why something didn't work, as to know why it did.

ADHD individuals try hard to avoid having to come face-to-face with themselves. One of the most loving gifts we can bestow upon ourselves is one of accurate self-observation and honest self-disclosure. You may be disappointed in what you observe and hear, but you will certainly feel doomed if you stop trying. The sad reality is most people only face themselves when they're forced to. Nothing like an emergency, trauma, or loss to get our attention.

With a patient and sensitive approach to an ADHDer's inner world, emotional wounds can be cauterized, cognitive distortions uncurled, adrenaline-infused behavioral escapades defused, spiritual understanding and acceptance restored, and familial and relational rupturing repaired.

If you keep telling yourself that things suck, and nothing is going to change, you steadily increase your chances of being right. On that same token if you don't expect much you will probably receive just that. However, believing you have the capacity to control your own affairs is a powerful motivator. The desire to live a better internal life translates into external changes. How you see yourself defines what you will accomplish. In the long run, teaching an ADHDer to cultivate, then nurture an attitude of peaceful confidence and persistent determination, is more effective and sustainable than any behavior modification plan or a handful of narcotics (medications). They actually learn to regulate themselves through their own volition.

We all hope for something better to come, but if we don't nurture that hope, we've already lost. Thomas Monson, a spiritual author, wrote, "Hope is putting faith to work when doubting would be much easier." We can all get better!

CHAPTER 7

Tears: Completing the Past and Our Body's Instinctual Data

> *"Tears come from the heart, and not from the brain."*
>
> ~ Leonardo Di Vinci

Human beings need to cry. Sadly, many view crying as a symptom, not a solution. Individuals with ADHD often find their tears very close to the surface. ADHDers possess a deep intuitive empathy and can relate to another's feelings and struggles. Some non-ADHD people who I've worked with in therapy, and were hurting tremendously, prided themselves by saying, "I never shed a tear!" I respond by saying, "I'm not sure there is going to be a medal in heaven for such self-deprivation."

Our lacrimal glands produce three types of tears. The first are "basal" tears, which are always present, making our eyes moist. Thank God for basal tears or our eyes would dry out. We produce five-ten ounces of basal tears a day. To envision that, (in your mind's dry eye,) imagine a half-to-full can of coke. Put basal tears on your gratitude list. These tears drain through our noses, which is why after a good cry we need a tissue.

The second type of tears are "reflex" tears. These protect our eyes from harsh irritants, like smoke or dust. To produce these, the cornea communicates discomfort to the brain stem, and the brain dispenses hormones to the glands, which then produce tears, ridding the eyes of irritants.

The third type of tears are "emotional" tears. The cerebrum is the part of the brain where we register our emotions: sadness, anger, loss, disappointment, betrayal, etc. When the cerebrum registers these emotions, the endocrine system triggers the delivery of hormones to the ocular region, causing tears to form. These tears bring about physical and emotional relief, ridding the body of toxins that build up while experiencing elevated levels of stress and distress.

The area of your brain that is activated through physical pain, like banging your knee against a table, is the same area that gets "lit up" when feeling emotional pain, such as rejection, disappointment, and disapproval. Therefore, emotional pain is also experienced in the body. We feel it physically. It's literally embodied. ADHDers seem to embody emotional pain much stronger and deeper than the average individual. Or maybe they're just not as good at understanding, metabolizing, and disguising their pain.

ADHDers have a lot going on inside. Our five senses (touch, smell, taste, sight, and hearing) bring the outside world into our awareness. Emotions swirl around inside their mind and body as if it were a blender; the mind being the blades and the body, the vessel. Being able to slow things down and become aware of what's going on internally is called <u>interoception</u>. It's our seldom mentioned sixth sense, interoception, that provides the instinctive ability to mentally perceive the internal state of our mind, body, and soul. This heightened awareness helps us detect irregularities where tears might be pooling. Developing this sixth sense for ADHDers is a vital tool for creating emotional balance and well-being. Lamina 1 is the layer of the spinal cord that carries these internal messages and data upward, transferring the information into our body's interior world, where it passes through the insula. The insula is like the Internet in that it's a superhighway to the limbic region. The limbic system is the area of the brain that deals with emotions, memories, and arousal. It delivers an identifiable message to the brain stem through our senses telling us, "What's up."

I cried hard when my first dog, Emil, got hit by a car. I cried when I was cut from the baseball team that all my friends made. When I got canned from my first job as a dishwasher, I bawled. When my girlfriend, Paula, dumped me for a guy with a car and sideburns, I was devastated. At funerals, the ones left behind always affect me deeply.

I cry when I see an athlete succeed, then run to the crowd to embrace their parents. I cry at the end of plays, when the cast comes out, holds hands and bows. When I see an individual tearfully thank their parents or significant people in their life during an awards ceremony, or a soldier surprising his loved ones when returning from overseas, I'm a blubbering mess. Having listened to or watched almost every Royals game, and when the season ends, I sniffle, then fall into a two-hour depression. Heck, I see a dog food commercial with the kid, the dad, and the dog, and I'm weeping, missing my own young boys and dogs.

In college, I worked at a couple of different hospitals as a respiratory therapist and an EKG technician. Behind the curtains of the emergency room or in the intensive care unit, when we lost or were losing a patient, tears came, but I knew that we were doing everything medically possible to save their life. What ripped me to shreds, sending me back to the far reaches of the lab to sob abdominally, was when I would pass a little old lady, or a weary old man with tear-stained cheeks, clutching tissues, looking at me for an update on the condition of their loved one. Or when I pushed my machine past the emergency waiting room and would see two little kids playing on the floor with cars, while their mother held a baby in her arms not yet knowing that she's a widow and that her children no longer have a father. I'd be torn to pieces. On those nights, I would go home and kiss my daughter in her sleep. Witnessing the fragility of life, and my evolving awareness of its temporary reality. I would whisper in my daughter's ear "Daddy loves you, Addie." She would nod and smile in her sleep as if to say, "I know you do, Daddy."

I'm telling you this so you can begin to explore the crevices in your life, where you've been affected, afflicted, and conflicted the most. The place where your tears may have become frozen or calcified. When the light of truth shines in through the cracks, we discover that our tears are primitive, petrified in the past, and what affects us on the surface of today can dislodge tears from long ago, that were held captive and never released. When we adults come to grips with what's been ailing us from the past and make sense of it and explain it to our children, it gives them an opportunity to know us from a different perspective and avoid some of the pitfalls they recognize from our lessons.

Before I attained full custody of my sons, taking them back to their mother's following a weekend of fun, frolic and laughter moistened my eyes. When the Ninja Turtles or the Ghostbuster toys that were bursting with life less than an hour ago lay motionless on the floor when

I returned, I would tearfully place them in their toy box. I believe that our tears are truly the better parts of us.

There are tears of loss, tears of joy, and tears of anticipation. When Betty or I waited for the other to disembark from an airplane, anticipating the first eye contact, knowing that love, hugs, and kisses awaited us tears formed in the eyes of us both.

Some of my deepest tears have been over the loss of pets. Lopez, my 21-year-old cat, who I scooped up from under an eighteen-wheeler at a truck stop in Salina, Kansas, and who slept on my shoulder for the next hundred miles ... what a loss. He slept in my arms every night for the following 21 years. His reign covered the span of my life between ages 19 through 40. It was a damn good thing he couldn't talk.

Satchel was a beautiful, loving black lab who accompanied me on well over 1800 miles of running and posed with me on the award stand with my medal draped around his neck. He eventually developed cancer. Schumdley was a beautiful white Himalayan cat whom my sons referred to as "a strange little man." He simply wore out. Little Miss Snuggles, a sweet and gentle Lhasa Apso, was so lovingly submissive, that when approached, she would roll over on her back and wait for her tummy to be rubbed. I put to rest my cat, Grace, of 19 years and again tears flowed. And then there was Roscoe. Affectionately known as "Lil man." He was another Lhasa Apso who left us quite recently. I have tears just typing this. Roscoe has now been joined by his best friend, Tucker, Newfoundland, who was simply one of the nicest spirits I have ever known.

The tears released by sad or joyful experiences are often instructions from wiser parts of us that are not interested in impression management or stilted personas.

And some of our tears may emerge from implicit memories, ones that live below the surface of our awareness.

When an ADHDer allows themselves to cry deeply, a part of them gets up, dusts themselves off, then moves on. Tears and laughter are equally good medicine for our mind and body. Crying is a safety mechanism, a valve that releases then flushes the body of stress-producing hormones and toxins. It's a form of mental hygiene, a cleansing that changes our brain chemistry. When we continually plan our life around our pain and keep our feelings in, life can feel like a never-ending pregnancy. Our body presents its bill for all the feelings we keep locked up inside. The anxiety that comes from unresolved grief is like fertilizer to the ADHD system. Heart disease, hypertension, colitis, depression, and anxiety disorders are just a fraction of the ways our bodies get thrown out of balance by a lack of healthy emoting.

In "Lady of the Lake," Sir Walter Scott wrote, "Love is loveliest when embalmed in tears." I couldn't agree more.

CHAPTER 8

Medication Beware

> *"I never disliked a kid enough to fill them full of medications."*
>
> ~ Patch Adams

"I lost one of my friends this summer," Josh choked out between sobs and gasps. "He was a really good guy. He was kind and funny. We both understood each other. We didn't have to talk all the time to know what the other was thinking. We would just start laughing." Josh cried even harder while I consoled him.

"What happened?" I asked. "Was it sudden and unexpected or a long painful struggle? What did he die from?"

Josh looked up at me and through his tear-stained gaze, he said, "He's not dead, but he might as well be they put him on medication. He's not the same anymore."

Most families try and reinforce vertical identities—lives that are forever on the upward trajectory toward success and accomplishment. Families with an ADHD child, or children, struggle with horizontal development—the child whose trajectory follows the path of a ball in a pinball machine. ADHD is often treated as a horizontal defect, an abnormality; a deviation that needs to be arrested and subdued by medication, like a stun gun. Once narcotized, strict behavioral and emotional constraints can be enforced.

One out of five Americans takes some form of psychiatric medication. Richard Friedman, M.D. wrote in the *New York Times,* "Even though 25 percent of Americans suffer from a diagnosable mental illness in any year, there are few signs of innovation from the major drug makers." Friedman points out that often clinical trials of new and novel medication fared little or no better than placebos.

It's important for doctors and the public to be aware of the side effects of medication—not just the physical side, like heart palpitations, gastric difficulties, suppressed appetite, and such, but real-life emotional consequences, such as relational, academic, and mental functioning. Just as no ice cream manufacturer is going to warn you that eating too much of their product is going to make your butt the size of a washing machine, we can't rely solely on the optimistically carefree ads where in one frame a kid is sitting in a cold damp alley, then after taking meds is running through a field, holding hands with his family, clutching a picnic basket while chasing butterflies. Drug companies will tell you the downside, but it's a sped-up litany that sounds like The Chipmunks on meth. Like the advertisements say, "If you experience a dry mouth, rectal bleeding, or suicidal ideations, stop taking it and call your doctor immediately." Such symptoms would surely curtail the fun and frolic typically depicted in ads for medication.

The most common side effects of ADHD medications are loss of appetite, weight loss, sleep disturbances, and mood swings. Hell, that right there is enough to tilt all sorts of measures of wellness. That's a steep price to pay in exchange for the ability to tether a state to its capital or conjugate a verb. What's truly more important: a test score, or a well-rested, emotionally balanced, well-liked kid with a healthy diet and sound body image? Just these few side effects alone have been known to impair both short and long-term outcomes.

Parents and practitioners find it easier to take a pill and narcotize that little bugger into compliance rather than engage in the long difficult process of emotional and behavioral renovation. Medications possess the power to suppress feelings and modify behavior, taking away an individual's free will and volition. Some will say, "That's exactly the point. This population is too willful." Medication doesn't make you more rational. In fact, it can compromise levelheadedness and personal responsibility. Of course, we all want our children to be determined, self-sufficient, original, and predictable. But with ADHD children, spontaneity rules. This can certainly be both good and bad. There's a fine line between spontaneity and impulsivity. Impulsivity can be tamed, but spontaneity should never be washed away or crushed. Medication can do just that. Taming impulsivity requires consistent quality control, emotional awareness, relaxation, and meditative therapy.

Medication can be effective in some situations, but it's never the whole answer. It's the ugly side you may not hear much about. For instance, *akathisia* is a drug-induced neurological disorder caused by medications. It's been known to drive people to suicide and violence. *Akathisia* is characterized by the inability to sit still and paranoid delusions. Delusional racing thoughts spawn and drive compulsive tormenting beliefs and behaviors. This dysphoric state produces, then breeds, hostile words, and actions.

When you suffer from *akathisia* there is a spellbinding effect. The technical name for this mesmeric effect is *anosognosia*. This is where the individual doesn't recognize the mental and emotional impairment they're demonstrating caused by the toxic effect of medication. This can range from mild to severe. One can be drawn toward depression, become apathetic, with no sense of humor or interest in anything life has to offer. Conversely, they can choose to preach on a street corner the virtues of their extra sensory attributes and the onset of a new horizon that only they have been anointed to see. Some might view the former, as an improvement, a blunting and dampening of the manic emotions and agitated behaviors that are often equated with ADHD. But masking the symptoms doesn't solve the problems. Drugs don't help the individual understand the origins of the issues they're struggling with. They often hear, "Take this, it should make you feel better in four to six weeks. We will meet then and see if it worked."

When children are drugged, they fail to sense the degree of their emotional turbulence. Sadly, the actual impairments and delusions that are quite clear to others, go unnoticed by the child. They aren't aware of how impaired they've become or the continually disagreeable state they exhibit.

Dr. Peter Breggin, the author of *Medication Madness*, writes that Substance-Induced Mood Disorders (S.I.M.D.) S.I.M.D. can be caused by the short-term effect of certain medications that cause patients to go into withdrawal between doses. Antidepressants can cause mental overstimulation. The effects can range from mild to torturous, from insomnia and minor anxiety to psychotic levels of mania and compulsive behavior.

Children and adults who possess little confidence and self-awareness may believe they "need" medication in order to function effectively. Or, conversely, it might be an astute self-awareness that tells the individual, "I do need some, but not an elephant size dose."

Dr. Marcia Angell, a former editor of *The New England Journal of Medicine* and a Senior Lecturer at Harvard Medical School, wrote in 2007, "The FDA also refuses to release unfavorable research results in its possession without the sponsoring company's permission." From this, Breggin extrapolates, "Americans need to know that the FDA is not their friend. It's the friend of the pharmaceutical industry." Through years of my own observations and the validation of such experts as Breggin, I think I'll adhere to Breggin's research, as opposed to the FDA, to whom Breggin is not beholden.

Some M.D.s say that ADHD is a life-long battle and that life-long pharmaceutical treatment is necessary, even crucial. This claim is not supported by scientific research. You can outgrow your impairments, learn strategies to streamline your behavior, and increase productivity through heightening your awareness of your awareness, now commonly referred to as mindfulness. At the same time, you can strengthen your capacity to manage your emotions through meditation, exercise, talk therapy, caring social support, deep spiritual grounding, and even volunteering-type endeavors.

I once heard a very prominent doctor, author and researcher tell a room of 500 other practitioners that if you have diabetes, you have it forever, just like ADHD. "You wouldn't stop giving insulin to a diabetic just because they are older." He stated the same is true with ADHD. "You'll have it forever, so why would you ever stop taking medication?" Much of this gentleman's research is sponsored by pharmaceutical companies that are more than likely footing the bill for his workshops in the Bahamas, as well as the new deck on his lake house.

The media and big business can frighten you into believing that ADHD is an epidemic. This simply isn't so, according to Dr. Keith Connors, professor emeritus at Duke University. Connors was quoted in an article from *The New York Times,* December 15, 2013, entitled, "The Selling of Attention Deficit Disorder." As Dr. Connors stated, "It's preposterous. This is concocted in order to justify the dispensing of medications at unprecedented levels." The rise of ADHD diagnoses and prescriptions directly corresponds with a financially fruitful and amazingly effective marketing campaign over the past two decades. Pharmaceutical companies have broadcasted the ADHD condition alongside photographs and videos of despondent vacant-looking youth. They claim that an antidote has been born in a lab. So, bring your gold, frankincense, and myrrh, along with your insurance card and a check payable to "The Savior."

The public has been bombarded with promises of quick and easy medical fixes. The pharmaceutical industry has mesmerized doctors, educators, and parents by trumpeting the assurance of academic prowess, the pledge of rapid compliance, and potential for characterological transformations. In some cases, the benefits to parents, teachers, and stockholders have outweighed any benefit to the child. Parents are extremely susceptible to what their doctors recommend. If a doctor says it, it must be right.

Drugs should literally be the last option. They are most effective when combined with talk therapy. However, the American Academy of Child and Adolescent Psychiatry now lists a plethora of medications available for troubled kids, but talk therapy is seldom mentioned. I can see a stark difference between when the person is talking or when the pill is.

The list of available drugs suggested to treat ADHD individuals includes stimulants, mood stabilizers, sleep medications, antidepressants, anticonvulsants, antipsychotics, and anti-anxieties. That's not even considering more specific drugs to deal with impulsivity and post-traumatic flashbacks. We even have drugs to counteract the side effects of the aforementioned drugs. The majority of these meds have been approved for adults only but are being distributed "off label" for younger and younger patients. Children are not little adults. You just can't cut a pill in half, believing the dosage is matching a "kid's menu measure." Children metabolize medications much differently than adults. For years, kids have been used as guinea pigs in medication trials, disregarding the side effects while not tracking the results. Because of this, the usage of medication has exceeded our knowledge base.

When it comes to helping our children, it's difficult to accept the obvious; we are still waiting on the healthcare system to get well. Most of the children who are receiving their medication are not getting it from specialists in psychopharmacology or psychiatry. Some family physicians are recklessly wielding their prescription pads, at the cost of the children's well-being. Many family doctors and pediatricians don't perform the extensive evaluations and screenings necessary for proper diagnosis. I once knew of a boy whose mother got all his prescriptions through her gynecologist, who was also a workout buddy. The boy and the gynecologist, as you might guess, had never met.

Note below that some of these medications have been very helpful and, in some cases, lifesaving and should not be discounted because of my experiences. The reality is that I don't see those kids in my office. But I have collaborated with doctors and conscientious and insightful parents who know the importance of psychotherapy while taking medication.

For your edification, here is a list of the noted side effects of ADHD medications. It's to be noted, not everyone has these experiences.

- Adderall is a once-a-day amphetamine that works by putting the brakes on the areas of the brain responsible for organizing thoughts. The side effects can include rapid heartbeat, high blood pressure and overstimulation. It can also produce dependency and addiction. Treatment centers are full of Adderall addicts.
- Concerta soaks the neurons in norepinephrine and dopamine which reduces hyperactivity and inattention. It's known to cause headaches, stomach pain, sleeplessness, and overstimulation.
- Strattera is the first non-stimulant drug for the treatment of ADHD, and it enhances norepinephrine levels in the brain. Reported side effects include decreased appetite, nausea, and stomach pain.
- Ritalin's active ingredient is methylphenidate, which stimulates the brain to filter and prioritize incoming information. Reported side effects are headaches, lack of appetite, irritability, nervousness, and insomnia.
- Meth patch delivers continuous low doses of methamphetamine through the skin. The side effects are occipital discomfort, headaches, suppressed appetite, anxiousness, irritability, nervousness, and sleep disturbance.
- Prozac is the first antidepressant aimed at regulating serotonin, the neurological chemical that involves mood. The side effects are sleeplessness, anxiety, nervousness, weight loss, and mania.
- Zoloft also enhances the level of serotonin in the brain in order to maintain feelings of satisfaction and stability. Again, the poor stomach can get upset, the mouth becomes dry, agitation increases, and appetite decreases.
- Paxil raises the level of serotonin, which, if you'll remember, helps manage moods. Side effects include nausea, drowsiness, and insomnia.

- Effexor targets two of the brain's chemicals that regulate mood: norepinephrine and serotonin. Coupled with ever-present nausea, you can now throw in constipation, nervousness, loss of appetite, and drowsiness.
- Depakote is an anti-seizure medication that is effective in treating the grandiose, over-the-top, hyper-agitated states of mania. Unfortunately, it also affects the liver and white blood cells, causing abnormalities, headaches, nausea, and drowsiness.
- Zyprexa is a mood stabilizer designed to balance levels of serotonin and dopamine in the brain. Instead of having no appetite, you can potentially gain weight, coupled with drowsiness, dry mouth, and seizures.
- Lithium has been around for years. It brings you down off the emotional pedestals associated with mania. Nausea and lack of appetite are common, as well as trembling hands.

The administration of meds in emergency situations is driven by a dire need. It's certainly not fair to withhold meds when a child is emotionally tormented or suicidal. But meds aren't solution-oriented. It's like putting a bandage over an infected wound, even though that may be what you have to do in order to keep the wound sanitized. But it seems to me most things get better with sunlight and air.

There is a high correlation between untreated cases of ADHD and substance abuse, dropping out of school, and legal entanglements. Many deaths are caused by self-medicating and interrelated behaviors with alcohol and drugs.

It's important to understand that these individuals with ADHD need to talk, brainstorm, problem-solve and employ critical thinking where they learn to utilize both inductive and deductive reasoning when dealing with their emotional makeup. They need to be free to express their feelings in a safe, shame-free environment. The ADHDer needs to know that they matter, and their anger and sadness is as important to you as it is to them. Good therapy is like lancing a wound and draining the infection. We heal and get unstuck when we allow ourselves to be as mad or as sad as we really are. We can then examine why we feel that way. When we do this, transformations take place, and we can shift. We learn that we have inner freedom and inner strength that can keep us from being overwhelmed by our own experiences.

We get better by allowing ourselves to express what's happening in our "inner world." We, humans, are dynamic animals. We were meant to move and express, interact, howl at the moon, swing our bodies to music, and spend a good night with close friends. That's what aliveness is. Sadly, when one is filled to the gills with medication, it can take us away from the very things we need the most—friends, authenticity, and access to our true self.

Early in childhood, some ADHD kids have a fateful choice to make. They must ask themselves, "Am I crazy, am I bad, do I have what it takes to be okay?" Or "Are my parents and teachers senseless and insensitive; do they have any idea how to provide for my developmental dependency needs? Can they be patient with me till I get it right? Do they have any idea what I'm going through?" A child needs to learn how to discover their own natural goodness with sensory acuity and then learn to call it up. The misuse of medication can block an ADHDer's ability to get on their own side.

Throughout the spectrum of ADHD disorders, there are innumerable pharmacological success stories. But there are also tragic accounts of the misuse of medication and squandered opportunities to repair the moment. By installing mindful strategies, they can learn to fill their toolbox with resources that help them get better and move on. Just because a drug can change your state of mind, doesn't mean that's the best state to be in.

I've seen many cases where parents and physicians unintentionally meddle with a child's normal development. Kids with moderate struggles are being subdued or muted when they aren't depressed or hyperactive, but rather a bit restless or squirmy. Certain repetitive behaviors that are designed for comfort but are not obsessive can easily be classified as an obsessive-compulsive disorder so that a prescription can be thrown at it. The popular mindset is that these behaviors must be halted, transformed, and fixed immediately. The goal is to make a child look and act like everybody else. Imagine how mundane and monotonous life would be if every eccentric and carbonated personality were medicated.

The brain doesn't fully mature until the mid-to-late twenties. So, if you're medicating the child for years, it means that you're turning the prefrontal lobes into cerebral clay. The the prefrontal lobes have a tremendous responsibility. It organizes thoughts, perceptions, and behavior and plans and governs movement. The frontal lobes regulate attention, control impulsivity, spur critical thinking and problem-solving, while also managing the unconscious display of empathy and responsiveness. Medication might help oil the gears, but the ADHDer doesn't feel it's from their own volition.

The prefrontal lobes house other portions of the brain such as the basal ganglia, which controls anxiety levels and coordinates motor behaviors; the cingulate gyrus is critical to adaptation, cognitive flexibility, and cooperation; the hippocampus helps formulate memories and higher learning, and the amygdala (that little bitch) is the reservoir of fear and emotion. Do these medications help strengthen control by analyzing what a situation needs, helping to foster adaptation? Or do they just take the wheel and steer the mind throughout the duration of the dose?

It's apparent that there are just too many unanswered questions regarding the child's underdeveloped brain that's being bombarded with chemicals. It's like putting way too much pesticide in the vegetable garden in order to save the vegetables.

Over and over, I have seen how certain medications thwart the access, acquisition, and development of specific emotional skills. One example might be anxiety drugs being given to a child who has not yet learned how to master the experience of successful stress management. The pill alone doesn't teach this. We learn from what hurts us. Don't get me wrong, it's horribly unfair to deny a child medication who is suffering horribly, but what do they learn ... "I need a pill to be okay." Whatever happened to the timeless adage, "This too shall pass"? I assume it's still around, but this passage is just way too slow for some. They are willing to bypass the learning in order to obtain immediate relief.

Dr. James M. Swanson, a psychologist at the University of California, Irvine, states, "There are no long-term lasting benefits from taking ADHD medications." He points out that mindfulness seems to be training the same areas of the brain that medication blasts. Mindfulness, or what I've been calling for years, the awareness of our awareness, helps reduce and minimize ADHD symptoms. Quality talk therapy with a kind and sensitive mindful approach gets to the root of the frustrations, rather than masking them for the duration of the dosage.

CHAPTER 8

Alan Schwarz, a Pulitzer Prize writer for the *New York Times*, wrote a startling front-page story that shocked some but was painfully familiar to those of us who have worked with addiction and the misuse of medication. Appearing in the Sunday, February 3, 2013 edition of *The New York Times*, the article was titled "Drowned in a Stream of Prescriptions."

It told the tragic story of Richard Fee, a handsome, articulate young man, a popular college class president, a fine baseball player, and a medical student-to-be. While in college, he acquired Adderall from some friends in order to help him with his studies. He immediately became addicted to the medication and was a master at skillfully lying to doctors, convincing them of his desire to study medicine and become a doctor himself. He persuaded them that his goals were being hampered by his distractibility, procrastination, and other symptoms that placed him solidly under the ADHD diagnosis.

Because of his confident and eloquent delivery, the majority of the doctors he met skipped well-established diagnostic procedures and renewed script after script, sometimes spending as little as five minutes with him.

Richard Fee deteriorated rapidly, and his parents were in the crosshairs of his addiction. After returning home, his mother noticed that he was becoming paranoid and delusional, putting tape over his computer's camera and his fingers in order not to leave prints for fear he was being spied upon. Following horrific conflicts with his family, hospitalizations, and erratic and aggressive behavior, Richard Fee hung himself in the closet of his apartment two weeks after his prescription had run out.

Ambitious and driven young adults are the fastest-growing segment of people consuming ADHD medication.

The data company I.M.S. Health found that "Nearly 14 million monthly prescriptions for the condition were written for Americans ages 20-39, two and a half times the 5.6 million just four years before." According to Schwarz's article students take stimulant pills to enhance school performance. For some students selling their meds are a real money maker during finals week. Anyone with a script can quickly fatten their bank balance. Are these not performance-enhancing drugs, the same ones that are forbidden in other venues?

In his article, Schwarz cited a study by Dr. David Berry, a professor, and researcher at the University of Kentucky, who co-authored a study comparing two groups of college students. One group was diagnosed with ADHD, and the other was asked to mimic the symptoms. When given a standard questionnaire that screened for ADHD, the two groups were indistinguishable from one another. Which means that any good actor can get a script.

Again, Adderall and its stimulant cohorts are classified by the Drug Enforcement Administration as a Schedule ll drug, the same as cocaine, due to their highly addictive properties. Even with supervised use, medications can trigger psychotic behavior or suicidal thoughts in 1 out of 400 patients, according to a 2006 study in *The American Journal of Psychiatry*. And to think, that was 15 years ago, imagine what it is now.

Before prescribing these drugs, Dr. Keith Connors from Duke emphasized that a detailed life history must be taken along with other sources of information, from parents, teachers, and/or friends in order to understand the distinctions and intricacies of a patient's personality, character, and difficulties.

If there is another way to help individuals deal with the frustrations that ADHD perpetuates, then let's exhaust those options. What we all need, especially children, is time and patience, as well as heavy doses of love, direction, and redirection. Again, medication should be the very last alternative, and in many cases, never the first option. We must treat the whole individual; ADHD is seldom found in an isolated area of impairment.

Stephen Hinshaw, a specialist in developmental psychology at the University of California, Berkeley was quoted in the *New York Times*, May 13, 2014, saying, "The time is ripe to explore the utility of nondrug interventions like mindfulness." Well, what do you know? I have been saying this for years. But I didn't use the word mindfulness. What I called it was awareness. Becoming aware of your awareness. I guess you could say in order to be hip with the times, "be mindful of your mindfulness."

Medication does not change our narrative, or the story we repeat over and over to ourselves. Medication might help us solve an academic issue, but it doesn't help with emotional flexibility. Flexibility and being open to new experiences are central to the idea of wellness and balance. We ignite change by challenging, then changing, our beliefs, habits, and expectations that don't serve our higher good. We need to add new experiences, not petrify our brains with a synthetic substance. We need to help ADHD children believe that they themselves are the source point of their change, not the medication.

CHAPTER 9

When Sleep Isn't Restful

> *"A ruffled mind makes a restless pillow."*
>
> ~ Charlotte Bronte

When treating ADHD, we often look for all the classic symptoms. For instance, procrastination, forgetfulness, impulsivity, disorganization, lack of attention control, etc. When we treat an adult and see these symptoms, we might assume they've limped along their whole life with untreated ADHD. But chronic sleep deprivation can mimic the symptoms necessary to meet the criteria for an ADHD diagnosis.

In American society, workdays have become longer while sleep schedules have shortened. Children today sleep less. And the quality of deep restful sleep is diminished. For many children, sleeplessness doesn't cause weariness or fatigue. For some, their systems get ratcheted up in order "not" to succumb to fatigue, the feeling that low energy brings. As a result, this loss of sleep can trigger hyperactivity.

The National Sleep Foundation found that 85 percent of teens lack adequate sleep. Today's adolescents sleep at least an hour less than they did 100 years ago.

Twenty percent of teenagers get less than five hours of sleep a night, while the average is six and a half hours. Most days are filled with 14 hours of non-stop activity. And when you add the narcotizing effects of the all-consuming electronic options (phones, tablets, computers, and video games), the effect is staggering. Sleep-deprived teens are at a higher risk for self-harm or suicidal thoughts. This sleep loss trend grew more extreme in the late 1980s and into the 1990s—a trend that paralleled the explosion of the ADHD diagnoses. Today, sleep deprivation, anxiety, and depression are at an all-time high for both teens and young adults.

Different studies have indicated many kids who are diagnosed with ADHD also find their sleep disturbed by breathing irregularities like apnea or snoring. Restless leg syndrome also disrupts and keeps children from dropping into delta sleep, our deepest sleep, not to mention worry, fear, and generalized anxiety.

Children with sleep deficiencies have been misdiagnosed with the all-encompassing ADHD tag. Sleep is a physiological drive that removes waste from the brain. We spend a third of our lives sleeping. Allan Rechtschaffen, one of the world's foremost sleep researchers, stated, "If sleep does not serve an absolutely vital function, then it's the biggest mistake the evolutionary process has ever made." If the only purpose for sleep is to cure sleepiness, then we've all been tricked. But more recent research has proven that restorative sleep is necessary for the optimal functioning of biological processes. Proper sleep promotes the healthy inner workings of the immune system, hormonal balance, emotional and psychiatric wellness, learning, and memory. As a bonus, throw in the cleansing of toxins from the brain. W.C. Fields said, "The best cure for insomnia is a lot of sleep." Wouldn't it be wonderful if it were just that easy?

Lack of proper sleep can result in loss of nerve cells in two regions of the thalamus, which is found in the brain's mid-region. The thalamus acts as a waystation for arriving sensory data to be inputted. The thalamus regulates emotional memory and produces what's called sleep spindles. Spindles are an important pattern of waves in the sleeping brain, that are evident on an electroencephalogram. One night of complete or even partial sleep loss can interfere with various bodily functions, one being a hormonal activity that protects against infections. For the ADHDer, the gumming up of the thalamus due to lack of sleep, added to the already compromised ability to absorb information during class, is doubly frustrating.

Sleep deprivation's greatest impact occurs in the brain. Sleeplessness affects how emotional memories get consolidated and then installed in memory. Sadly, sleep deprivation increases the installation of negative experiences. ADHDers already magnify their frustrations which increases the likelihood of depression. Studies of sleep apnea, a disruption of breathing, characterized by snoring and a gasping for air, can make the likelihood of major depression more probable.

I have seen that sleep deprivation doesn't always cause ADHD children to be sluggish and listless. Rather it induces them to become more hyperactive. When you're in deep water and you're not treading it with an active consistent stroke, you will go under. To stay afloat, you must energetically stir the water downward in order to stay upward. As it is with tired children, in order to stay awake they ratchet up their energy output, causing them to become unfocused, anxious, and quite disruptive. So, maybe what looks like ADHD sometimes isn't.

The increased expectation of physical and mental exertion, restrictive time commitments from over-scheduling, have decreased the amount of time kids and adults sleep. I was talking to a kid the other day about his baseball team's record. In my day we'd play 16 games a year, unless you made the playoffs then you would get a few more games. I asked him what his team's record was so far. He said that his team was just average. "We're 34 and 32." I turned and asked his mom, "How many games do they play?" She said, "Close to 75 and sometimes three games in one day if they are playing in a tournament out of town. But that's on the low end. There are some teams that play close to 100 games. Those are the elite teams." I'm sure this holds true for other sports like soccer, gymnastics, basketball, cheerleading, dance competitions, and numerous other activities.

Many children participate in a nonstop inexhaustible cornucopia of lessons, practices, tutoring, entertainment, community services, and religious studies. Where is the downtime? When do they get to hang around and just be a kid? Unfortunately, their downtime is on screens, or fast action electronic games, that don't give the mind and body much of a rest. I saw a picture of a 13-year-old female golf prodigy sitting on a curb, after placing high on the world stage. She was competing against women three times her age. Out of the spotlight, she sat eating an ice cream cone and playing in the dirt with a stick. An obvious difference in pressure and decorum. These routines of incessant activities really began to tilt life in the 90s, the same period where the tsunami of ADHD diagnoses began to swell.

When working with a family, I always insist on meeting with the parents or parent before I ever meet with the child. This is for a couple of reasons. First, I don't want the child sitting in the waiting room while he/she is being talked about like some specimen in a Petri dish. And second, I want to gauge how sound and stable the parents are. This way I can determine right off the bat whether or not this kid was blessed with loving, patient, and understanding parents or had been genetically assigned to what I refer to as "symptom escalators." As I mentioned, family weirdness and dysfunctionality are like stimulants or fertilizer to the impairments.

In our first sessions, I always inquire about sleep and often hear three predictable reports. The parent says, "He/she drops like a rock. When they hit the pillow they're out, there is no waking them." Secondly, I hear, "This poor little guy can't shut down his mind or body. He can't ever adjust himself enough to get comfortable." I refer to this as not being able to, "find their spot." Thirdly, I hear, "We just give him a pill, and by 8:30 or 9:00—*boom!*—the little rascal is knocked out, down for the count." Sleep isn't the answer to all ADHD frustrations but why not evaluate its effects. It might just help level the playing field.

A lot goes on in our brain and body at night. If a good percentage of your night is spent in unrest and turbulence, then the benefits of deep delta sleep are hindered. Memory and cognitive performances correlate strongly with delta sleep. A study from the February 2013 issue of *Nature and Neuroscience* showed that those deprived of sleep might not report that they feel any sleepier or less rested, but there is a clear indication that their cognitive skills and performance drop proportionately and continue to decrease over five nights of sleep loss or restriction. When an ADHDer lacks restorative delta sleep, then almost everything else may be compromised. We need to take seriously the role sleep disorders play in the creation or exacerbation of ADHD symptoms.

We can help ADHD kids learn how to steer their attention and direct the flow of mental energy toward a place of intentional rest and relaxation by teaching them about two of their *neurodevelopmental functions*.

The first neurodevelopmental function is the <u>awareness control system.</u> In the classroom, the ADHDer needs to be aware of "taking in and holding on" to instructions and lessons. But at bedtime, there needs to be more of a letting go rather than a holding on. When trying to drift off the ADHDer needs to drop the reins of their mind and let go. We can teach them to become interested in the space between thoughts where relaxation can occur.

When the dark cloud of mental weariness begins to hover over the ADHD kid, they do one of two things; they become manic and over-reactive, kicking off the covers or depleted and listless. Most ADHDer's brains don't want to surrender to the night even though they are besieged with weariness. Sometimes just helping a child turn off their regulator and slow things down, gives the hamster on their mind's wheel a chance to step off, lie down, decompress, and get some rest.

A second neurodevelopmental function is the ability to learn how to govern <u>sleep and arousal</u>. The relaxed confident belief that you "can" regulate restful sleep and wakefulness, is crucial to controlling and directing your mental energy. Achieving delta sleep is what reenergizes the brain and body. Delta sleep can be attained through relaxation, meditation, and guided imagery. The ADHDer needs to become mindfully aware of what's going on in the upper reaches of their mind. This intuitive sense of knowing what's happening is the first step in letting go and dimming their mind's overhead lamp. This form of letting go can be learned, developed, and installed so they can make the intentional effort to flip the switch so rest can begin. But as we know, things are hard before they become easier.

The ADHDer has a difficult time dialing down their mind and body, not just due to their wiring, but to the unanswered questions, baffling observations, and troubling encounters from earlier in the day. These problems begin to rumble, shoving their way onto the mind's center stage now that the body is trying to be inactive and decompress. It's hard to quiet down and contain an angry, sad, or rebellious mob of thoughts and concerns. Teaching the ADHDer to use their breath as a friendly guide, is an ancient practice that welcomes friendly fatigue.

For an ADHD individual, drifting into a peaceful night's journey can be anything but peaceable, especially if medication has been involved. Kids have told me that it's very uncomfortable to let go at night, especially if their minds have been bound by medicine all day. Now they are expected to let go. Kids have told me that when falling asleep the dropping into relaxation can sometimes awaken them with a jolt. Thus, they wake themselves up by falling asleep. The question for the ADHDer is, "How do you return to and sustain a restful state?" The answer is to restart the process of letting go peacefully and gently through prayer, breathing, imagery, and other sensory decompressors.

At the base of our brain, in the brain stem, there is something similar to a sleep thermostat that allows us to wind down. We can learn to activate and adjust the thermostat through relaxation techniques. Stretching before bed, comforting readings, a grateful and surrendering prayer, deep cleansing breaths, and numerous other approaches can help us decompress. Such practices provide us the chance to let go and disengage all cylinders. Nighttime is when the ADHDer should lay down their burdens. Nighttime is not the time to figure it all out. Not much gets solved late at night.

Also, let me suggest that boring and tedious reading can be a great sleep inducer. I've always been able to fall asleep relatively fast, but when I couldn't, maybe I should have pulled out an article on sewer district proposals in

Czechoslovakia. That would surely make my energy levels plummet rapidly, sinking my brain into a giant vat of sorghum.

For some ADHD children, sleep is like driving on a bumpy road with no shocks. Rocky sleep produces mental fatigue, which is often hard to recognize. In order for these children to battle their weariness, they shove their bodies into full throttle. When asked to complete tasks that require them to slow down and focus their mental energy on specific problems (e.g., mathematics, grammar, etc.), the brain sputters to a halt and a black cloud of lethargy and apathy enfolds their mind and body. Consequently, fatigue caused by a poor night's sleep forces the body to produce extra adrenaline to keep itself moving, like throwing gas on a spark in order to light a candle. To interrupt this cycle, I highly encourage stretching, or push-ups and sit-ups before getting in bed. A fatigued muscle is a relaxed muscle. Breathing exercises, soothing music, white noise machines, reading (something boring,) counting backwards at bedtime have all been known to help children drift off to sleep.

Parents need not despair. Children who experience sleep-arousal imbalance may be the next generation's night shift, writing novels late into the night, working in the ICU at a hospital, shipping overnight freight or doing talk radio. Throughout their childhood though, these future night-shifters are sentenced to daytime school with no parole until the age of 18.

CHAPTER 10

The Magic Balloon

*"The world is
full of magic things,
waiting for our senses
to grow sharper."*

~ W.B. Yeats

Years ago, my then five-year-old son, T.J., and I were driving along when I noticed he was in a particularly despondent mood. I pulled the car over and asked him what he was so upset about. He couldn't articulate his distress, but his eyes quickly filled with tears. I asked, "T.J., do you need a balloon?" Confused, he stared at me. I then pretended to pull an imaginary balloon from my shirt pocket and stretched it a few times. Placing my fingers on my lips I blew into the imaginary balloon. My other hand pretended to steady the balloon, indicating that it was getting larger with every breath.

I acted like I was holding the balloon in my hand like a big watermelon. I said, "TJ when I get really mad, I take a balloon and blow all my anger or sadness into it. Then I tie it up, throw it out the window and let the wind carry it away." I looked at the imaginary balloon in my hand, then back at him. "Would you like to try doing this?" He nodded, his cheeks now showing trails of tears. I got out of the car and joined him in the back seat. Then I looked into my pocket while asking, "What color would you like?" Pretending to fiddle around until I found the color he requested, I then proceeded to pull it from my pocket and stretched the make-believe inflatable, and held it up to his lips.

I asked, "Are you mad at mom?"

He said, "Yes." So, I told him to blow all that anger at Mom into the balloon. He pursed his lips and blew hard. "Are you angry at your little brother?" Again, the answer was a resounding, "Yes."

"Keep blowing," I said, moving my hand around to show him how much the balloon was inflating. "Are you angry at me, for not doing what you want sometimes?"

"Yes!" he yelled.

"Then blow," I pleaded, "blow!" I pretended the balloon was inflating as I made my hands look as if I was now holding a basketball. "Now tie it quickly," I demanded, "before any sadness or anger escapes."

This he pretended to do. "Now hold it," I said, handing it to him. He reached out his little hands and held the imaginary balloon out in front of him. I reached across his body and opened the window next to him.

"Now quick, throw it out, quick!" This he pretended to do, and we both stretched our necks out the window and watched the imaginary balloon sail up and away, far off into the sky. T.J. looked at me with a baffled but intrigued smile and asked, "Dad, is that magic?"

Children like analogies, examples, metaphors, and magic. Children understand things more clearly when you explain ideas in pictures. I've taught kids to chill out by turning down the heat in their brain and body, by using their ears as a dial. I tell them that this cools down inflamed parts of the brain. I've seen that stop a freak-out in its tracks before it ever fully blossomed.

Teaching ADHD kids to become aware of their own capacity to cool, compose and delay their reactions empowers them to return to a safe emotional baseline and take control of their emotional lives. To some, it might feel like pure magic. To a parent, a miracle.

Last November 2021, I visited my now 36-year-old son Air Force Sargent T.J. Scott, his wife, and my one year old granddaughter Elizabeth who is magic to me.

CHAPTER 11

The Dart Game That Isn't Fun

> *"For every minute you're angry, you lose 60 seconds of happiness."*
>
> ~ Ralph Waldo Emerson

Bad things happen when we leave a kettle on the stove for too long. It can boil over and scald whatever it meets, or evaporate and turn the kettle a fire red. The brain may be likened to a cauldron that contains our thoughts and emotions. When we ruminate over troubling thoughts and scenarios, we've essentially turned up the heat in our brain and body. We can also adjust the heat and let things simmer by intentionally reducing the temperature through relaxation, imagery, deep breathing, developing a language of comfort, exercise, prayer, or a mantra that reboots our brain. Whether using any or all of the aforementioned, it's important for the ADHDer to understand the origin of their discomfort, and what they can do to relieve it.

Some mental and physical discomfort is easier to avoid, some unavoidable. ADHD individuals experience a disproportionate amount of discomfort and frustration.

Some ADHDers learn more easily than others and are relatively happy-go-lucky because learning is working. Sadly, many others aren't so fortunate. They can't do the old "fake it till you make it" soft-shoe shuffle, and it's obvious. The social spotlights are glaring. If you're not making it academically, socially, or emotionally, everybody knows it. Coming face-to-face with our shortcomings can be startlingly painful. But when we accept and learn to tolerate the discomfort this awareness generates, we can respond by acknowledging that any change worth making will require some discomfort. Everything is hard before it gets easier. When we recognize our mistakes, we know what we need to work on. Oscar Wilde said, "Experience is the name we give mistakes." Our shortcomings and mistakes can be the connection between inexperience and wisdom. This awareness provides us the opportunity to fine-tune our thinking, normalize our perceptions and upgrade our behavior.

The inescapable physical and mental distress we all experience by simply living on this planet is what the Buddhists refer to as the "first dart." As long as we're alive, first darts will land. Sadness, disappointment, frustrations, anger, loss, and betrayal are all unavoidable. It's the rent we pay for occupying our wee bit of space on earth. We all will experience some form of this just because we exist. But it's the "second darts" that cause the real harm. Second darts are the ones we throw back at others, life, or ourselves. Second darts are what we do when we don't know what to do. This is where a majority of our suffering comes from. The second darts are our reactions to the first darts. But sometimes the second dart is not provoked by a first dart but triggered by some internal reaction that snags a memory. ADHDers believe they must react with second darts in order to guard their fragile dignity and self-worth.

The more anxiety, the more second darts get launched. For example, if something upsets or startles us, it triggers an emotional and physiological response in the body. Just the anticipation of a challenging or threatening event can have the same physiological impact as if the event were actually happening. This is because of the powerful effect the brain has on the body.

The brain's limbic system houses emotions, motivation, and memory, and is home to the <u>amygdala.</u> The amygdala responds to fear-evoking stimuli and is overly involved in the expression of anxiety. The amygdala is particularly reactive to social uncertainty, playing a vital role in social and emotional decision-making. The amygdala is an irascible little character, constantly sounding alarms and activating sirens in response to emotionally charged situations and provocations, whether real or imagined. Imagine a part of your brain that works like the robot from the TV series *Lost in Space*, rolling around the spaceship chirping, "Danger, danger!" Now imagine that robot rolling around your brain and throughout your body shouting out the same thing. The process works a little like this: The amygdala senses a threat, falls off-balance, freaks out, and sends signals to the <u>thalamus.</u> The thalamus is like a relay station that provides sensory information in the form of a warning to your brain stem. The brain stem then orders the release of <u>norepinephrine</u>, a neuromodulator that alerts and arouses the mind and body with, "Beware, beware." Anxiety then flushes through our body by way of the <u>sympathetic nervous system</u> (SNS) and the <u>hypothalamic-pituitary-adrenal-axis</u> (HPAA). These are cohesive systems, housed in the <u>endocrine system</u>, which sends signals to the major organs and muscle groups to announce, "Trouble is on the way." The hypothalamus regulates the brain's endocrine system, prompting the pituitary gland to signal the adrenal gland to release the "stress hormone" epinephrine (adrenaline) and cortisol. Epinephrine and cortisol aren't good for your system. Both increase your heart rate, moving blood in greater quantities throughout your body. The pupils in your eyes dilate as do the bronchioles in your lungs increasing your gas exchange thereby forcing your brain and body to respond more intensely. More intensity is exactly what an ADHD kid doesn't need. It's as if the gas pedal is stuck to the floor with no one at the wheel.

There are two important branches of the <u>autonomic nervous system</u> (ANS). The first is the <u>sympathetic nervous system</u> (SNS) which operates below the level of consciousness in order to regulate many bodily systems. It helps you adapt to changing conditions that you face throughout the course of a day. The SNS is responsible for readying the body for action.

The other branch is the <u>parasympathetic nervous system</u> (PNS). This is where we build the mind, body, and spirit connection. When you stimulate your PNS, you affect your physiology. You lower your stress level, calm down and assess the emotional and visceral storms in both the mind and body. Learning to intentionally relax comforts and quiets the anxious readiness of the SNS. The PNS conserves energy and creates feelings of peacefulness, calm, and contentment. Some call this the "rest and digest" system.

Obviously, it's quite valuable to our overall well-being to learn how to activate the PNS. The two branches—PNS and SNS—can be likened to a seesaw, both sides cannot be up at the same time. The SNS is like a dry bale of hay. A small spark can set it ablaze. ADHDers need to learn to detach themselves from the fray by taking deep breaths, inhaling slowly and deeply through their nose, and exhaling through pursed lips. Doing a three-count inhale and a six-count exhale increases bi-lateral stimulation. Breathing to this count relaxes and stabilizes the sympathetic nervous system because the parasympathetic system is pumping the brakes bringing the seesaw to an even balance. Relaxed breathing is much like gently rocking your mind back and forth as if you were soothing a baby. This mild activation aids in the restoration of peace, the desire for achievement, the rekindling of enthusiasm, and the restructuring of wholeness and contentment. And for an added bonus, it creates a distancing effect between the ADHDer and their problems.

Teaching an ADHD child to steer their own mind is better than telling them "Take this pill." Threatening strict behavioral consequences in a harsh tone doesn't help anything. By assuring an ADHD child that you are with them for the long haul and that you won't abandon them even in their worst moments, creates a space inside them where the parasympathetic system can prevail, preventing the impulse to fling second darts.

CHAPTER 12

Healing the Spirit

> *"All the world is full of suffering, but it's also full of overcoming."*
>
> ~ Helen Keller

ADHD personalities respond well to emotionally focused therapy that emphasizes feelings, problem-solving, relaxation, and guided imagery. They particularly like releasing and rewriting the self-talk and internal narrative that's both baffling and battering. I help ADHDers learn to break their rotating narratives of self-doubt by helping them identify explicit indictments that maim and deplete their spirit.

Make it clear to the ADHDer that other people's external points of view that torment their internal makeup are not valid, and we waste a great deal of time believing and giving them credibility. Letting go is liberating. Learning how their spirit's been diminished and how they can resuscitate it is hopeful and redeeming. We all need to ask ourselves, "Do these specific thoughts help me or hurt me? Do these relationships nourish and fertilize my spirit or weaken it? Are the people telling me these things operating in my best interest?"

ADHD kids need to be consistently reminded and exposed to the riches of both their mind and spirit. Doing so is grounding and nurtures a basic faith in themselves which they can carry around privately and pull it up when they need it the most. We all need moment-to-moment-to-moment emotional restoration. Here in Kansas, we say, "If you don't like the weather, just wait an hour." The same is true for the ADHD individual's mood and mind. Although they can get stuck in un-nourishing mindsets, they are soon off to the next batch of incoming stimuli. Unfortunately, with every frustrating or humiliating moment, a bit of neural residue is left behind, taking the gloss off their spirit. I've talked with kids about cleaning up the biohazards of other people's insensitivities. They very much like the idea.

People have come up to me following a talk asking, "Do you ever get depressed?" The answer is, "Maybe, but not very long. I know at the end of each baseball season I descend into a deep depression for, maybe a few hours. My mind is usually on to the next slide." By helping the ADHDer interpret their narrative, the story they tell themselves about themselves, the dialogue that loops around inside their head, they can learn to reboot their brain before it defaults into a gloomy and doomful place. Learning to engage in a language of comfort that pacifies, forgives, supports, and revives one's sense of worth and value, in that very moment, is the beginning of healing the spirit.

Each stage of development has escalating risks and responsibilities the ADHDer needs to be keenly aware of. Awareness can be enhanced with a combination of emotional, spiritual, and meditative practices. All of this balanced proportionately then seasoned with just the right amount of cognitive therapy, encourages inner peace. Helping the ADHDer get down in the subterranean level of their emotional being, helps peace last longer and makes it easier to retrieve when it flees. Peacefulness, joy, contentment, and persistent hope encourages a growth mindset.

It's important to teach ADHDers sayings or mantras they can use as an emotional or situational disinfectant. Certain words can right the canoe when things get a bit turbulent. I've always loved this rhyme penned by W.W. Bartley, an American philosopher born in 1934. He wrote:

> For every ailment under the sun
> There is a remedy or there is none
> If there lay one try and find it
> If there be none, never mind it.

Just think of all the unnecessary weirdness that could have been avoided if we had been taught how to "never mind it" when we were young. Our spirit would have been much less challenged.

The ADHD spirit yearns for peace, pleasure, and involvement. Of course, we all want peace, and the pleasure that comes from getting what we want is nice but somewhat temporary. But if you experience something pleasurable, that's unexpected, the reward lasts a bit longer, but not much. However, if you wanted and expected something good and got it, the reaction is more one of relief, and then you're on to your next pursuit or responsibility. But for the ADHDer being involved, being part of, connecting with, and experiencing inclusion, runs deep, and has a much longer shelf life than things that can be repossessed, stolen, or burned. We value ourselves to the degree we feel valued. In studies on happiness, it's been concluded that the two most important components that lead to contentment are feelings of connectedness and reciprocity. ADHDers feel that if they give and give, then people will like them. Sort of like buying your way into a relationship. ADHDers cater to others because just being themselves has never been enough. People enjoy being catered to, but they eventually despise the neediness of the ADHDer. You can't just give and pretend you don't need something back. Healthy and kind reciprocity fuels the spirit.

The spirit is fed when the ADHDer learns to cultivate and harvest their own peace and pleasure. Once learned, it takes a lifetime of practice, refining, and upgrading this intentional act of self-compassion. Teach them how to suspend and lengthen the experience of "a good feeling." Holding it longer in their window of awareness consolidates the good feeling and encodes it into the cells and neurons of the brain. These new neuronal pathways toward wholeness feed and fortify their spirit. Be sure to teach them that heightening their awareness is not a one-time event, but a delightful, sometimes difficult journey within. It takes a lifetime of gentle midcourse corrections.

Dr. Richard Davidson, a professor of psychology and psychiatry at the University of Wisconsin-Madison, teaches about "affective styles." Affective styles refer to how we go about regulating our emotions. It varies greatly from individual to individual. There are two types of positive affect. The first he refers to as the "pre-goal attainment positive affect." This is the satisfying feeling you earn as you make progress toward your goal. The second is the "post-goal attainment positive affect." This arises once you have reached your goal. Often, with the ADHDer, the "post-goal attainment" effect, doesn't seem to provide a sense of satisfaction lasting long enough to consolidate and install into their memory bank of accomplishments.

You can see, hear, and feel an ADHD kid's spirit swell when they know they are heading toward accomplishing a goal. But oddly, when they reach it, their reactions and receptiveness to their accomplishment can appear quite underwhelming. For many ADHD individuals, they base their assessments on whether or not the goal they accomplished was fun or not fun, hard, or easy. They must learn to ask themselves, "Am I better off by doing it, or was I trying to satisfy someone else, and keep them off my back," which are both good reasons to "do it." The mental energy required to meet a goal or change a habit is hard to summon for the ADHD spirit unless of course it's entertaining and engages the senses. If there is no visible gain or pleasurable bump on the ecstasy scale, then the spirit tends to stay dormant. Though our spirit has no bounds, our everyday level of happiness is said to have a set point determined by our genetic inheritance. So, no matter how high we soar into the cosmos riding upon the wings of glee, we inevitably return to our brain's default level of happiness, a set point determined by our genes. But just because we have a certain set of genes, doesn't mean they'll be expressed. And there is no rule that states, "This is where I must remain." Though each of us has a distinctive level of happiness, our spirit can oscillate up and down, back, and forth. We can learn to raise the set-point of both our spiritual and emotional world.

Sure, who isn't drawn to the experiences which provide us joy, pleasure, and happiness. But there is a shelf life to these sensations. ADHD individuals are known to try and squeeze the last drop from every event or sensation, then immediately feel empty when it's over. Their spirit needs to be constantly replenished. But the sooner the child learns to accept the inevitability of beginnings and endings, the easier it will be for them to recalibrate their spirit, believing much good still lies ahead. Understand, our spirit is never static; it always wants to grow toward fulfillment

CHAPTER 13

The Best Time of the Week for 13 Straight Years

> *"Children understand and remember concepts best when they learn from direct personal experience."*
>
> ~ Joseph Cornell

For 13 straight years, I facilitated a support group called "Running, Relaxation and Support" designed for children with ADD, ADHD, and other emotional and social frustrations. The group met twice a week on Monday and Friday, for eight weeks. There would be a two-week break between sessions, then another group would form, often with many carrying over from the previous sessions. Childhood is like practice offstage, and I created a safe place for them to practice life. At the start of each eight-week session, I would tell them, "Through the course of the next eight weeks, I will see you in some of your best moments and some of your worst. Not one of us will finish ahead, there will be no first place, and no one will be left behind. We will all finish together, with no judgments or evaluations."

Everyone contributed in their own unique way. We created a safe place and space, that was loving, supportive, and at times very difficult. In this community, all the members were valued, tolerated, celebrated, and listened to. Imagine that—being listened to. We met from 4:00 to 5:15, but more often 5:30, since no one wanted to leave, and time management was never one of my greatest strengths.

Each group would begin with all of us meeting in the front room of a fitness facility called Health Plus. I enthusiastically greeted each child as they arrived. In turn, the early arrivals would welcome each member who followed. I could easily read the tenor of their school day or sense the tone and atmosphere in the car ride over with their parents, by just observing their expressions. The countenance etched on their faces said it all. The moods ranged from bland, mad, and exhausted to turbo-charged with joy and excitement. Most of them were very happy to see one another. They would burst into dialogue as if they were finishing a sentence from the previous session. Some of these kids received very little attention from their peers throughout the school day. It was so cool just to see them experience "welcoming" and the sense that their presence was valued.

Once the group had gathered, we'd transition (walk first, shuffle fast, then burst) into the gym. Here they could have free unstructured time (15-20 minutes) where they could kick balls, shoot baskets, hang out, talk, huff and buff, glower, walk the perimeter or just celebrate the moment. They could do whatever it was they needed to do in order to decompress, except being mean, nasty, or rude. This was a great opportunity for me to observe them interacting unstructured, like a big laboratory. When I would detect someone's frustrations, I'd try to help them dislodge themselves from the mindset they were stuck in. The kids whose medications were wearing off benefited the most from this unstructured time. By movement, they were able to fast-forward the discomfort of withdrawal their bodies and minds were experiencing. The gym time helped them feel unencumbered. They had free and unstructured time to either sit or frolic. Some children entered the gym like bucking broncos, immediately engaging in something or with someone, while others would cautiously circle the group, seeking out a comfortable and indiscreet place where they could merge with the pack.

The medications that contained and suppressed them throughout the day were now being challenged by their natural zeal and in some cases volcanic energy. You could visibly see how contorted and captive they likely felt inside. It took some kids quite a while to trust their own instinctual data and untie themselves and merge comfortably with the freedom offered them in an open gym.

When 20 minutes of gym time came to an end, they all would sit against the wall, under the basketball goal. Here, I would see how many free throws I could make in a row. This small bit of time gave them a chance to get it together, before transitioning to the group room. By shooting free throws, I modeled for them optimism, mood management, and determination. I would pick someone to rebound for me, which was always a popular job. During many sessions, there was a ten-year-old boy named Tucker. When my count of made free throws started to rise, Tucker would get so excited he would spring to his feet and start dancing. He soon earned his own space where he would do what became known as the ever-so-popular, "Tucker Dance," which was meant to bring me good luck. Some kids couldn't contain themselves witnessing Tucker's infectious freedom. They would jump to their feet joining Tucker in his free-form tribal stomp. What I wanted to model for the kids was the optimism that I've always felt. I would anticipate doing quite well, out loud, so they could hear my approach. But if I didn't make very many in a row, my demeanor wouldn't change either way; meaning I wouldn't slam the ball down, belittle myself, forecast never-ending defeat, or give up on myself and life. Some days, I couldn't make five shots in a row, other days I could nail 15-20. But on this one day, this one day, the heavens rained free throws. I got on a roll setting my all-time record of 36 free throws in a row. You talk about excitement; the crowd was in a frenzy, and Tucker was coming up with dance moves that were foreign to all mankind.

I believed that I was going to make the shots. I asked them to encourage me by using the same words they would want to hear. Some kids were quite inspiring saying, "Good job, Tom! You can do it; you can do it!" Occasionally, an individual or a small temporary faction would form, attempting to hex my efforts with uncensored pessimism and gloom. The majority would pounce, immediately squelching such insolence. They would expose the recalcitrant members like a raw pig soufflé at a vegan picnic. The group refused to let the positive and grateful atmosphere that we'd created be hijacked by negativity. We created an environment where it was okay to feel down, and even non-expressive, but never okay to be mean or rude.

The group would transition often from one setting to another throughout the hour and a half. Anyone who is even vaguely familiar with the personalities of ADHD kids and their behavioral idiosyncrasies knows that getting them all to move in one direction simultaneously is like trying to push pudding. Before we would transition to another space, I would assign someone to lead the line and another to pull up the rear. They took this momentary sense of leadership and responsibility quite seriously. If they were leading the line, you can bet that no one would pass or cut them. Those who brought up the rear made sure no one dawdled.

We would shift from the front room to the gym and the gym to the aerobics room. Entering the aerobics room, the members would be instructed to pick up a mat and either get in a circle, if we needed to talk first or find an isolated spot in the room for meditation and relaxation. Invariably, a kid or two would start swirling in circles, mats extended from their outstretched arms like a helicopter propeller. This was a very predictable phenomenon; a sort of motor ecstasy that provided a fleeting little buzz.

Once seated in the circle, we would start with a silent check-in. One at a time, each child would go around the entire circle and make direct eye contact with each member of the group. They had to stay connected for no less than five seconds. No scanning was allowed. Interestingly, when someone felt they weren't looked at long enough, or deeply enough, they would demand that a connection be made, even if it was someone they weren't particularly connected to. They all wanted to be seen. Once they had rounded the circle and had connected with everyone individually, they would then say, "I'm in," conveying that they were present and committed to one another and the process. We then shared thoughts, feelings, and events of the past few days and the previous 20 minutes in the gym. We would deal directly with our immediate concerns by sharing, not the "rainbows and shadows," but "what was good and what sucked." We celebrated and praised the good, while also offering support and concern for another member's plight. Kids would offer advice on how to "un-suck" things. I would ask them to share a couple of things they were proud of. This could include any action, thought, effort, or accomplishment they felt good about, <u>except</u> video games. I quickly discovered that there was no end to that dialogue once it got started.

When sharing in a group, one must be sensible and not dominate the time by infusing one's opinion into every silent moment. While sitting in the circle, each member had the option to pass, though I don't recall many who did throughout the 13-year span. In fact, prattling on and on is a characteristic that needs to be harnessed before the group members would glaze over like a donut and lose interest. Keeping the interest of an ADHD crowd isn't easy unless of course, you match their eccentricities and weirdness. If they could keep the group's interest, you'd see immediate relief because they were "feeling felt." "Feeling felt" is what we experience when we're being listened to and taken seriously by others. This often came after a day of feeling marginalized, shunned, and sometimes just blatantly rejected by their peers.

If two kids had gotten into an argument or scuffle during gym time, I would immediately assemble a kangaroo court, witnesses, and all. I'd give each kid an opportunity to state their case, and as they would scramble to uphold their innocence, it was often immediately clear as to who was responsible, especially if the truth was corroborated by witnesses. I'd help the guilty, without shame, blame, or humiliation, accept responsibility for their destructive or insensitive role in that moment. I taught them how to feel the freedom and relief that came from promptly admitting when they were wrong. Lord knows, there were plenty of opportunities to practice getting over things. I showed them how to audibly say, "Let's move on." Hanging on to uncomfortable thoughts and feelings until everything goes our way was not a solution. I reiterated that learning to become comfortable with our discomfort provides us with the opportunity to move our uneasiness to a place of evaluation. I'd ask, "Do you want to be solution-oriented or problem-bound?" Some kids have had their esteem diminished and their character assassinated for so long, it's as if they had become card-carrying professional victims. Feeling happy and in control felt foreign to them. We all made an agreement not to tolerate being a victim. After determining who was responsible for the scuffle or disagreement, the responsible party, while making direct eye contact would apologize and say, "I'm sorry, will you forgive me?" Sincerity was paramount. If it wasn't, then we wouldn't quit until it was. Group members would orbit around these corrective moments, riveted by the goings-on. You could feel a collective sense of relief when the two combatants shook hands. The forgiver would then be instructed to say, "It's okay, I forgive you." We immediately completed the past.

For some, this was the first time frustrating interactions and emotional discord ended on a positive note as opposed to holding themselves or others in scorn. It was so gratifying watching the kids, their dignity still intact be able to erect healthy boundaries and be vulnerable at the same time. It was as if they were maturing right in front of my eyes. Even if it was fleeting, and they age-regressed three minutes later, the flavor of peace was tasted, the seeds were planted, and the negative weeds uprooted in their mind's garden. Repetitively practicing these teachings of forgiveness helps it become expected and more naturally accepted by the ADHDer. Peaceful settlements are so restorative and feel darn right good. Such treaties literally change the brain's chemistry, clearing out the old and creating more room to install the good.

As I said, with ADHD kids, the opportunity to practice what they'd just learned would occur immediately. But what always amazed me was watching two kids work through a difficult moment, then run off together to play, imbued with a new sense of safe vulnerability and respect for one another. Vulnerability creates closeness. The other members and I would give the two adversaries a round of applause for letting go of whatever it was that stunk up the place, thanking them for creating a better atmosphere for everybody involved. We seldom get an ovation for doing the right thing, but such kind acknowledgment always made them feel a bit sheepish as the relief and pride would begin to shine across their faces. They both had repaired the moment, which I would illuminate with reinforcing praise.

The swifter justice is applied the more effective the consequence and influential the lesson. This seldom happens within the course of a school day due to other kids vying for attention while acting out or simply trying to manage their own personal dysfunction and dissatisfactions. Then of course there are the kids who want to pounce on the ADHDer's vulnerability while trying to prevent them from ever getting a foothold of peace and contentment.

The same goes for family settings, where life is often rushed. Incompleteness runs rampant and individuals are left frayed when difficulties are never resolved, just stored. With ADHD kids, things need to be broken down and explained in manageable, discernable, palatable portions. The ADHDer needs to verbalize why, how, and what. "Why" things got broken? "How" things got fixed? And "what" they felt once the situation was resolved. Our groups proved to themselves over and over that resolution was possible.

Teaching kids how to detach from unhealthy entanglements, even when not immediately resolved, is a victory. If a kid was on a rant, and everyone had given proper time and attention to his/her story, I trained group members to raise their hands and say, "Enough is enough. Complete the past and move on." In no way was this interpreted as rude or insensitive. Rather, it was learning how to put a cap on things so that others could contribute and feel welcomed. The goal was for everyone to collectively return to baseline and resume the business of simply being and enjoying themselves with no impression management necessary.

Following circle time, we would place our mats throughout the room for relaxation and meditation. I'd turn off the lights, and the kids would block any incoming light from the windows with the extra mats, ensuring a peaceful ambiance. This special time provided them the instruction and opportunity to create a safe space inside, a refuge if I may, to relax, breathe, and let go. We'd then baste anywhere from 15-25 minutes in peace, hope, and the goodness that each of us possessed. They experienced an atmosphere of safety and a heightened awareness of the transformative significance of that very moment. We'd focus intently on our breathing, inhaling hope and exhaling despair, inhaling peace while exhaling anxiety and revenge, inhaling confidence while exhaling doubt. These self-supporting and community-building meditations cultivated compassion and peace, within themselves and toward one another. Their bodily awareness, their interoceptive-ness enhanced as they learned to listen to messages their bodies were sending their brains. Their minds were like frequent fliers, but during the meditations and guided imagery, their thoughts became grounded as they learned to tether themselves to their very next breath. Some kids would fall asleep, and some kids would fake being asleep when it came time to rise. Imagine that ... an ADHDer pretending to be asleep. That's a great exercise within itself. Due to their agitated brains and bodies, some kids would have a hard time finding a spot, "their spot," they would call it, and struggled to get comfortable, flipping around like a fish out of water. Many of them would experience the withdrawal that takes place when coming off their medication. You could see those neurons just firing away throughout their brain as their bodies would respond accordingly. It was sad to see how accustomed they were to such discomfort. These were meant to be serene, cathartic times, and our efforts were intended to override the agitated amygdala with the loving and soothing prefrontal cortex. It was calm, and it was peaceful until one member would decide to bring down the house by dazzling the masses with a rip-roaring fart.

Imagine 15 ADHD kids all lying on mats, in a variety of restful poses, setting aside their frustrations, overriding any impairments or opinions of others, and just breathing. All of them had been schooled in the wonders of neuroplasticity. They knew that in these moments they were literally rewiring their brains. I'm sure I could have won some bets with their teachers and peers as to the likelihood of young Mary or Billy demonstrating such control, after spinning around like the Tilt-a-Whirl at the state fair an hour earlier. It was a precious and treasured sight.

In no way do I even pretend to know the Bible, but I have caught the main gist of some passages. There's a passage that I found soothing in my worst times. Philippians 4:8-9 suggests: "Whatever things are true, whatever things are noble, whatever things are just, whatever things are pure, whatever things are lovely, whatever things are of good report, if there is any virtue and if there is anything praiseworthy meditate on these things." That we did.

We focused on the good and the positive, not just that which was present in that moment, but the good that was yet to come. They needed to convince both their mind and body that they "can learn to relax," despite some of their unsolved problems. This is what they needed to believe and then feel. This was hope management in action, as opposed to being battered by a litany of what "Should be," "Ought to be," and "Must be." What "they weren't," never made it into our meditative practices. If by chance some negative thought would slip into their mind, I'd have them challenge the thought by asking, "What is your message?" They got it, illuminated it, learned from it then ushered it right out the backdoor.

Humans are more willing to talk about drama and tragedy rather than the nice gentleman or lady at the store, or the beautiful walk in the park, or the great song they heard on the radio that moved them to tears. That's why it's so important to inspire all kids to first notice, then embrace, the things they're grateful for. You never notice your nose until it gets plugged up. Thank your damn nose right now if it's working properly. Notice the good by going on gratitude hunts. I'm not talking about searching for million-dollar moments of success and victory, but experiences as simple as common courtesy, affection, respect, patience, dignity, and gentleness. These sensations need to be illuminated and held in conscious awareness for an extended period of time in order to be consolidated and filed in long-term memory.

While in the circle, the kids were encouraged to identify topics that pushed them into emotional quicksand or a defensive posture. For instance, like having a mean big brother or sister, or a teacher who doesn't understand that you "are trying" and you "do care." A mom or dad who will not allow certain video games; a mother who won't allow sleepovers; a friend who chooses not to be one anymore; a parent who refuses to let you wear the clothing you believe defines you. There was never a shortage of material.

The kids helped each other learn to steer their minds away from despair and stuckness. I taught them that stuckness was a developmental arrest, and when they get stuck, they become rigid and inflexible. We practiced becoming flexible and accepting. I reiterated over and over, that being flexible, and patient just might be their saving grace. We imagined putting up signs along the roadside of their thinking. "Discomfort and Despair-Ville 1/2 mile." "Resist and Retaliate Township 1 mile." Or "Warning—Bridge Might Be Covered with Bad Memories—Proceed with Caution." "Mandatory Homework Ahead: Just Do It." Another sign might read, "Danger: Unfair and Non-Negotiable Parent Around Next Bend—Detach Immediately." While another might read, "Explosive Topic-Don't Go There." They learned what experiences triggered them. And how to become vigilant, not adhering to the lure of the signs. We worked to stay on the "good" highway. If they found themselves traveling down one of those ramps, they would learn not to travel deep into these townships, but to hit the brakes, make a U-turn and get back on "Hope Highway."

I taught them how to immediately sense, locate and identify triggers in their bodies. For instance, the heart starts to speed up, they hold their breath, they feel driven to act either verbally or physically, the head gets hot, their fists and teeth clench. Or they sense the fear of exposure and the rush of shame and cortisol flooding through their systems. Whatever it might be, the kids were taught to imagine warnings, like tornado sirens or fluorescent double lines in the middle of their minds' highways that were not meant to be crossed. With such advanced notice, it became hard to justify traveling in that direction knowing it would bring no positive results.

Nonetheless, ADHD kids constantly do the wrong things for the right reasons. One of their favorite refrains is, "It's not fair." The number one thing Bill Gates shared at a graduation commencement in his highly publicized list of the "Ten Things You Didn't Learn in High School" was, "Life is unfair, so get used to it."

Following circle time and meditation, it was time to run. If it were inclement weather, we'd go upstairs to the indoor track. But if it was nice out, we'd travel along a beautiful running/bike trail. We seldom ran, walked, or jogged less than two miles and the beautiful running trails wandered along the side of a creek. The kids referred to the water as the "babbling brook." Everything was handled in a democratic fashion. Votes were held by a show of hands whether to stay in or go outside. The "babbling brook" always seemed to win out.

After heavy rains, the brook didn't just babble but became a rushing creek. The water was like a magnet that drew bodies into it. The kids would, or would not, peel their shoes and socks and wade up and down the canal. Some kids would squat down and get chin-deep, some would just insert a toe or two, while others never entered. I had the privilege of enjoying some of the members from third or fourth grade all the way to high school. How cool is that!

Once we were finished jogging, we'd return to the front room of the fitness center, reuniting the kids with their parents. There would be a quick synopsis of the day's joys and frustrations. Due to strict confidentiality, no names were ever mentioned, and no parent was to ever punish their child outside the group, for what occurred inside the group. Again, I reiterated, "I will see you in some of your best moments, and some of your worst moments and we will make it through all of them." So, if the group or an individual had a particularly tough day, I would ask the kids in front of the parents, "Would you like me to share with your folks what went on today?" In these cases, I would get a resounding "NO," and their confidentiality preserved and their trust in me enhanced. When there were outstandingly hilarious moments, breathtaking acts of kindness and compassion, or extraordinary efforts made, I would brag all over the child using his/her name, specifically praising their deed or effort. That would be followed by resounding applause directed at that child. Just acknowledging how far they ran generated applause from members and parents.

Sometimes walking back into the facility, a kid would approach me and quietly ask, "Would you say something good about me in front of my mom?" I would assure them that I would, so they could count on something positive coming their way. ADHD kids so badly want their parents to believe that they're inherently good. A child's self-esteem is dependent on whether or not they're the type of kid their parent approves of. How often does an ADHD kid get drenched in approval? How often have your goodness and efforts ever been acknowledged with a round of applause on Monday and Friday around 5:15 p.m.? The kids would lap it up like a kitten would cream.

Friday was the day we feasted. At the beginning of Friday's group, while in the waiting room, before entering the gym, I would assign two kids to take everyone's order and deliver it in advance to Winstead's, a famous Kansas City hamburger joint (since 1947), which was right across the street. This is where we would finish our runs. Fries, ice cream, onion rings, and drinks awaited us. Such delicacies were well-earned following what were usually emotionally, academically, and behaviorally challenging weeks. Two days of group therapy and running a total of no less than four miles was no easy shake. The rule was that no one could spend more than two dollars. This was to avoid having "the privileged" devour a triple cheeseburger, fries, onion rings, and a banana split in front of everyone else.

The food portion of the week, just like free time in the gym, was a laboratory for me. Here, I could observe their interactions with one another in a public setting. "Please and thank you" was mandatory language directed at the servers. Occasionally, a kid would have a tantrum or meltdown in the restaurant due to getting the wrong order or concerns over seating arrangements. I was moved by some of the young servers, who were so compassionate, polite, and accommodating when a kid would have a freak-out. They would comfort the child with words, show concern, and often deliver a free therapeutic order of fries for the kids. It was very touching.

Customers who thought they would be enjoying a late lunch or early Friday evening dinner, were either amused or aghast, when 15 hot, hungry ADHD kids would come traipsing through the door in what I'm sure seemed like a never-ending procession of winded, proud, and happy sweaty bodies. It seemed like every Friday was a mini holiday for us. We were celebrating ourselves for the accomplishments achieved and efforts extended. On Mondays, I would announce, "Today we run, and Friday we FEAST." This would always be followed by fists pumping, high fives, and extended celebration that had to eventually be squelched since most ADHD kids don't recognize their fatigue point.

Two of the group's goals that I shared with them over and over throughout the eight-week session were, first, they were going to learn to make sense of their illustrious thoughts and overly sensitive minds, while intentionally relaxing and steering their attention. Secondly, they were going to learn to sense, study and gain jurisdiction over their thoughts, bodies, and motion. It's a great relief for an ADHD kid to understand that much of the anxiety, panic, and anger they experience was not always the result of a neurochemical glitch. But the life they're experiencing and their place in it played a major role. However, it was their responsibility to figure out what's going on, so they don't believe themselves to be crazy, flawed, or defective. I told them, "Don't believe everything your mind tells you. Listen more to your heart, and with practice, you'll learn to get your mind on your side."

On the last day of each eight-week session, we'd meet at Pizza Shoppe. At the beginning of every eight-week session, I would choose a group leader from the previous session to help me manage the herd. To be selected as a leader, the member would have needed to model self-regulation, respect, patience, and fortitude. I'd pay them five dollars a group, which was ten bucks a week for a total of $80 bucks. It was on this last day at the pizza parlor I'd bring the leader to the front of the room and present them with a check for $80 dollars. I would suggest they not save a penny and thank them for their help. While families and group members feasted on pizza, I would bring each kid up individually, to the front of the room and spend a few minutes sharing moments of triumph, flashes of brilliance, bursts of humor, kindness, and recovery from a freak-out or just a bad day. Members would eagerly wave their hands while bouncing in their chairs, wanting to be the next one called up. They all wanted to be seen and bragged on, which for some was quite transformative in itself. I would decorate them with honor, approval, and praise. All this was witnessed by their parents and siblings, who might seldom experience the positive interactions that I described. I would then thank each kid publicly for the patience they had with me and my ADHD.

It felt so good to watch the kids absorb admiration and recognition. When a plant leans toward a window to absorb any light, it can, it's called phototropism. These kids were the same way. They would lean into me, lapping up and absorbing my verbal tributes.

The kids who experienced a tough time managing themselves and merging with others, who I had to continually monitor, were praised for putting up with my impatience at times. But deep down, they realized that my words were delivered in the spirit of love and support, emphasizing constructive growth and preventative measures, to make now better, so that later is easier. We fortified one another's strengths, italicized our goodness, and expressed appreciation for our individual uniqueness.

One kid said to me, "Mr. Scott, you can be so mean in such a loving way!" I had to stop and reinterpret that as meaning direct, and sometimes blistering, but always in the context of respect and admiration. Most all interactions ended with a smile, forgiveness, and a hug of encouragement.

We ran, relaxed, celebrated, honored, meditated, shared, quarreled, negotiated, resolved conflicts, forgave, laughed, cried, comforted, held one another accountable, problem-solved, made gentle inner corrections, fixed ruptured moments, feasted, showed vulnerability, swam, apologized, waded in creeks, and uncovered the goodness in one another.

Humans gravitate toward the sources which help them feel accepted and hopeful. In this case, it was me and the other members. The group allowed one another to grow at their own pace. The goodbyes were long, and the kids demanded a promise from one another. The promise was that they would gather again in two weeks when the next session began.

Hal Higdon, a well-known writer from *Runner's World,* flew to Kansas City to spend the day interviewing me and observing the group. He wrote a very nice article, "Getting Their Attention," which appeared in the July 1999 issue. Higdon witnessed the group in action and wrote of their goodness, innocence, and effort, reporting that by the end of each eight-week session most of the kids had run 35-40 miles.

This wasn't just exercise but biweekly adventures within themselves and with others. We were all momentary stars. The excitement, authenticity, sincerity, humor, kindness, growth, and compassion these kids exhibited, and the respect and appreciation they bestowed upon me, has been one of the most wonderful and gratifying parts of my professional life: twice a week for two hours and 30 minutes for 13 straight years, I got to love them.

CHAPTER 14

The Limbic System and the Wonderful Prefrontal Cortex

> *"In any given moment*
> *we have two options:*
> *To step forward into growth,*
> *or step back into safety."*
>
> ~ Abraham Maslow

The part of the brain called the amygdala, located in the limbic region, is responsible for our emotional life and the management of memories. Memories affect your entire body, especially in regard to the fear response.

I can't emphasize enough the importance of helping the ADHD individual understand the limbic system. Kids enjoy learning about new and fascinating aspects of their bodies and being. It just needs to be presented in pictures, in a way that's clever and interesting, or you'll lose them.

The limbic system is the brain's emotional center. When upheavals arise, they can result in horrible and sometimes irreversible consequences saturated with fear, anxiety, anger, sadness, and trepidation. When we are in a place of peace and calm, experiencing a sense of equilibrium, our mind and body feel well-oiled and flows smoothly.

When we freak out, become agitated or depressed, our mind's crankcase springs a leak and splatters limbic oil all over everything, grinding to a halt the gears of wellness and balance.

The amygdala, which resides in the land of limbic, is forever over-reacting, ginning up anxiety, stoking fear, fetching indignance, while becoming hypervigilant, on guard, and persnickety. The amygdala often incites an immediate survival response that's disproportionate to the real or imagined threat. It's like the robot from *Lost in Space*, rolling around yelling, "Danger, danger!" The last thing the ADHD child needs, much less any of us for that matter, is for the amygdala to constantly be running the show.

The amygdala will look for and register negative events, information, tones, and facial expressions faster and more acutely than the positive ones. When entering an unfamiliar setting, ADHD children have shared with me that they immediately scan for people who look unfriendly or unsafe. "I look first for people who probably won't like me." That's the amygdala's doing.

The limbic system is responsible for informing you whether something is safe or not. "Is this good or bad?" The limbic region is pivotal, determining how we form relationships and our emotional involvement with others. It plays a key regulatory role that distributes and receives hormones throughout the body.

Traumatic, shameful, and demoralizing events activate limbic responses. Even minor frustrations can quickly spread like a brush fire becoming a major cortisol-infused freak-out. Cortisol is a steroidal hormone produced in the adrenal gland, that's released into the blood during times of stress. Cortisol puts our entire system on "high alert."

The amygdala is the brain's early warning system that from birth has memorized the emotional tones of our life's experiences. It files and stores anything that could serve as a warning of trouble ahead. So, when repetitive frustrations accumulate, as they do with ADHDers, the limbic system prepares the amygdala to react, often stronger than needed. It is hard to regulate your mind and body when you're constantly on guard. That's why I spend a lot of time doing relaxing, letting-go, peace-producing guided imagery. For some, these moments are the first time they've ever stepped into their mind and body in a soft compassionate relaxing manner. They learn to accept themselves in that very moment despite some of their unsolved problems. Even in the times, we feel most stuck, we are never alienated from our open loving heart. We learn to move toward difficulty when we operate from our hearts.

Helping an ADHD kid learn to recognize and sift out the emotional memory produced by the amygdala, then compare the memory to the actual event, provides <u>them the choice</u> to decide if the memory and event are worth entwining and reacting to. By learning to heighten their awareness, they can consistently begin to label "old learned habitual reactions" as just that. Again, the good news is that habitual reactions can be unlearned. Old reactions from our implicit memory bank become traditional ritualistic responses. "If this happens" or "this is said," I must follow form. These subconscious thoughts stirred up by the amygdala are often of no use in the present moment.

The good news is that the amygdala first releases signals into our awareness that are informative, protective, and legit. The bad news is that this information gets sensationalized then sucked into our mind and body like a pneumatic tube at a bank's drive-through window. We think it, and the amygdala runs with it broadcasting fear, doom, and gloom throughout every crevasse of our mind and body. Either an offensive or defensive posture is assumed, fast-tracking a call for action throughout the call centers of the body. In the beginning, the amygdala's voice is insistent and convincing. It talks over, drowning out hopeful, reasonable, and solution-oriented ideas that might neutralize the moment providing response flexibility. Good news and solution-oriented advice emanating from the brain's Emerald City, home of the great and powerful prefrontal cortex (PFC) needs to override the amygdala.

When the amygdala gets its cells and synapses all up in a wad, it thwarts the potential effectiveness of the prefrontal cortex's regulatory functions. Instead of the PFC influencing the bodily processes with empathy, compassion, and facts, the amygdala just rants and raves like a guest on *The Jerry Springer Show*. This makes it difficult for the prefrontal cortex to decipher and construe what's happening in our mind, at that very moment. Once we become aware of the amygdala's toxic influence, we can then tap into the expertise and experience of the prefrontal cortex. The prefrontal cortex will help us form images that protect us in that moment and project our thinking into the future. This way we can make plans. The prefrontal cortex must override the amygdala with kind and gentle reasoning, though there are times when the PFC needs to just grab the amygdala by the back of the neck and say, "Snap out of your unreasonable and irrational snit."

Imagine the prefrontal cortex hearing a commotion outside the gates of the Emerald City. Being a kind and concerned grandmotherly-like presence, the prefrontal cortex peers through the gate only to see the amygdala dodging traffic on the central nervous system's super information highway. The amygdala's arms are filled with files of frustrations, grievances, and exaggerated concerns. "Grandmother Prefrontal" comes out and convinces the amygdala to come inside where it's safe. The amygdala notices the sign on the gate reading, "Welcome to the Land of Well-being." Imagine when this distressed being is greeted with kind, loving grandmotherly understanding. Then visualize your irascible amygdala, dripping of cortisol, being led to the kitchen table where it spills the files, frantically explaining past defeats, looming frustrations, and doom that lie in wait right around the corner. Then imagine this grandmotherly-like voice wrapping the amygdala (our troubled mind) in a shawl, placing a plate of warm cookies and a glass of cold milk in front of it, then putting a darling limp sleepy puppy on its lap. I would think it would be hard to stay upset very long. The prefrontal cortex doesn't eliminate frustrations, it just neutralizes them by smearing warmth, wisdom, and intuitive insight over the conundrum. Like a soothing balm, the PFC inhibits the amygdala from acting on its first impulse keeping the ADHDer from going over the edge.

We can learn to recognize and forewarn ourselves when the amygdala is steering us down the low road toward a freak-out. The prefrontal cortex so eagerly wants to share our minds' and bodies' intuitive wisdom. Such learning allows us to pump the brakes, rather than careen down the "low road" while freaking out.

What the prefrontal cortex does for us is:

1. The PFC regulates biological functions such as heart rate, respiration, and digestion. It synchronizes activity in the autonomic nervous system (ANS). When the ADHDer goes down the low road, their minds stop regulating these functions. There are two divisions of the ANS the prefrontal cortex regulates: Sympathetic and Parasympathetic. ADHDers' minds can be considered frequent fliers, and the sympathetic system can be considered the throttle and steering

mechanism of the airplane. It accelerates and steers the mind, lifting it off into skies sometimes haphazardly creating less than a smooth take-off. The parasympathetic decelerates the mind, pulling back on the throttle, slowing down the aircraft, hopefully bringing the mind and body in for a safe landing. Without self-awareness, there is a lack of coordination between the sympathetic (throttle) and parasympathetic (brake.) Without an intentional pursuit of balance, our mind and body can be trying to lift off while standing on the brakes. As you can imagine, this is very hard on the ANS, as the ADHDer sits at a desk, trying to pay attention when their mind is continually trying to lift off.

2. <u>The PFC helps us attune our inner world to connect and resonate</u> with another person's inner world. When the ADHDer feels aligned with themselves and someone else, they "feel felt," and they "feel understood." If this plays out consistently, that's how friendships are made. When we freak out, we disconnect from ourselves and others. Being close to someone who's freaking out is like trying to hug a cactus. The prefrontal cortex helps us attune to others in a non-destructive way. It helps us make our presence desired by others.

3. <u>The PFC also helps us recover and maintain our emotional equilibrium.</u> It helps the ADHDer navigate through life's "china shops" without stumbling into all the delicate displays. The prefrontal cortex wants us to feel alive but tempered and balanced. When our emotional life is satisfying, we are more apt to involve ourselves in a variety of experiences and endeavors. Without

a sense of balance, the ADHD individual vacillates between over-the-top exhilaration and severe dejection. We need to teach the ADHDer the gray area, the middle ground. A middle ground can be taught. Skills such as breathing, relaxing meditations, reframing, cognitive restructuring, emotional understanding, installing the positive, and releasing feelings, all bring us back to a steady-state that can produce a welcoming sense of internal symmetry. Even if it's only for a few fleeting moments, when practiced enough, these seemingly transient states can become steady traits. Such balance helps the ADHDer stay clear and attentive in the face of life's uncertainties. This sensation begs to be repeated by both the mind and body. When we freak out, become unhinged, or just plain "go off the chain," we lose that comforting sense of equilibrium the prefrontal cortex provides. When the ADHDer's emotions are well-founded, healthy, and resilient, you can bet their prefrontal cortex is at work. Aristotle referred to this state of being in balance as the "golden mean." This is when the ADHDer's reactions are neither excessive nor minimal. They aren't tweaking out, nor are they flat and indifferent. One hundred and eighty degrees from wrong is still wrong. It's not productive to plant yourself on either polarity. The soil found in the middle ground contains the healthiest nutrients. Learning to activate and then be open to the healing properties of the prefrontal cortex, helps the ADHDer stay clear, focused, and balanced in the face of upheaval when trying to learn new stuff.

4. <u>The PFC offers us a "pause,"</u> where the ADHDer can learn to build a dam, divert, stop, and deliberately reroute the overflow of energy their

mind and body is producing during a freak-out. A freak-out usually follows a well-practiced and subconsciously developed predictable pattern of thought, sending the ADHDer on a headlong slide into rushing water. This habitual mental script gets etched into the brain like a stream flowing down the side of a hill, creating a furrow. The turmoil and emotional mayhem that these thoughts and feelings cause can come on rapidly like a flash flood.

5. <u>The PFC helps us filter out the inflexible and fruitless mental arrangements.</u> This is referred to as response flexibility. What a nice useful attribute the prefrontal cortex offers. It's a wealth of grandmotherly insights and nurturing, providing a space where social and emotional intelligence can form. The ADHDer then comes to believe that the choice of how to respond is theirs. Being flexible creates options, helping the ADHDer learn to avoid their first impulse. Flexibility is the key to becoming unstuck.

6. When utilized, the PFC can inhibit and even gag the incessant prattling of the fear-evoking amygdala. Managing fear is important for all of us to learn, and doubly so for the ADHD individual. When we freak out, fear infuses the belief that urgent action is necessary. Some have said, "My ADHD child is fearless" when it comes to jumping off playground equipment. But the fear they experience when faced with relational issues or challenging academic exposure can create emotional and cognitive paralysis. The prefrontal cortex region has direct connections to the limbic area. Learning to be "consciously aware" of the flavor and trajectory of their thoughts cascading

incessantly across their mind's screen, helps them determine which thoughts will serve them best, and which are harmful. Again, we can train ourselves to use the prefrontal cortex's penchant toward kindness and compassion to override the amygdala's anxiety and agitation. Kindness and understanding calm our lower limbic system, overriding the distress the amygdala has ignited. Such an awareness creates a pause, which creates the space where anxiety can be understood and modulated. Since the amygdala has a hard time listening, a sprinkling of soothing verbal directives might not get its attention. Imagine the prefrontal cortex having to resort to a fire hose to get the amygdala's attention and quell the riot, by pummeling it with a drenching of gamma-aminobutyric acid (GABA). GABA is a neurotransmitter that inhibits subcortical firings and limbic tsunamis, like a taser you see on cop shows. The prefrontal cortex has an ample supply of GABA, but when the ADHDer becomes overly fearful and their reactions run amok, the limbic system becomes inflamed, and GABA can then dry up quickly.

7. Empathy is one of the greatest strengths of the PFC. This is where you sense the flavor and thoughts that shape another person's mindscape. You're able to attune to their emotional posture and see beyond their defenses. Empathy is when we learn to sense another person's mind and emotional experience. When the ADHDer freaks out, they become blinded, unable to sense or take into consideration the emotional and mental status of anyone but themselves. Lack of empathy means lack of attunement. Life can become emotionally motionless and stagnant when empathy for

others is absent. The prefrontal cortex empowers us to sense another person's dilemma by removing ourselves from center stage.

8. The PFC possesses great <u>insight</u> into our emotional world. It can travel back through the dim reaches of memory and connect the past to the present, while at the same time anticipating the immediate future. The prefrontal cortex puts us at the wheel, allowing us to choose the direction of our unfolding journey. When an ADHD individual freaks out, insight is lost, and they fail to consider the other person's experience. The prefrontal cortex helps us find the better parts of our thinking and responses that have been displaced. Doing so allows us to recalibrate the moment. When we learn to turn vision and hearing back on ourselves, the toxic narrative looping through our heads is exposed. We all want to be the ones directing our own responses. The last thing any of us needs is to allow the amygdala to choreograph, produce and direct our inner world. When the amygdala takes over, empathy and insight are the first to go. When the food starts to fly, it's insight that provides a perspective that helps us interpret the mindset beneath our behavior. The prefrontal cortex helps us find and comfort the mind we "lost."

9. The PFC has a strong and accurate <u>moral compass</u>. Functional magnetic resonance imaging scanners (MRI) have shown that the PFC becomes highly active when even just imagining actions that serve the greater good. The PFC wants the ADHDer to experience a sense of inclusion and cooperation, starting internally. The PFC wants to override the amygdala's impulses that

don't feed and nurture a more noble and humane purpose. When the ADHDer freaks out, they are not making their inner or outer world a better place. When they offer the universe the better part of themselves, you can bet their prefrontal cortex is highly active and at work. Doing well is good for your mental health in more ways than one. Your prefrontal cortex always wants you to do what is fair and just. Successful recovery programs don't just ask for moral awareness, but for us to search our moral inventory fearlessly and thoroughly, how we're living inside. The prefrontal cortex is very helpful when taking that inventory. What the prefrontal cortex does is remind us that there's something we still need to look at.

The prefrontal cortex, influenced by the flow of insight and wisdom, also sends the brain information from the body. This is where the ADHDer experiences a deep, wholehearted sense of intuition that is referred to as a "gut feeling." When we access our intuition, we are heightening our awareness skills and making wiser decisions. In turn, wiser decisions are made by honoring our feelings and sanitizing our thoughts.

The key is knowing when the amygdala is on a roll. Whether it's a subtle low-level insistence or screaming provocative terror, the ADHDer needs to recognize how and why something is happening. This way they can put a kibosh on the hurtful rampage. Once halted, then contained, a space or pause is created. This is where the ADHDer learns to consciously resuscitate the moment, reconnecting themselves to the grandmotherly PFC's wonderful Emerald City, where dreams really do come true.

CHAPTER 15

ADHD and Addiction

> *"Sometimes you find heaven by slowly backing out of hell."*
>
> ~ Carrie Fisher

In addicted individuals, brain scans reveal disruptions in regions that are important for the normal processing of motivation, reward, and inhibitory control. All addictions, drugs, alcohol, shopping, religion, golf, sex, or video games share the same brain circuits and produce the same brain chemicals. The goal of addiction is to create an altered physiological state through biochemical means. Addiction is never solely psychological; there is always a biological component that must not be overlooked. And conversely, you can't solely focus on brain chemistry or circuitry while ignoring sociological and psychological factors.

ADHD and addiction are both disorders of self-regulation, formerly known as self-control. It turns out that self-control is more effective when trying to establish good habits, rather than trying to break bad ones. I've always taught that learning to regulate your behavior and thoughts is not just to get through adversity, but rather to help avoid it.

Dr. Gabor Maté, a renowned expert on addiction, asks, "Instead of asking why the addiction, ask why the pain?" Most addicts substitute addiction for the nurture and connections they never received. We need to learn what has hurt the ADHDer so deeply that they're willing to pay the devastating price that addiction demands. To think that they can only feel peace and a semblance of control when they're using, just imagine the excruciating discomfort when they're not. Every traumatized ADHDer doesn't grow up to be an addict, but every addict has had some trauma in their developmental years. When addiction is focused only on the disease model and the genetic predisposition, it makes it easy to ignore the emotional, social, and academic trauma many ADHDers experienced growing up. So instead of looking at addiction as a solution-based choice or some inherited disease, how about seeing it as something that worked in the beginning. There's comfort, distraction, soothing, and postponement of stress and pain. So rather than looking at addiction as a central brain disorder, maybe we should start off by seeing it as an attempt to solve a problem, a life problem that involves emotional pain, anxiety, and depression. Addictions are what people do when problems are unresolved and there are no immediate solutions for them.

Addiction has always been a big part of my life. Even something as innocuous as baseball cards, I constantly wanted more. Some great uncles on my father's side had been known to put down a few drinks. On my mother's side, there was an addiction to a learned pious self-righteous, critical mindset. My dad was a prolific and accomplished journalist who was an alcoholic. Through AA, he died 21 years sober at the age of 69. My older brother's demon is food. My younger brother's drug of choice was alcohol, and I'm pleased to report he's been sober for 33 years. Me, it was pot. From the moment I smoked it I was hooked. Being ADHD and fully carbonated, it slowed down my mind, sort of de-fizzing my brain and body. As my fingers hit these keys, I'm going on twelve years of pot-free living.

I have worked in the alcohol and drug treatment field during different segments of my life. In graduate school, I worked for a couple of years at the Community Addictive Treatment Center. I helped bring in the first chairs and set up the program. I also got canned when during a fundraising car wash for our center, a patient found a small film canister of pot when vacuuming under the seat of my car. Of course, he brought it to the attention of the director. Boom, out the door. Following that, I was the Intake Inpatient Coordinator/Therapist for a federally funded alcohol and drug treatment program. One of my responsibilities was going into the Kansas City, Missouri jail to screen inmates and determine if they would be interested in alcohol and drug treatment. Some were sincerely committed to getting out and making a change. Others would agree to treatment just to get out of jail. Others would tell us to go "f__k" ourselves, and stay locked up, rather than get out and get help. Following that, I was the assistant director of a substance abuse program at a mental health center, facilitating groups and doing individual therapy. During most of my life, I'd make sure to keep a joint hidden in the car below my ashtray to puff on during my drive home. Dealing with all those addicts can be incredibly stressful.

I knew I was an addict, but it really wasn't a concern since I wasn't one of "them;" those addicts in jail or treatment. I was training hard, running fast, winning, and placing high (no pun intended) in extremely competitive road races. I had good relationships with my kids, friends, family, and I was making good money and paying my bills.

I remember asking patients who had been clean and sober for good stretches of time, in a very professorial, compassionate, and therapeutic timbre, "How does it feel to be clean and sober?" What I was really asking, in a yearning desperate curiosity, was "What's it like? I have no clue; I have been buzzed for years." My friends and I were proud that we "never ran out" of weed. When the whole county was dry and searching for buds, we were fat and sassy.

But in retrospect, most of the addicts that I worked with during the early 70s and 80s had been symptomatically classic undiagnosed ADHDers. Whereas today, the average addict has been tagged with the ADHD diagnosis in childhood and has been stuffed full of medications, with very little explanation as to how to manage their emotional life. Most medication didn't work. Hence, more shame, disappointment, and hyperactivity permeated their minds and bodies. When the "legal" drugs didn't work, they tried to self-medicate into fleeting states of okay-ness, until, of course, that wore off, and they had to repeat the act over and over.

Know that most people with ADHD taking antidepressants and anti-anxiety pills are still depressed and anxious. They still have ADHD. Their difficulties have less to do with the stories they're told about their "broken brain," "faulty wiring" and "chemical imbalance," and more to do with their emotional, social, and academic needs not being met; not living the life they had hoped for.

In the case of abusing stimulants, such as meth, cocaine, or Adderall for that matter, it's tricky to diagnose ADHD, because these drugs themselves drive both physical and mental hyperactivity. It's sometimes difficult to ascertain which came first the addiction or the ADHD. But more likely, the ADHD symptoms for most addicts have been there since childhood, predating any drug use.

Remember, ADHD is a major predisposing factor for addiction. A study at Yale revealed that if you just treat the addiction and not the predisposing ADHD, the patient doesn't do as well. It was reported that 35 percent of cocaine users and as many as 40 percent of adult alcoholics were found to have underlying ADHD.

People with ADHD are twice as likely to descend into substance abuse and nearly four times as likely to graduate from alcohol to other psychoactive drugs. Craving risk, novelty, and excitement, ADHDers are more likely to smoke and gamble, while hosting many other addictive behaviors.

The link between ADHD and a predisposition to addiction is obvious and, in some cases, inevitable. The connection has little to do with genetics, though some will argue that ADHD is the most heritable of all "mental disorders," second only to autism. Without fueling the debate, ADHD and addictive tendencies can both arise out of stressful early childhood experiences. Although there is a more probable genetic predisposition toward ADHD, a predisposition is far from being a predetermination. As twin studies have revealed, two children with similar predispositions will not automatically develop the same way. I believe that the environment is often the most decisive factor, and scientific findings confirm that pre-and postnatal distress and anxiety are factors that may lay the groundwork for a future ADHD diagnosis.

An article in *Child Development* by B.R. Van den Bergh and A. Marcoen in 2004, stated that 22 percent of ADHD symptoms in eight-and-nine-year-old children can be linked to maternal stress and apprehension during pregnancy. And abused and neglected children are far more probable than others to be diagnosed with ADHD. The ADHDer also exhibits a similar brain structure, found in children affected by childhood trauma. Abuse is not the cause of ADHD, but it increases the risk for it. Early childhood stress and anxiety on the brain, make ADHDers vulnerable to addictions. Such a disruption can lead to permanent alterations in the dopamine systems of the midbrain and prefrontal cortex. These disruptions aren't just because of "bad parenting," but the increasing pressures on the parenting environment seem to increase with each new generation and its technological advances.

ADHD and addiction are strikingly similar in both their characteristics and neurobiology. As I wrote earlier in this chapter, they are both disorders of self-regulation involving abnormal dopamine activity. The medications used to treat ADHD are stimulants. Their effect on the brain is intended to raise dopamine activity in important brain circuits. The character traits of people with ADHD and addiction issues are often indistinguishable: poor self-regulation, deficient impulse control, need for action and stimulation, defiant disposition, and a constant compulsion to distract themselves from the pain inside. It's no wonder that people with ADHD are predisposed to self-medicate.

Again, whether it's an addiction to substances, thoughts, or behaviors, all share the same brain circuits and brain chemicals. The purpose of addiction is to create an altered physiological state of mind. So, addictions are never purely "psychological," there is a biological dimension. It's impossible to understand addiction from just one perspective. All addictions spring from multiple sources: biological, chemical, neurological, psychological, medical, emotional, social, economic, and spiritual. Simply assuming that addiction is an illness from an inherited gene narrows it down to a medical issue that some believe you can throw a pill at. Addiction is about many things, and such a limited approach can cause you to miss the entire picture.

The implications are twofold. First, it's important to distinguish ADHD from "normal frustrations" and to treat it appropriately in childhood. Treatment doesn't have to include medication, and in many situations, meds prolong the healing process. Just because you can't tether a capital to a state or handle trying realities doesn't call for medication. And in no case, should medication be the only treatment. ADHD is not a disease but mainly a problem in growth and development. The quest is not to govern the symptoms, but to help the ADHD child develop correctly. Studies are clear: those ADHD children whose developmental dependency needs are not met, are at higher risk for addiction later in life. Developmental dependency needs clearly state that the child is dependent on their caregivers to get those needs met.

Second, when treating adults with any addiction, it is important to look for untreated ADHD. It's not possible to treat addiction successfully if we ignore obvious ADHD propensities. Addiction exacerbates the underlying disorder. Addressing ADHD issues can be a great help, adding clarity for those struggling with addiction.

Addictive substances and behaviors—whether it's cocaine, fixations, or shopping—temporarily suspend the individual from having to listen to an unhealthy or non-supportive inner dialogue. Addictions have a short shelf life that offer us temporary relief, but there's at least a momentary reprieve. A false sense of well-being and control, intellectual and emotional mobility, and temporary grounding seem to be the lure. But repeated mind-altering addictive behaviors lead to long-lasting changes in the parts of the brain and its structure that rob the individual of voluntary control. Addiction changes the part of the brain that is responsible for decision-making. Addictive compulsions actively disrupt the self-regulation circuits. These circuits are needed in order to say, "No," to interrupt the practicing of our addictions.

ADHDers need to be taught to turn their vision inward so they can activate these regulatory circuits in order to recognize a fatigue point that's likely screaming, "Enough is enough." Moderation has never been considered a boastful attribute among the ADHD population.

No moderation, no balance. Living on any extreme is disproportionate, too much food, not enough food, too much exercise, completely sedentary, too much sleep, not enough. I remember hearing one of my mentors, John Bradshaw, so poignantly state, "180 degrees from wrong is still wrong." You can't live on the polarities and learn to master the middle.

Either extreme can create a chaotic mindset that breeds bad habits. Faced with confusion and inconsistency, we look for ways to stabilize. When addicted we're driven toward people, substances, and behaviors that help us not notice our greatest inadequacies. We lose self-respect and a bit of dignity whenever we can't say "no" to ourselves. It's difficult to resist something that has tricked us into believing it brings us relief.

Leonardo da Vinci said, "It is easier to resist at the beginning than at the end." When we're submerged in our pain, addictive tendencies and ideas begin to foment. This can begin when the ADHDer is quite young. But when the individual is in the throes of addiction, these same ideas need squelching and the idea of starting over isn't an option. It's the hardships and adversities that re-introduce us to ourselves. Shouldn't we learn to accept ourselves on easier terms? You can't completely judge yourself by a small sample of who you "aren't," or by who you "should" be.

Without moderation, the life we desire is usually the one we don't lead. How many years must we be a slave to addiction before gaining our own assurance that we're capable of leading the life we choose.

CHAPTER 15

Ben Franklin said, "There is no little enemy." That's so true for the ADHD addict who spends a lifetime seeking to minimize insecurities with things from the outside, in hopes of making the insides feel better.

Eliminating addictions will help alleviate ADHD symptoms. Dealing with ADHD symptoms will help with the process of eliminating addictive behaviors.

CHAPTER 16

Parenting Toward Peace of Mind

> *"Patience is sometimes bitter, but the fruits are sweet."*
>
> ~ Unknown

It's amazing how our best intentions can generate a reaction or response that's the exact opposite of what we had hoped for. Though intentions and reactions differ from kid to parent, and parent to kid, they both need the same things: love, patience, support, patience, structure, patience, guidance, patience, forgiveness, patience, tolerance, patience, and protection. It's just that ADHD kids need a lot more of "this" and much less of "that," and with more repetition than the norm. It also needs to be brought to the child's awareness when their parent is providing these things, in order for them to practice gratitude.

Here are some ways to immediately and effectively help your ADHD child:

- Accept the obvious; if some of your approaches and strategies aren't working, you'll need to learn something different.

- Understand that discipline is modeled and can be used as a verbal as well as a silent guide to teach, not just imposed as a punishment. Discipline is a process, a procedure, not just some levying of consequences.
- Be open to new approaches. Be willing to let go of "Well, my parents used to ..." Just because something worked for you doesn't mean it will work for your ADHDer.
- Learn to respond in ways that fortify their opinion of you as a reliable, comforting guide, not an inflexible dictator.
- Explain why these new skills will help them both now, and throughout life. Give examples of what you've learned through some of your own bumbling exploits, not just your successes.
- Help the ADHDer understand the difference between managing their emotions and stifling them.
- Demonstrate that feelings should be understood, expressed, and completed, as opposed to muted and blocked.
- Believe in yourself as a parent. Your children will sense it if you don't.

You hear parents say, "I just can't relate." But you don't always have to relate to connect. When we help the ADHDer understand and express their emotions, they can then redirect their behavior. When this happens, learning is taking place.

An angry child won't be receptive until they feel they've been understood. They will use their anger to guard their feelings and exploit your insecurities, taking advantage of your need for peace and coherence. Or they'll turn their anger in and hurt themselves in immeasurable ways.

One of the greatest sorrows I continually witness in my office is the sadness, regret, and guilt parents carry knowing they weren't a good effective parent. I'll never forget this girl telling me at the beginning of her senior year, she hoped she could work things out with her parents. Because if she couldn't and she went off to college, she'd rarely want to come home, even to visit.

Our kids are this age only once. We have such little time with them, it's vital not to blow it. Children change quickly relative to adults. Unfortunately, adults become fossilized, inflexible in their latter years. The secret is to stay loose, current, and flexible. This is what allows kids to approach us. There is much more change from ages three to ten than between the ages thirty to forty.

Drs. Daniel Siegel and Tina Payne Bryson published a great book (2014) titled *No-Drama Discipline*. It suggests that before you respond to misbehavior, pause, and ask yourself three simple questions.

Why did my child act this way?

What lesson do I want to teach at this moment?

How can I best teach this lesson?

If we expect our ADHD children to learn how to avoid their first impulse, we must model that for them. When we overreact, our primitive brain takes over, driving us to respond in primitive, unthinking ways. By learning to override our first impulse and create a pause, we can redirect our intention in ways that benefit both parent and child.

There are good reasons why children misbehave, foremost to get parental attention. Misbehavior isn't the method parents prefer, but it certainly works for the kid. Most ADHDers can't act developmentally appropriate because they aren't developmentally ready. They simply lack the skill set necessary to locate and understand the origins of their disruption in order to calm themselves down and make an intentional decision. Misbehavior is a default strategy for expressing big frustrations. It's what you do when you don't know what to do, yet.

Skill building, like anything worth developing, takes repetitive practice. If we all were able to delay gratification with swift reason and logic, we might very well never have misbehaved. With a non-ADHD child, testing the limits feels safe because their attachment to their parent is secure. Conversely, the ADHD child has experienced so much disapproval and frustration by spontaneously but unconsciously obliterating boundaries, the parental attachment can become frayed. They don't sense or recognize limits, and in some, fatigue points don't exist. Even in a secure relationship, the ADHD kid can act out.

Parents need to ask themselves, "<u>What is it I want them to learn through my instruction in this moment?</u>" Maybe it's how to handle disappointment when people and life don't meet their expectations. Maybe it's learning to manage themselves within time in order to get out the door on time. Maybe we want to teach them that frustrating moments are surmountable and how not to get bogged down by anxiety and doubt. Maybe the kid needs to learn to be responsible for their feelings and how not to blame others for their entanglements. Whatever it is, parents need to be specific and crystalize exactly what it is they want their kid to learn at any given moment.

Also, accept the fact that "this particular moment" might not be the best time to have a "teaching/learning experience." Sometimes just waiting a few moments provides the ADHDer the space to make sense of their frustrations on their own. We don't need to rush in with bandages and balm nor will a flamethrower help produce the behaviors and answers we hope will evolve. Knowing when the lesson will stick, even if the timing is off, at least you're heading in the right direction. But timing is truly everything. I recall a cartoon in *The New Yorker* where the daughter and mom were at an art gallery holding hands viewing a painting. The daughter turned to the mother and asked, "Can we now have an eating experience?" Everything doesn't need to be a moment of learning.

To ensure the ADHDer that their messages are being received, make direct eye contact, audibly paraphrase, and affirm them. This establishes a sense of equality which is necessary when convincing the ADHDer that you're sincerely committed to understanding them. Showing them that you are truly connected by giving them your full attention, helps calm their brain. This provides for them the experience of being talked with, not at. By simply acknowledging that you know through your own experience that, "It's hard to calm down sometimes, isn't it?" provides them the sensation of being heard and feeling felt.

If a freak-out occurs, ask them if they want a "do-over." If you're the one who flipped out, then ask them if they would grant you one. This way you both get to start over, like hitting the rewind, and splicing and editing the immediate past. We can reboot our minds and our moments just like we can reboot our computers. Tell the ADHDer we can redo this whole last scene. Remember our brain is shaped by experiences, and we can redo experiences. Be explicit about how you both want this situation to look once the two of you have "fixed it." It's never helpful to tell an ADHD kid, "If you would have listened to me the first time, you wouldn't be freaking out now." I doubt you will receive an appreciative grateful response, such as, "You were right, how silly of me not being receptive to your first overture or direction. I should have listened the first time. How could I have been so imprudent?"

If you want to change a child's behavior and belief in himself or herself, you have to start with the parents. Believe me, that's the last thing most parents want to hear. In fact, they think that the reason they are paying me is so I can "fix" the kid. I always tell parents the kid is not broken, but the communication is, and their immediate expectations might be too lofty. It's a package deal. You change, and they'll change. They change, and you'll change. It's a contextual reality.

You hear people say, "love your child unconditionally," and I concur. It's easier to love them unconditionally than it is to like them at times.

Here are a few things that can aid in everyone getting better:

Forgive everything that lies behind you. Forgive as completely as you want to be forgiven. When I act upon this belief it releases me from regret, sorrow, and revenge. The transformative powers that forgiveness offers, make peace possible. When we forgive, revenge is no longer an issue, there is no need to strike back. We wish no harm on others. Lack of forgiveness chains us to the past. ADHD kids need to learn how to unshackle themselves daily by practicing forgiveness. Mark Twain said, "Forgiveness is the scent the flower leaves on our heel, just after we crushed it."

Openly show affection. Who doesn't love affection? Receiving affection makes us glow inside. It makes us feel secure in that moment when experienced from someone we love and respect. David Viscott, M.D., an American psychiatrist, who taught at the University of Boston Hospital, said, "To love and to be loved is to feel the sun from both sides." I've always liked that.

Demonstrate that having fun is an important part of life. Everything doesn't have to be a teaching moment. We seldom seize the opportunity to play, until there ceases to be one. The way to enjoy your child is to be less serious and more soulful. Show them that you enjoy them immensely. You cannot imagine yourself into playfulness, you must actually actively do something. We must join them in their world, on their map of development, no matter how whacked-out it may seem. We must participate in the fun, not just provide it.

Encourage relaxation because relaxing is letting go. Relaxation loosens our grip on life. Relaxation and regret don't mix. Regret is only good for wallowing. It's hard to comfortably settle into ourselves and the present moments with a load of regret. Explain to the ADHDer that relaxation is important and has many restorative properties. Explain and model for them that relaxation is the opposite of worry. When you relax, you're consciously choosing not to spend time in unpleasantness. Relaxation provides the ADHDer inner support for the moment. Repetitive efforts to relax can form a surplus of peace that gets stored up and can be called upon later. Acts of purposeful relaxation are a preventative exercise that prepare the ADHD child for whatever circumstances life might throw their way—and for that matter, in the next few minutes. Relaxation creates a clear distinction between how we are, and how we want to be. Things are better resolved when approached from a relaxed state of mind.

Live in an orderly environment. Structure and predictability are very reassuring for a child. Show them you are proud of how you live. Express to them the comfort you feel from the predictability that comes from order. Lack of internal order feels like a city whose walls are broken down and have no boundaries. For ADHD kids, disorganization and lack of structure demonstrate a lack of self-governing. Such disarray keeps them from fully living in the present moment.

Encourage balance. As my five-year-old son, TJ, taught me, "Sometimes it is and sometimes it isn't." Personally, nothing throws me more off-balance than witnessing or being the target of rude, insensitive treatment. Though my disgust doesn't change the facts, I feel I need to express these emotions directly to the discourteous person, so I don't internalize them. Though it can ratchet up the intensity, somehow it wrings it out of my system like a sponge. In no way do I want to fight, but when I externalize my discomfort, it moves me back to the center. Holding it in and accepting inconsiderateness as just my lot in life has never been good for me. I'm still working on learning to pause so that experiences go through me, not to me. At 67 I'm getting better at it.

The mind is what the brain does, and both are connected to the body and spirit. They work together and compensate for one another when one part needs support. It's not just our brain that processes complex information, but the heart does also. The heart sends messages up to the brain through a vast network of nerves, keeping the body in balance whether we are awake or asleep. Balance flows more readily from our heart, whereas our mind can be a whirlwind of weirdness, doubt, and frustrations. When we live our lives through the filter of our heart, peace, kindness, and acceptance leads the way.

Set good examples. Does my ADHD child witness me telling the truth? Do they see me having fun and enjoying myself? Does my child see me in a loving relationship? Do they see and feel me offer both them and others empathy and concern? Do I focus less on material things and more on intrinsic rewards? Do they see me with outside interests or hobbies? Does my child see me read for pleasure and knowledge? Does my child see and hear me pray?

Encourage open communication. I remember my son walking out of the kitchen when he was five, saying,

"In a minute, in a minute, in a minute." Obviously, I wasn't listening. I told him from now on TJ, if you are asking or telling me something and you don't have my attention say, "Dad, you're not listening!" This he has done, and it's been really good for both of us. We can help our ADHDer by graciously answering questions with a happy demeanor. I've heard parents reprimand their ADHDer, saying, "Do you always have to be asking so many questions?" I encourage the kids to say, "Yes, I do need to ask questions! That's how I learn." Show interest and be intrigued by their curiosity and inquisitive nature. Be able to accept the mild with the wild. Don't let their words become weapons in your hands when you're mad, or they will learn never to tell you anything. To the ADHDer, there is no such thing as "too much information." They will offer you, in vivid detail, every thought, observation, and motive they had concerning their morning bowl of cereal.

Encourage independence. Parents need to respond appropriately to their child's frustrations, instead of disabling them with disgust and exasperation. ADHD kids develop learned helplessness when they must continually endure painful, negative treatment and evaluations that they can't otherwise escape or avoid. Also, if a child is continually rescued from responsibilities and expectations that might make them uncomfortable, they'll miss the opportunity to endure, learn, and then change.

I once heard a teacher in an Individual Educational Program (IEP) meeting say, "I wish they would put medication into the drinking fountain so my day would be easier. I don't have time to help certain students that can't seem to navigate through the material." I turned to her and said, "Then have the school district remove the wheelchair ramps and tell the physically disabled students to try harder on the stairs." As parents, teachers, and therapists, we can be their mental and emotional "wheelchair ramp", but they have to be the ones who turn the wheels. Some parents have an unhealthy need to be needed. By not encouraging independence, an ADHD child learns to roll over, play helpless and let somebody else do it. You can't do anything that you believe you can't. Make them responsible for their own responsibilities. Never underestimate a child's ability to do things for themselves but be willing to give them a little jump start, and possibly more than a few.

Make a clear statement of your expectations. This sure helps a child preview what lies ahead, and what the situation requires. I would tell my sons, "Okay, we need to run into the store for a few minutes, this is what you guys can do to help me." Help them see themselves as part of the solution, part of the team, not separate. Including them in the plan helps them contribute to the necessary flow in order to get things done. Tell them what you need from them, not what you don't. When we retell the ADHDer over and over of their past blunders and chaotic inconsistencies, they believe that's all they really are. And, what if the ADHDer begins to believe that who they really are needs to be constantly suppressed. It's difficult to trust that it's okay to be who you really are if the feedback you receive is frustration and exasperation.

Provide opportunities where the ADHDer can make their own decisions. Whether it's something to wear, an item for the grocery cart, the choice of music, a full tray at a buffet ... little choices like these encourage them to believe they themselves can affect their own world. So much of a youngster's life, especially an ADHDer, and for good reason, is choreographed and directed by others. It's important to provide opportunities where they can freelance a bit, having it their way without the judgments, coercion, and pressure to automatically comply with everybody else's blueprints.

Set a time aside for quality interaction. I will always remember my good friend, Chuck, who passed away a few years back. I would go to his house after school, and his mother would literally sit us down at the kitchen table and provide a whole package of Chips Ahoy cookies and big glasses of milk. She would then rest her chin on her folded arms and become fascinated with the details of our school day. Hell, when I got home, I was lucky to get eye contact and was told to go outside. Most ADHDers would much rather go on an adventure with the parent, tromping through a creek in old tennis shoes, sharing time and experiences, rather than sitting by themselves in front of a TV. You might say, "Not my child, they'd much rather go electronic." And that might be true, but it's because they haven't had a consistent taste of you and adventure. Now if you're playing with them that's different but being out in nature doesn't create competition or an obsessive desire to win. Albert Einstein said, "Look deep into nature and then you will understand everything better." Though we as human beings often create our own weather, we all have the ability to bring our own sunshine.

Praise good values. Catch the ADHDer being good. Praise them when they display consideration, kindness, and respect to you and others. Describe to them the effect you saw on a person's face when your ADHDer extended kindness to another. Tell them how it made you feel to see them being kind and considerate. Ask how it made them feel. Then the two of you hold that goodness in consciousness for more than a few fleeting seconds. Stretch out that good feeling in your awareness. That way the experience can be installed as a neural trait, as opposed to a fleeting state. Inquire how it made them feel to affect someone so positively. But don't overly praise them or pile on how smart and competent they are, just point out their thoughtfulness. Such incessant fawning and babble create a lot of pressure, and the child begins to doubt your sincerity if it's over the top. Comedian George Carlin used to say that if your child brings you a paper with some scribbles on it and says, "Look mommy/daddy I drew a horse," tell them, "That's the worst drawing of a horse I've ever seen. Please don't show me things like that and tell me it's something that it's not or I'm going to have to get you tested." We don't want the bar so low that we're praising the way they scratch their ear. Don't exaggerate the criteria for okay-ness.

Eliminate criticism. Point out the causes and effects of their words and behavior. Give examples of "<u>how not</u>" to act, request or behave. Don't just bash them and leave it at that. Explain constructively, "You're not going to get what you want when you ask like that." Show the ADHDer how to do things over and over until they "really" get it right. Sometimes you may have to be a bit direct, but the message here is to get your point across constructively. The world is not so accommodating for an ADHD individual, but it doesn't have to be harsh in your household.

Don't expect superstars. Perfectionism is a curse, not an attribute. Most forms of stardom have a short shelf life. As a parent don't try to appear perfect with the hope of being respected and admired. Shoot for sincerity and authenticity, that's what your child will love and respect. Gloria Steinem refers to perfection as "internalized oppression." When the parent and the ADHDer believe they don't have to be perfect, they can enjoy being okay.

Demonstrate that feelings are important. Words do hurt, and animals do feel. Adopt the Buddhist philosophy of "Do no harm." ADHD kids are much more sensitive than most, and feelings do matter. Teach them not to get stuck in their feelings but never minimize the messages feelings deliver. Learn a few thoughts or mantras that help dilute the intensity of the feelings. Making sense of your feelings, and then integrating them into a cohesive narrative, restores balance if you don't deny their meaning. Everyone feels better when they know that their feelings are felt and understood.

Withdraw from conflict. When you take away the other person's audience then there is no one for them to argue with. ADHDers feel entrapped when someone is perpetually trying to tattoo a lesson into their emotional and behavioral psyche. If you insist on getting the last word in, make it an apology for your part in the matter. When in conflict, maybe instead of aiming to win, our aim should be to end it. Imagine waging peace, kindness, and acceptance. It's better to be happy than right. If you're wrong, promptly admit it. It's okay to have differences, but it's not okay to have such a gap that it keeps you and your ADHDer from coming together on common ground.

Assign meaningful responsibilities. Don't try to do everything yourself, then become resentful when they aren't helping. Assign responsibilities, then acknowledge, praise, and explain how their help made it so much easier for you. Point out how their contributions aid the flow of the family system. Sometimes you'll have to demand, direct and prod for the completion of a task. You may have to ask over and over again, but keep your cool, because in the end there is a payoff. With enough repetition, they'll get tired of hearing you. You might even hear them say, "Okay, okay, I know what to do, you don't have to keep telling me." Of course, it may get done theatrically, but it gets done, and you haven't come out of your face. The ADHDer must know that the results of their efforts need to meet your specifications, not theirs. ADHDers are often satisfied with an incomplete, half-assed effort, especially if it gets them done more quickly and sticks a cork in the parent's pie hole.

Read to them and let them read to you. I can't emphasize the importance of this. With young ADHDers, find small details in a picture and ask, "Where's the bird's nest?" "Which trees don't have nests?" "Where is the boat that's way past the house but on the left side of the lake?" They feel smart when they get things right. It's not hard for most of us to find the sun in the sky, so ask for details, ones that are a bit harder to find so they see the entire picture. When my children would lose interest in a story and start to wander away, I'd feign amazement and say, "Wow, look at the size of that hippo," and they'd come running back to see what I was so astounded by. Show your ADHDer that you get really excited about things also. Know that their excitement level usually gets ratcheted up a few more notches above the mean. Model genuine curiosity for current events, new discoveries, and literature. Reading shovels in brain food for the imagination. Teach them to be hungry for knowledge. It will make them more interesting individuals.

Let go of suspicion. Not everyone is out to get you or expose your secret frailties. ADHD kids are hypervigilant. Sadly, some are accustomed to not being liked. We can teach them to turn vision back on themselves, so they can see how they act and sound. We can help them recognize the circularity of their inner dialogue that keeps them stuck. The ADHDer can let go of suspicion by stepping out of obsessive mental loops. We can teach them to get on to better thoughts and avoid the loop altogether. By helping them cultivate more trust in their instinctual data, they begin to experience a sense of wholeness with less fear from a perspective they're not used to. We can't feel whole unless we have our own approval. Believing they "can make it through anything," keeps them looking ahead instead of behind or anxiously scanning the periphery.

Let go of resentment. ADHDers seem to have a tough time escaping their past. When my father would get mad, he'd recite every screwup of mine dating back to second grade when I got caught taking a candy bar from Safeway. Some significant people in the ADHDer's life have the tendency to nurse grudges against the ADHDer, thus keeping both parties stuck in the past. To respond to life's numerous demands, we all need to stay current in our inner world. Letting go isn't easy for some ADHDers because others' resentments and disapproval cut deep. ADHDers hold on to negative memories and churn the feelings those memories generate well past normal shelf life. Sadness can be washed away by the rains of time. But the ADHDer needs to be taught the temporariness of everything. It's hard to see farther than our knowledge reaches, but if we could, we would let go of a lot more, a lot sooner. Think of all the things we have perseverated about, and in the whole scheme of things mattered very little. Providing examples of unnecessary ruminating in your own life gives your ADHDer the permission and wisdom to let go of resentments sooner.

Don't live in or dwell on the past. Picking at the scabs of old mistakes, disappointments, and screwups keeps us bleeding. Teach the ADHDer that they can't reach back for happiness. We must learn to make now better, so happiness will happen organically. Having the mindset that everything should be "great" all the time, and if it isn't there's something ghastly wrong with you, sets anyone up for disappointment in the present. This creates both fleeting and potentially devasting bouts with anxiety and depression. You can learn from the past, but you can only reconstruct things in the present. When we as caregivers demonstrate the belief that "The best is yet to come," it usually does. And even if that doesn't "always" hold true "all the time," what a nice direction to err. Miguel de Cervantes said, "Ne'er look for the birds of this year in the nests of the last." We were meant to move on. We can't let yesterday suck today dry.

Learn and embrace the Serenity Prayer. ADHD kids waste a lot of time and energy ranting and raving over conditions and events they can't change. Cooperate, accept, and explore some of life's basic rules, on life's terms. Be leery of people whose attitudes limit the idea of growth and self-improvement. When we teach the ADHDer how to step back and examine the flavor of their thoughts, they can learn to let go of what isn't flavorful. Martin Luther King, Jr. said, "We must accept finite disappointment, but never lose infinite hope." Change what we can and become acutely aware of what we can't. It's written somewhere, "To appreciate the beauty of the rose, we must accept the thorns." But this doesn't mean we need to be pricked by them.

Realize self-pity gets us nowhere. It's so very unattractive when someone plays "poor me." You talk about an instant repellant. It's easy to fall into a self-pitying mode because, in the beginning, it draws people closer. Some ADHDers develop learned helplessness, generated from so many experiences of powerlessness. Self-pity poisons life, but a good healthy dose of self-compassion can be the antidote. Courting self-pity says that you're willing to sink. The cure for self-pity is to do something now. ADHD individuals get very little done when they are constantly feeling sorry for themselves. I love to help people go on gratitude hunts. Start off by thanking your nose if it's now unplugged.

Do you know who I feel sorry for? I feel for children who don't have enough to eat or youngsters born in Syria who haven't had a peaceful night for 19 straight years. I feel really bad for animals who are abused and neglected and never receive the love they so badly deserve. I feel sorry for over one billion animals killed in the 2020 fire in Australia. And of course, I feel very sorry for our planet earth and all the things we've done and continue to do. Plus, a whole bunch of other stuff.

Cultivate the old-fashioned virtues: love, honor, compassion, loyalty, generosity, integrity, hope, and accountability. An ADHDer needs to believe that they, too, possess the ability to cultivate these strengths. Happiness or even just okay-ness is still pretty good. Hope and accountability can be difficult for the ADHDer. The social spotlights are glaring. Who wants to be accountable for a shoddy everything. It's hard to feel hopeful when their confusion and frustrations can't be privatized. Such daily exposure eats away at one's basic faith in themselves. The good news is that the ADHDer can learn to grow strengths through patient repetition and good therapy. Strength and willpower are not virtues that you either have or don't have, but strengths that can be trained and developed. We can teach the ADHDer how to untangle their thought distortions and rectify their falsehoods. Virtues can be diminished and challenged by life, but more good news, they can be resuscitated and resurrected. Our basic goodness cannot be repossessed, stolen, or burnt, rather I believe it to be intrinsic, lasting, and contagious.

Don't expect too much of yourself. When there's too wide a gap between self-expectation and your ability to meet these goals, a feeling of inadequacy is inevitable. Perfectionism disables development. Keep it realistic. When we believe "Everything must always be right," then something isn't. William Faulkner wrote, "All of us failed to match our dreams of perfection." And dreams are the only place where perfectionism exists. When we are little and our dreams don't come true, it's usually for just one day. The older we get, the longer we hang on to disappointment. Be satisfied with doing a good job, as opposed to a "great job," "fantastic job" or a "superlative job." This doesn't mean you live small and play it safe. It means you've made a noble effort and have done well. Good efforts and results add up and eventually tip the scale of life in your favor. Unfortunately, life usually doesn't adhere to our schedule. There is nothing wrong with just being darn good.

Find something bigger than yourself to believe in. Self-centered and egotistical people score lowest on any test that measures happiness. When we pray in gratitude, to whom or whatever, we flush out our spiritual enemies. Samuel M. Shoemaker wrote, "Prayer might not change things for you, but it for sure changes you for things." Again, become more reflective and less reactive.

It's essential to know when it's time to work or time to play. Differentiating between the two is difficult for an ADHD individual. When they're playing and know they should be working, then they probably should be. When a non-ADHDer puts off un-fun responsibilities they experience stress. They find relief by being responsible and getting it done. For the ADHDer the relief comes from "not doing it," avoiding the un-fun. The Nike slogan needs to be consistently installed in the ADHDer's mindset. "Just Do It." Unfortunately, they can't but they would if they could. But they can and will learn once they understand and feel the consequences of "Just Not Doing It." Enumerate peacefully the ramifications and repercussions they'll experience if they don't do it, then gently redirect them back to the "Just Do It" mindset.

It's essential we become aware of the type of emotional experiences we are providing for our ADHD kids. Our child's experiences of us will shape their private narrative and dialogue. Their accounts of these interactions and perceptions will loop around in their minds. To provide better material for their mental footage we as parents should ask ourselves these questions:

- Does my ADHD child witness me having fun, relaxing, and enjoying myself?

- Do they see me get excited about learning?
- Do they see me embracing beauty?
- Do they see me taking good care of my body?
- Do they see me laughing plentifully?
- Do they hear me express appreciation and gratitude for what we have?
- Do they witness me involved in healthy meaningful relationships with family members and friends?
- Do they see me experiencing renewal from partaking in a spiritual community?
- Do they see me exercise and decompress the stress I encounter?
- What aspects of my life are my children inhaling?
- If they modeled my life, would it inspire them to learn and grow?
- Do they witness me neutralizing negativity?
- Do I promote, model, and cultivate a nurturing spirit of wholeness?
- Do I display the importance of being open to the grace and calm that's available?
- Do they see me as forgiving?
- Do I share with my children my illustrious and creative thoughts?
- Do I share with them my frustrations and past fears, and how I've worked to overcome them?
- Do they know I have any?
- Do I?
- Am I interesting to them?
- What do they see me get enthusiastic about?

There has never been a study that extolled the lofty benefits of living too seriously. When we don't let go, imagine, or play, there are tremendously harmful effects on our biochemical makeup, and if it's affecting us, it's affecting the kids. Though some of these suggestions are as old-fashioned as grandma's apple pie, they're still just as appropriate, tasty, and satisfying.

CHAPTER 17

What Matters Most: Friendships or Plankton?

> *"No person is a friend that demands your silence or denies your right to grow."*
>
> ~ Alice Walker

When you're young you spend a lot of time and energy trying to make sense of your inner world. We do this by observing the outer world and studying others. You're constantly trying on different personas to see what fits and how to fit in. This requires sorting through racks of identities and interests that would help you merge with specific subgroups. It necessitates learning to manage the impression you produce in order to fashion an appealing distinctiveness. This is difficult for ADHD kids because sometimes it's their uniqueness and seemingly odd proclivities that keep them from fitting in. Often the ADHDer just wants to appear adequate. For many ADHD individuals, happiness seems to be right over the horizon. Being able to "maintain" without freaking out in social situations and relationship encounters can take a herculean effort for the ADHDer. ADHDers fear exposure, while at the same time, have a hard time protecting their vulnerability.

Other children offer little charity to their ADHD contemporaries. In fact, some are like sharks circling the social waters ready to strike and exploit their classmate who's visibly struggling with smoothness and social agility.

Numerous factors aid in the social success or failure of a school-age child. Being "cool," or at least trying to look "cool" is more desirable to some than appearing to be smart. Having an attractive body, displaying self-confidence, and being likable brings more powerful emotional rewards, easily trumping the proficiency of conjugating a verb. (I'm not sure I even remember what conjugating means.)

There are <u>three important developmental tasks,</u> or missions, if I may, that need to be accomplished at specific times originating solely in the social realm. Unfortunately, ADHDers don't predictably match developmental milestones or specific timetables. These specific missions are major in helping the ADHD child connect with others in socially satisfying ways. This merging and connecting with the pack involves learning how to reciprocate with others.

The first is <u>The Friendship Task:</u> What is more valuable to any of us than a friend. Inside true friendships, we find support and protection. It's called bonding. I've always loved Kahlil Gibran's belief about friendship, describing it as "A sweet responsibility, never an opportunity."

To have a friend, you must be a friend. Aristotle considered friendship "A slow ripening fruit." But ADHDers often rush to intimacy because they are so starved for connection. But they have a quality, a warm welcoming magnet in their core that can attract true friends. Good friendships are based on feelings of compassion and concern, equality, and active reciprocation. You can't be intimate with someone unless there's a sense of equality, parity, and safety. When you feel free from judgment, you open up and share your feelings and experiences. Knowing that your words and feelings won't become weapons in someone else's hands is a wonderful luxury. Most of the time we find our most significant friends outside our family. I once read on a sweatshirt, "A Family Is a Close Circle of Friends Who Care." Good friends are the family we choose.

Boys often build friendships around activities. With ADHD boys, spontaneity and impulsivity never prevent a shortage of creative options, pranks, or adventures.

Girls on the other hand feel less propelled to rally around an activity to feel connected. Girls are much more interested in sharing thoughts, feelings, and emotions and less interested in scoring, winning, or dominating the other. But ADHD girls are different. They can be dominant and forceful needing an event, activity, or prop to entice other girls to show an interest in them. Knowing what to share, and how much is difficult for them to gauge. ADHD girls frequently display a more urgent need for a connection, linking them to a group or individual they can matter to. Such visible neediness and rush toward intimacy can quickly ostracize a young girl. Girls are much less accepting of other girls who appear different and noticeably vulnerable. Girls are less trusting of other girls than boys are of other boys. Girls compete amongst themselves with greater fervor and on a much different playing field than boys. I once read that if you want to find out about a girl's faults, compliment her to her girlfriends when she's not there. I always thought that was sad.

The second mission is <u>The Popularity Venture:</u> Remember how important it was to be popular? It takes a lot of work to strategically position yourself in the right places with the right people at the right times.

When it comes to popularity, ADHD kids fall into two social camps. In one camp, they can display their unbridled and befuddling ADHD tendencies and inclinations. But if they're attractive, funny, athletic, or talented in a unique and marketable way, a lot of social blunders and miscalculations will be overlooked. Being considerate of others and performing well on life's daily stage can take you a long way. Unfortunately, even for the popular ADHDer time reveals inconsistencies and the paint begins to peel when learning and academic expectations aren't happening. The ability to slide by sideways on charm, sexual allure, talent, and deliberate tactical maneuvering can only work for so long. Life forces the popular ADHDer to become less funny and more accountable. You are expected to produce acceptable work and demonstrate mastery over the material. And, of course, this needs to be done within specific time parameters. Sadly, the ADHDer gets accused of not trying, when really their excruciating effort isn't working. They need to be open to new ways of learning. Therein lies the struggle. Learning new ways.

On the other end of the spectrum, if you're not genetically blessed, nor possess a quick wit, or your playground dexterity is shamefully deficient, or you're completely oblivious to the length of time your finger is lodged in your nose (God forbid your finger finds its way to your mouth) you ain't hanging with the popular kids. On top of that, if you can't privatize your emotions, disappointment, and pain, everybody knows it. The social spotlights are glaring. "Popular" kids seem to naturally perform properly, where the unpopular ADHD individual continually stumbles over their lines. They humiliate themselves by being themselves. Sadly, being themselves is what they learn they shouldn't be. And remember there are pills that tell them the same thing. Take these and you'll be different. Sometimes it works, and sometimes it doesn't. I once heard an ADHD girl tell me, "I exhaust myself all day, trying not to be me." That was so sad to hear because she was wonderfully cool.

Popularity is about having a positive reputation that reaches a larger sphere of kids, outside your inner circle of friends. I've seen individuals who are vastly popular but feel very alone because they lack a few close friends. Conversely, I've seen kids who are ranked low on the popularity charts (of course by the popular kids) who possess a deeper sense of intrinsic contentment, with fewer, but closer friends. Aided by others' research and my own observations, I have found a child's reputation in school can be subdivided into general groupings.

<u>Subgroups and Characteristics</u>

Admired/Popular Kids—Well-liked, approachable, respected, and revered by most of their peers.

Notorious Kids—Liked and respected by some groups but disliked by others.

Good-natured Kids—Visibly obscure, not well known, but socially acceptable.

Excluded Kids—Actively rejected, possibly bullied, or verbally abused.

Ignored Kids—Almost non-existent, neglected, and unnoticed by anyone (some by choice)

ADHD children tend to pool at either extreme: A popular ADHD kid demonstrates the ability to "pull it off." They are intuitive enough to sense what the moment requires and when to dial it down. These kids are quite likable, considerate and their exuberance well-calculated.

But there is another subgroup where most ADHD kids are being choreographed by nature and neurons and less by conscious choice. These kids are controversial and provocative. The individual is well known but not accepted due to their obvious weirdness. These ADHD kids seldom go unnoticed and are hard to ignore because they constantly need to be corralled and steered, drawing both wanted and unwanted attention.

When talking about the rejected ADHDer, a subgroup of the excluded and ignored kids, the number is much larger. This group of kids subconsciously provides ample kindling for insensitive bullies to sniff out, sparking and igniting their vulnerabilities. They are then left to emotionally burn in public. Behavioral spills are made worse by their flailing and floundering theatrics, much to the delight of their oppressors. School life can leave the ADHDer so crushed and defenseless that the only place they can retaliate is at home. They target the people they know will never leave them: their parents and siblings.

When you're consistently falling behind, victimized, and humiliated by a system that isn't designed for your type of mind, it's difficult to return home from school and graciously fall in line with the flow of the family. This is especially true if your brain and body are beginning to withdraw from medication. Oppositional defiant and belligerent indifference is often what rebel ADHD kids do when they don't know what to do. They certainly don't want their family to know how bad things are at school. Sadly, they can deceive themselves into believing that family members don't see their social and academic failings. When so much energy is used throughout the day trying not to publicly explode or privately implode, it's no wonder they shatter the moment they walk through the door.

I've heard parents say, "The moment they get into the car or return home from school, they fall to pieces or aggressively lash out." I saw this happen often when a parent would bring their kid to my group or office right after school.

CHAPTER 17

To me, there's a difference between a meltdown and a freak-out. A meltdown shows hurt. It consists of an emotional and spiritual collapse. You become very vulnerable during a meltdown, more tearful and needy. You need to be listened to and understood from your point of view. Comforting is welcomed, but only after you've drained yourself of frustration and hurt. Meltdowns can have a balancing effect. They can lance, drain, and sanitize our systems. Unlike freak-outs, there are teachable moments during meltdowns where the ADHD individual will offer us "an in." But your entrance needs to be timed perfectly, and at the kid's accord. Rushing in too quickly to "fix" things keeps them from "feeling felt." This prevents the needed emotional drainage that normalizes the brain's chemistry. Nothing gets completed if the kid is fast-forwarded through their disappointment and pain or bribed into "sucking it up" in order to make the adult feel better,

There are messages in meltdowns that parents and practitioners need to hear in order to utilize the plasticity that allows the brain to rewire. Sometimes it's the last few blubbers that hold the relief, the cleansing, the cathartic moment where the past begins its completion and clarity and liberation set in. That process should not be cut off.

When you connect too late, the ADHD individual feels you weren't truly interested in the first place. The child may feel as if the parent's attention was a begrudging obligation when they feel shooed away. A little pat on the head won't suffice. It's as if the parent looked at their watch and read that the statute of limitations has expired on their child's right to blubber.

On the other hand, a freak-out may be verbally and physically destructive. There is a lashing out that needs plenty of room. It's hard to cuddle a cactus or influence the tide of a juvenile tsunami. But matching anger with anger has been known to involve the police. Listen for the underlying messages and themes throughout the tirade, while ducking and dodging the verbal assault. It's important not to take things personally or try to out-escalate them. As a parent, sibling, or friend you become the easiest target. They know that there is the promise of forgiveness and acceptance following the storm. Detach to the greatest degree possible. Melody Beattie implores us in her very influential book, *Codependent No More*, to search inside ourselves and develop a "healthy neutrality" that keeps us safe from the storm.

A good meltdown can bring the ADHDer a sense of relief and closure, where no apology from the ADHDer is needed. Conversely, following a freak-out, the ADHDer usually feels remorse and sorrow over the carnage left behind. Apologies are needed.

The third is the <u>Political Mission</u>: This is where you influence the influential people in your life. ADHD kids vary quite a bit in this realm of interaction. Some ADHD children and adults are naturally charming. They exhibit an authentic, engaging spontaneity and sincerity that people enjoy. On the flip side, some ADHD individuals consistently bring out the worst in others. Their cadence of speech, choice of verbiage, tones, postures, etiquette, and lack of eye contact creates a first impression that garners little interest from others. When meeting others for the first time the ADHD child is hobbled by the belief of never-ending defeat and anticipates rejection and disapproval. Subconsciously, some partake in self-sabotaging interactions, fast-forwarding the inevitable outcome they've learned to expect. To prophesize anything better only sets them up for disappointment. ADHD children, by no fault of their own, often make simple things complicated. Our goal is to help them learn ways to make complicated things simpler. I'll never forget one kid telling me that when he enters a new environment, he will immediately scan the room for people who might not like him.

Children who are politically successful know how to influence the influential people in their lives. They have an acute sense of what it will take, and which individual is more likely to butter their bread and get them to Best Buy or Dairy Queen. Learning how to interact and be in favor with people who are in positions of power and influence, such as teachers, parents, coaches, bosses, and popular peers makes life easier.

For most children and adults, this strategic positioning is unconscious and is common courtesy. But for the ADHD individual, it's much more complicated. Instituting common courtesy can be baffling if the ADHDer has not felt it from the key figures in their lives. In some cases, gentility is nonexistent. Again, the good news is that political astuteness can be taught when loving parents, teachers and therapists keep the ADHDer's self-awareness evolving through truthful assessment, accurate interpretations, and solution-oriented action.

In earlier generations, children's books emphasized the importance of the political charge by offering chapters on how to get the upper hand in life. These chapters would emphasize mandatory protocol and decorum with an ulterior motive of societal approval as the goal. For example, "How to Get Your Teacher to Like You," was considered a primer that could just as easily have been titled, "How to Kiss Your Teacher's Ass," or "How Not to Rain Shame Down on Your Family by Being a Complete Schmuck." But to gain respect from the people you respect is the ingredient for a good relationship. Political dexterity provides steppingstones to better places.

Of course, to be politically savvy you must sometimes feign interest in someone who is not so intriguing.

ADHDers glaze over like a doughnut at Krispy Kreme when they're not intrigued. Again, this is where learning to privatize your emotions and check your impulses is a necessary lesson for the ADHDer to learn. You can't manipulate others as a strategy to get what you want. But being authentic and learning how to manage a moment to bring about a favorable outcome is good to know.

Sometimes the best political strategy with some people is to steer clear of them. But ADHD kids tend to gravitate toward the eye of the storm, trying to make sense of what's baffling or believing they can fix things with their kindness and innate goodness. Knowing how to respond to turbulence with a deliberate, thoughtful, and delayed analysis without personalizing the whole mess is difficult. Some ADHD kids will try to make things their fault, so they can do something to fix it. Realizing that it's not always you and that you can't fix everything, is a form of "Getting better." And that's very political.

CHAPTER 18

Intake Mechanisms

*"Learning can
be found on the other side
of frustration."*

~ Me

I will address the importance of our neurodevelopmental functions and how learning and productivity rely on getting the information in, and then, getting it out.

I once heard a kid in my running/relaxation support group say, "Things go right in one ear, and straight out the other." His buddy next to him said, "Cover the other ear." What a genius observation. The kid next to him leaned over and said, "Just make sure it's not the intake ear, or you won't hear a thing." This was a serious exchange among three kids who clearly understood one another and cared. They wanted to support one another in everyday life.

Attentional difficulties obstruct the ADHDer from taking in important information and vital instruction. One can't act on or respond to information that never arrives. ADHDers must precisely hear, consciously select then manage the material in order to process it. Learning to do this needs to take place at the point of performance. When they hear it they are expected to do it now. For the ADHD kid, just subpoenaing their mind to a state of readiness is difficult enough, much less remaining focused for the effective period of time. Next, they must endure the effort it takes to concentrate long enough to discover, absorb and act on exactly what it is they are requested to do. This requires sensing the proper order while extracting the most important aspects of instruction to be acted upon first. If you are unaware that your ear is covered, nothing's gonna get in and how will you know to uncover it. Helping the ADHDer develop effective intake control from the beginning gives them a fighting chance.

I'm going to share four neurodevelopmental functions that divvy up the responsibilities of the intake mechanisms.

The first is selecting the important data while filtering out distractions. It's the brain's responsibility to sort through and render particular data useless. This is very grueling and problematic for the ADHD mind. Making decisions is difficult because there is so much to choose from. Being confident in knowing what's necessary, and what needs to be parsed out, is hard to distinguish.

If I tell an ADHD kid that George Washington, our first president, was the Commander-in-Chief of the Continental Army, and he was a surveyor and farmer before he became President, and he was a member of the Virginia House of Burgesses, and his political party was the Federalists, and he served as President from 1789-1797, and that he liked horses, what do you think they might select as the most important information. You guessed it, "He liked horses." That is the most intriguing perhaps the most fun-filled aspect of what I laid out. The selection process that allows them to compare information is underdeveloped and at times quite confusing. You pick: the Virginia House of Burgesses or horses. One will get you points on a test, the latter most likely won't even be asked. One is more boring; the other is a blast.

It's hard to focus and retain important information if the delivery is too fast and condensed. An ADHDer's mind has difficulty filtering out, diluting then italicizing vital aspects of what needs to be known, because they're constantly battling visual and auditory distractions. They're missing out on something they're supposed to be learning if they're wondering why the teacher's pencil jar is empty when pencils are scattered across the desk. Such a conundrum might be more consuming and immediately impactful than the due date for an assignment that's clearly written on the board.

Auditory systems can be leaky and oversensitive. ADHDers have difficulty filtering out noises and distracting sounds. ADHD kids are oversensitive to hums, clatters, crunches, and faint jingles. It's not that these kids don't hear, it's often they are overhearing everything.

In college, I could concentrate if I were completely alone, on an upper floor in the library, sitting at a single desk, facing the wall, at the end of a row of bookshelves. No distractions. I could hear myself, and only myself, think. Conversely, I was also able to focus on my work at a table in a busy restaurant, with my back to the dining area. With so many different sounds, my mind couldn't and wouldn't attempt to filter out any specific one; unless, of course, someone sat down at the table next to me. I then found myself wanting to finish their sentences or substantiate their point. My wife will often ask me when we're in a restaurant, "Are you listening to me?" My answer has many times been, "No, but did you hear what that guy behind us said?" Also, little sounds will ignite my curiosity, derailing my focus. Moderate brain arousal from random environmental noise can produce loud internal noises.

I either needed no noise or "white noise." White noise happens when many sounds of different frequencies come together. Think of white noise as 20,000 tones all playing at the same time. For me, the white noise in the restaurant masked specific sounds. It would drown out individual voices that my brain would naturally latch onto. For the ADHD individual, the sound masking properties of white noise can bring calm, focused attention, and proper selection.

A study conducted in Belgium compared the behavioral and neurophysiological benefits of "white noise" for children with ADHD and for those without. Without going into an exhaustive description of the procedure, the study concluded that "white noise" does appear to improve cognition in some children with ADHD.

What if your intake is curious not just about sounds, but about touch or the feel of something? What if the girl's ponytail is beckoning you to rake your digits through it? Such finger safaris can land you in a heap of trouble, especially if you're supposed to be "intaking" something you will eventually be accountable for.

ADHD individuals need to know that they can increase, clarify, and solidify their intake by raising their awareness in order to remain in the moment. By testing different approaches, strategies, and techniques, they can try out different methods for learning what works best for them. Mindfulness training, guided imagery, relaxation, meditation, exercise, stretching and yoga type practices, can train the body and mind to stay connected to one another. For many ADHD kids, it's learning to peacefully endure the discomfort they experience when trying to bend their attention and channel their energy in a direction that might feel boring, confusing, and physically uncomfortable. It's not just learning how to stay engaged but knowing how to immediately disengage when their minds become hijacked by less urgent stimuli. William James, a Harvard-trained philosopher, and psychologist offered the first psychology class in the United States. He reiterated over and over that this vital awareness and the repetitive practice of reconnecting your attention, when the mind wanders offline is, "The very root of judgment, character, and will." James, who studied science at the Geneva Academy in the late 1800s, said, "Whether attention comes by grace or genius, or dint of will, the longer one does attend to a topic the more mastery of it one has." He is talking about the strength-building aspect of continuingly returning your attention to the proper material in order to take it in. Learning to strengthen and steer your selection control through intentional discernment, provides a comprehensive and enduring intake process. This is the first step in learning.

The <u>second</u> neurodevelopmental function necessary for quality intake control is <u>the depth and detail in which information is considered.</u> The information must travel down a narrow corridor, goring the part of our consciousness that recognizes, then reminds us, "Hey, this is important. I better pay attention to these details and then document within my awareness that something is expected of me."

The arrival of new information can leak out readily before it even gets a chance to enter into short-term memory, where consolidation begins to take place. A porous mind, like a leaky container, holds extraordinarily little for very long. It's hard to determine the ingredients of something that's draining out rapidly. Some ADHD kids can tell you the overall theme, the big picture, but not the details, where others might tell you the details and have no clue how they fit into the big picture. Knowing the details helps score high on tests. Few tests ask us to generalize a topic. For the ADHD kid, their mind is more a wide-angle lens, than telescopic. Their mind has the capacity to zoom in, but it often collapses upon the wrong material.

The ADHD mind has a hard time rewinding to past details and important instructions because it's constantly in a state of acceleration. When the ADHDer's mind successfully understands the complexity and details of a body of information, the <u>intake,</u> and the <u>selection control systems</u> high fives the <u>depth and detail department.</u> There is a physiological sense of relief and gratification for the ADHDer when they "get it right."

The <u>third</u> neurodevelopmental function <u>regulates the mind's activity</u> by scurrying information down the narrow intake corridor.

I have pointed out that I was born carbonated, full of fizz, and very combustible, but in a good way. I was often bursting with joy and curiosity. My mind wasn't passive, it was quite active, but also very reactive at times. I daydreamed a lot. New information would flitter through my mind, snagging particles of memories and minutia on its way to the workspace, the tabletop of my active working memory. This is where I'd dump what my mind had accumulated over the last few minutes. This is where I tried to filter out then decipher what was just presented. Usually, something would pique my curiosity, reminding me of something else that had nothing to do with the present material on my mind's tabletop, sending me off on yet another mental excursion. My mental energy wasn't regulated.

I once heard a kid refer to his mind as a "frequent flier." I can certainly identify with their description. Within the course of my writing this morning my mind four-wheeled completely off the pavement. It all started when I got up to get a drink. I ended up rubbing the dogs, brushing the cats, playing a few songs on the harmonica (microphone and all), returned a phone call, fixed an extravagant lunch for Betty, guzzled a large coke, exercised, showered, started some laundry ... and oh yeah, got back to my writing. An active mind is good, but at times, like a bucking bronco, it needs to be contained if anything is to get done and lasting learning is to take place. But a good rider can teach a horse to obey. Unfortunately, the ADHD mind is like a rearing horse with no rider. The horse (mind) must be tamed and domesticated, to be enjoyed. The steed must be taught to decrease its activity and judiciously restrain its first impulse just like an individual's mind. When the mind becomes trained, it does what it should, rather than only what it wants.

When the mind is rapidly presented with new information that has no immediate meaning, nor is connected to anything familiar it can go into sensory overload and become overactive. Self-regulating means in this very specific moment that we calm down the overcharged mind and body. When this happens, peace and clarity ensue creating new neural linkages that pave the way for more productive future responses. Active processing consolidates information and becomes stronger and more proficient when the ADHDer is encouraged to continually ask questions of themselves and others. For instance, "What does this remind me of?" "Does this change my opinion about the subject?" "Who could I ask for clarification on what I speculate?" The answers to these questions feel satisfying because this is what learning feels like. Good feelings create new connections that long to be replicated.

Don't let anyone try to convince you that attention frustrations and distractions, resulting from an overactive mind can be eliminated completely because they can't. Distractibility can be greatly reduced, and its duration shortened by learning specifically about your own personal distractibility. This will help the ADHDer identify and then test new strategies that can immediately steer their mind back to the task at hand. Becoming aware of the unique triggers that lead to cognitive waywardness is the beginning of knowing how to correct them. Getting the wheels of your mind back on the road and your attention heading in the right direction is the most important strategy we can teach ADHD kids, over and over and over.

To understand how to get your attention headed in the right direction we need to understand the following: the brain is divided into two systems that control attention.

System one is instinctive: it's involuntary, automatic, always online, taking in and processing stimuli. System one makes automatic decisions for us. For instance, repositioning your legs if they feel cramped, or lifting your arm to reach for something or scratch an itch, or hitting the brakes when we see a stray dog approaching the roadway.

System two is contemplative: it's voluntary and focuses on factors and abstractions; it follows rules, chooses rationally, and sees and weighs options. System two will make the final decisions, choosing where to allocate attention. System two oversees anything that requires willpower and self-containment. We become distracted when system two begins to run low on the specific energy that manages and allocates our concentration and intentional attention.

The two forms of distraction that system two is forever battling are sensory (things happening around us) and emotional (things going on inside us).

System two wants to find relief and solutions to stressful thoughts and dialogues that loop around inside our minds, keeping us from fully concentrating. Remember, our minds have a natural bias, a slant toward the negative.

This way we stay on guard for the sake of self-preservation. Sadly, through an accumulation of frustrating experiences, this natural evolutionary negative slant becomes entrenched then reinforced in our emotional museum of memories and in our basic physiology. The good news is, through corrective experiences, emotional letting, and cognitive restructuring much can be unlearned.

Focusing and refocusing our attention over and over is very much like trying to strengthen a muscle. Consistent repetitive exercise can and will do that. Constantly corralling our attention and peacefully, but repetitively returning it to the task at hand strengthens our mental biceps. Unfortunately, ADHD kids will try all measures to avoid practicing something they've tagged as tedious, exhausting, and boring. They want immediate results. So, this is where we teach them that tolerating and enduring dull monotonous material is something everybody must learn to endure. They're the hoops everybody has to jump through. This may come easier for some, but for ADHDers, it can feel excruciating. But help them understand that by experiencing certain types of discomfort they become stronger. By doing just that, they make now better, so that later is easier. The byproduct: they feel much better about themselves, and the results are "felt" immediately. And accumulating this sensation of competency can make or break a child's belief in their future.

Here are suggestions that will help us bring a wandering mind back into focus:

- Meditation: Practice letting go while at the same time focusing your attention on your breath. You let go of distractions while accepting thoughts that will scamper across your mind's screen. It's just part of the deal. You can let them go by, like a car passing by your window, or you can tediously chase them in a circular loop in your head. By literally becoming aware of our awareness, we learn to steer our mind instead of our mind steering us. By openly and curiously observing our mind's activity, without getting snagged into exhausting ruminations, we can become consciously aware of when it drifts, and the themes behind those thoughts. When our mind wanders off, thinking about what we need at the grocery store, we can release that thought, then gently return our attention to our next breath.

- <u>Spend time in nature</u>: Nature can inflate our whole being. Nature has the capacity to wash our spirit clean, absorbing only what's natural. Nature turns off our mind to things that command our attention, while at the same time turning it on the beauty that's around us as well as below our feet. Nature has its own natural cadence. When we put ourselves in her enfoldment, we realize that patience is her secret virtue.
- <u>Immerse yourself in something you enjoy</u>: When we're doing something we love, the volume of our inner dialogue gets turned down. Search for something you'd like to become truly good at. Discover your passion and immerse yourself in it. Doing what you enjoy is restorative, and never really feels like work. We rest well when our actions naturally fit our desires. Feeling rested provides us the strength and fortitude to tackle difficult tasks. Everything need not be productive. Learning to disengage our minds is an art. Just because we spend time on something pleasurable, doesn't mean we're stagnating. Enhancing non-productive activities doesn't mean our brains are not engaged and being restored.

To improve "intake" a <u>patient and repetitive</u> approach help the ADHD individual become immediately aware of when they're distracted. Patience provides the time and space for things to get turned around. When the ADHDer is in the grips of distraction, learning to notice and then respond immediately affords them the opportunity to say to themselves, "Hey, I'm off track again. I need to get this done, so let's return to the material." This continual vigilance strengthens intake and decreases the interval of time between distractions, allowing them to regain their intentional attention and hone in on a specific task.

For intake to be efficient and effective, the <u>fourth</u> neurodevelopmental function that needs strengthening is the ability to stay focused and concentrate <u>for the right amount of time</u>. Nothing can be completed if your mind's off in the stratosphere. What we're talking about here is "attention span." Some ADHDers' attention spans are phenomenal, that is if they are interested in the topic or activity. Unfortunately, if they're not engaged, if they're not lasering in on the right material, the right action, for the right amount of time, then nothing gets done. It's crucial to know what you're supposed to be doing, and how long it might take, so you can mentally prepare yourself for the effort. "Sticking to it" for the necessary duration, to completion, is difficult for the ADHDer. When we can learn to shine our mind's spotlight, illuminating exactly what needs to get done, we won't need to continually ask ourselves, "Am I done yet, Am I done yet?" When the ADHDer learns to immerse themselves in their work for manageable segments of time, the end will come to them instead of them frantically trying to reach it. Being aware of time's passage and parameters helps the ADHDer start, stop, and restart important undertakings. At first, this is quite difficult because their mind is careening in all different directions. But like anything, with practice, it becomes easier. Again, the merging of time and effort is increasingly difficult if the task is laborious, time-consuming and there's little fun in sight. This is where they need to consciously widen their window of tolerance toward themselves and the task. "I will do this."

Talk about distractions, during this last sentence I heard my old dog Tucker come down the stairs. I got up, went over to greet him, laid down next to him and we talked for a few minutes. Suddenly I heard a voice coming from somewhere in my head saying, "Tom you're distracted, get up and go back to the desk and keep writing." So, I'm back. In the past, I could have been derailed easily for 30 minutes or more.

For ADHDers it's difficult to get excited and engage in activities they know won't provide them with a big shot of adrenaline, intense fascination or fun. If and when they do engage their intake mechanisms but find the experience to be complicated, perplexing, and laborious, then why continue. ADHD kids don't project themselves far enough into the future to know if what they're observing will be useful or advantageous later. What they do know is that "this is going to suck and will be both exhausting and potentially humiliating." What they see is a big load of "thinking" being delivered to their brain's "intake dock" for unloading. The cerebral cortex is the ADHDer's ultimate control and information processing center, critical for intake. This shipment must then be hoisted onto the "intake's conveyor belt" for orderly and sequential processing. If the processing doesn't run smoothly, the belt will shut down, immediately thwarting the cerebral cortex that sets thoughts and behaviors into action. The cerebral cortex is also responsible for higher-order brain functions such as sensation, perception, memory, association, thought, and voluntary physical action all of which support quality intake.

ADHDers often have a gnawing sense of insatiability. Such mild to severe sensations completely distract and obstruct intake, creating anxiety and obsessions. This in turn hinders the self-monitoring and self-regulation systems that control attention. This unappeasable state causes a restlessness that's satisfied only by something arousing. Often

"ADHD fidgeting" that others find so annoying is simply arousal trying to contain itself. For them movement is like a valve, constantly releasing steam. Though it helps them stay focused and stay present in the moment, it distracts others. What the fidgeting is really meant to do is help them manage the moment while trying to stay sufficiently present to re-engage the cerebral cortex's intake requirements.

Insatiability comes in many different forms. And there's nothing wrong with wanting things. But insatiable yearnings can completely block the intake of information and instruction that usually requires immediate attention and concentration. ADHDers' desires and requests often lead to exhausting extremes. Their incessant demanding and constant badgering wears down the people closest to them, thus causing others to give in, exhausted from the pestering. But their flighty minds quickly lose interest in what they've fought for and begin to insistently bang again on others to provide their intake with something new and riveting. These moments of urgency come often and are more prevalent to the ADHDer than they are to their non-ADHD comrades. Their minds and bodies are in constant need of immediate quenching for psychological and physiological survival. When they learn to say, "no" to themselves, intake opens back up and more options appear. They must be able to "get things in" in order to "get things out".

It's imperative that the mandatory importance of intake be illuminated over and over, and a commitment to strengthen its awareness is agreed upon. Here are a few suggestions that will help the ADHDer and will strengthen the cortex, so intake and productivity aren't so harrowing:

- Create a positive future story. Even if it's between ten and noon. Verbalize what that would look like if things went smoothly. Optimism raises the level of dopamine which energizes the brain.

- Invest in yourself with a vision of who you want to be in the next few hours, not what others want you to be.
- Learn to recognize, then disengage from the dramas of your own creations. Theatrical exchanges both publicly and privately fire up the irascible amygdala that derails the prefrontal cortex from utilizing its comforting and nurturing strengths.
- Move your body: Exercise, dance, do yoga, stretch, pedal, etc.
- Go on gratitude hunts. Finding ways to notice, then expressing gratitude, activates and increases the positive emotions and experiences which in turn activate the prefrontal cortex.
- Everybody loves hugs, except for a few rigid individuals. So, offer and receive healthy physical contact. Hugs soothe the brain with calming inhibitory peptides.

Develop a restorative sleep routine. Get in the habit of ending the day with a pleasant activity leading to a peaceful ending. An evening prayer as your head hits the pillow can be one way of putting a ribbon around the day.

CHAPTER 19

Output Mechanisms

> *"You can't produce output if there was never any input."*
>
> ~ Me

ADHD individuals struggle to get information into their heads due to weak intake control. But what if your intake isn't too shabby, meaning you can get information in, but your "output" falters and you can't get it out in a presentable or timely manner. You know it's in there, you're just not sure where you put it.

<u>Productive output is dependent on regulating the accurate interpretation and placement of what's coming through intake</u>. Productive output depends on correctly operating intake controls. These two aspects of attention management, intake, and output, depend on one another. This truly sucks for the ADHD individual, whose diagnosis, ATTENTION DEFICIT, doesn't seem to elicit much hope.

Getting information in and getting it out requires thought efficiency. Thought efficiency is developed through intentional repetition and patient instruction, which grates up against the ADHDer's impulsivity.

An ADHDer needs to be convinced that the material they're expected to "input" into their active working memory by way of short-term memory has some reality-based use. Mastering fractions was so difficult and rupturing to my esteem that it bled into many areas of my beliefs and behaviors, causing some severe disruptions. Due to algebra, I was ineligible for track my sophomore year of high school and cross-country my junior year. Same in college. I missed a spring track season due to a statistics course that has had no use in my adult life. I was punished for faulty input and output when it came to numbers, sequences, and analytical calculations. What I needed to experience more than anything was the success I derived from the discipline and hard work distance running and racing provided. I knew I had to do something about this learning business. Looking back what I had to do was learn to successfully input information, consolidate, and retrieve it in order to produce quality output, or I would never have been able to race. I'm fortunate that part of me refused to give up and I trained in exile while ineligible. This made my resolve to come back and show "them," even stronger. Which I did, resulting in a university school record.

ADHDers need to believe that with practice, practice, practice they can build and install a filter at the intake's entrance that will help produce a more precise and productive output system. Explain to them that the confidence and competency that comes from strengthening their input and output is learned and earned. And though seemingly unfair, they'll most likely need to work harder than others to construct and maintain these mechanisms. But it's worth it. The satisfaction of actually earning a good result after hard work, sacrifice, and diligence builds confidence and resilience.

When an ADHD kid is ruled by their impulses, input is obstructed and the groundwork for quality output is wobbly at best. Output has all to do with managing the moment while also planning ahead. Knowing what to do next, projecting your thinking and behavior into the future, even if the future is just 30 seconds away has all to do with what was taken in.

There are five neurodevelopmental functions when governed properly oil the gears of output.

The <u>first</u> neurodevelopmental function is <u>the capacity to preview what lies ahead.</u> It's to everyone's advantage to have an idea of what's coming next. ADHDers need to learn to ask themselves questions in the form of propositions. For instance, "<u>If</u> I do this, <u>then this</u> will happen." "But <u>if I don't,</u> then this will happen." These questions and answers allow the ADHDer to preview and anticipate a future outcome. Setting up mental scenarios helps the child anticipate life. ADHD kids often jump before looking to see if there is any water in the pool. Early on I had to build my wings on the way down. But you learn if you are not shamed and belittled. Remember what hurts us the most instructs us the most. Obstacles are part of the journey.

Learning to apply "if" questions and "then" answers can help the ADHDer avoid some grave consequences. Being able to preview what a situation actually calls for, in order to select the proper output instructs the ADHDer to refrain from telling the teacher, "Math is stupid, and your butt is a bit fleshy." "If-then" questions help to slow down the ADHDer's first impulse, effectively filtering output, so better choices can be made, and less time spent in emotional and physical detention.

When a submarine sends its periscope to the ocean's surface, it previews the situation by scanning, so the crew can gauge, then determine what to do next. Previewing moves your attention to the bow of your mind, making you acutely aware of what "is" going on in front of you in this precise moment. It also informs you of what "could happen," next or soon following if proper heed isn't taken. If previewing is enacted, and the kid looks ahead, the ADHDer can actually alter thoughts, beliefs, and actions which otherwise would have sunk their ship. This pause, this constructed moment of inhibition and intentional deliberation is where the ADHDer learns to wait, reflect, then project their thinking into the future.

Teaching the ADHD individual to pump their mind's brakes, in order to pause, they experience the empowering sensation of steering their mind instead of their mind steering them. As they become more aware of their awareness things start to shift inside and a balance is created in the central nervous system (CNS). The CNS, like a seesaw, has two sides. The sympathetic on one side and the parasympathetic on the other. Both can't be up at the same time. The sympathetic branch is like an accelerator, revving up the mind and body with anxious, cautious, and fretful warnings. The parasympathetic branch helps pump the mind's brakes. The etymological origin of "para" can be found in many languages. Para can mean to be alongside, to help, protect, to assist. So, the parasympathetic branch wants to balance the sympathetic branch's over-reactivity, allowing the ADHDer to pause so they can observe their thoughts and choose accordingly. Imagine that, having jurisdiction over your thinking, emotions, and behaviors. Enacting a deliberate pause buys the ADHDer more time to search their long-term memory bank for an action that may have worked in the past.

These mental mechanisms do not come standard in the ADHD mind. They need to be taught, installed then utilized over and over. As with anything worth learning, it will take loads of patience and a true and binding commitment from parents, teachers, and the child themself to accomplish what needs to be learned. That right there is the difference that makes the difference. And that difference is the saving grace.

ADHD individuals weren't designed with periscopes and their impulsivity thwarts their ability to look ahead. Often the ADHDer's output generates a response, opposite of what they were hoping for. Formulating in their mind an image and the sensation of how things might look and feel "if" they do "this" or sound like "that," can keep them headed in the right direction.

When writing a paper, I suggest that the ADHD students be required to write the last paragraph first. The final paragraph, the summary, would tell the reader, "In conclusion, what I hope you'll have learned is …" This process will provide the ADHDer with a clear route to their main objective; prepare, present, then deliver quality output. If you noticed, at the beginning of this book I have a chapter titled, "Last Chapter First."

The <u>second</u> crucial neurodevelopmental function that produces good and accurate output is being aware of options. Helping the ADHDer develop a list of options provides them the luxury of examining possibilities. Surveying, then plotting possibilities must be recognized as a deliberate act that produces a deliberate action. ADHD minds have difficulty with this step. Lack of inhibition of thoughts, speech, and behaviors are the hallmarks of their frustrations. The "gut response," "knee-jerk reaction," or "shooting without aiming" can produce perilous consequences for the ADHDer. That's why a list of options is critical to producing quality output.

For the ADHDer life is a series of relapses, rebounds, and recoveries. For the non-ADHDer, these shifts are short and manageable. But for the ADHDer, they can be long, chaotic, and repetitive. Life is an assemblage of possibilities, all of which have probable and often predictable outcomes. The ability to pause and choose what you're "outputting" is a luxury that can be learned then installed into the ADHDer's repertoire of action. Basic decision-making is more fruitful when the ADHDer mines, then excavates the realization that they have more than one option.

A <u>third</u> neurodevelopmental function with profound effects on whether an ADHD individual's output is interpretable lies in their ability to <u>find a comfortable and functional tempo or measure of regularity, that allows them to pace themselves.</u>

Many an ADHDer has experienced someone looking them squarely in the eye, shaking their head and asking, "Why did you do that?" in a tone assuming the ADHDer is crazy. Their output makes perfect sense to them but is received by others as a hastened grouping of incomprehensible utterances.

The ADHDer can learn to regulate the pace of their delivery to produce clear and organized output. ADHD children often display a frenetic urgency to harvest their thoughts well before they are ripened. If words from thoughts are spoken too early, they are too rare; if they're revealed too late, they are overcooked. Thoughts that remain unexpressed, left to char in their minds' ovens, create a lot of internal emotional soot.

Both intake and output can come to a screeching halt if the ADHDer becomes confused. Pacing requires establishing a tempo that moves in a methodical, meticulous, and deliberate direction. But it's much easier to shift if you know what the hell is going on.

For quality or even just adequate output, a lot needs to be orchestrated and coordinated at the same time. Thoughts need to flow in the same direction and at the same rate. For the ADHDer, becoming aware of their thought processes in that precise moment allows them to slow down, reflect and recalibrate so they can construct and eventually produce appropriate output. These <u>three neurodevelopmental functions previewing, weighing options, and pacing</u> are crucial for that to happen. Remember flexibility is the key

Many ADHDers are eccentric and creative in thought and produce intellectually intriguing and emotionally felt output. Unfortunately, society is less impressed with their imaginative output and more concerned with criteria that need to be met.

The <u>fourth</u> neurodevelopmental function that ensures effective output is <u>the quality control process</u>. This is quite teachable, but unfortunately for an ADHD kid, the desire to remain seated once the work is complete is like trying to keep a well-inflated beach ball underwater. Once they're done, a catapult thrusts them from their chair and their mind feels untethered as if it just got released from shackles. Remaining in the chair to review the quality of the output is emotional and physiological imprisonment when their mind and body are already out the door.

It's always good to know, "How you are doing," as well as "How you did." When the ADHDer can slow down (regulate their tempo) and ask themselves these questions in a non-critical fashion—"How am I doing right now?" "Is this making sense to me?" "Am I on the right track?" "Would a different approach be more fruitful?" "Do I know a different approach?"—like high beams on a car, the answers to these questions will allow the ADHDer to see past their own nose. The high beams will reveal not only what's directly in front of them but also what lies further ahead. This enables the ADHD child to "sense ahead" then turn the wheel before careening into a distraction. Learning how to intentionally steer their attention, at a very precise moment, is teachable. This not only gives them more confidence at the point of performance, but also increases the probability that their output is not just adequate, but acceptable.

The <u>fifth</u> neurodevelopmental function for output to be understood and mastered is <u>learning from previous experiences</u>. How is it that some kids learn immediately what to do and what not to do? How is it that past experiences make an indelible impression on some? But what you'll find with ADHDers, is what seems like one darn thing after another is usually the same darn thing over and over.

ADHDers have difficulty sensing, remembering, and connecting prior experiences, then summoning and connecting what thought or behavior had worked in the past. When things work there is less impact on their memory than when things don't work. When things don't work, their esteem can take quite a hit. Mild to severe trauma and shame can leave an indelible dent, influencing thinking and behavior. When an ADHD kid senses little connectivity between what's happening now and a previous experience, adults will assume they are consciously choosing not to make the connection.

To consistently produce quality output, the ADHDer needs to remember what worked, even if it was as far back as two minutes ago. There needs to be an identifiable and verbalized sensitivity to a result whether it's positive or negative. Something that says, "Hey, that worked, I'll try that again," or "Wow, that didn't work at all. I better avoid doing that." "It was a waste of time." Some ADHD children seem incapable of noticing such interior voices and in many cases, there might not be an inner voice at all. A typical retort is "whatever......" The good news an inner voice can be taught.

Some ADHDers view any unfavorable adult reaction as criticism or punishment. People who help ADHDers need to think out loud when modeling problem-solving. This way the ADHDer can pick out patterns and sequences because they need help distinguishing the mental direction their mind is traveling in order to problem-solve. In turn, the ADHDer needs to verbalize the steps and direction their thought processes are traveling. This helps them hear themselves so they can ascertain what steps move them forward and where they become confused and stall out. Actually, hearing things helps the ADHD kid encode the experience for future reference and self-guidance. "Do I replicate what I just did, or should I avoid it, and why?" This is a good question to ask, and an even better one to answer.

When attention controls tighten up and become more regulated and attuned, the ADHDer feels much more comfortable and confident offering their output into the world for observation and judgment. Even if they experience a less than favorable reaction, they must not assume their efforts are futile. When you're bright, eager, and industrious, it's very frustrating not being able to do what needs to be done immediately.

It really hurts when you know your output isn't refined and continually disappoints important people in your life. Our job as parents or practitioners is to help the child maintain a basic faith in themselves as they expand and contract. We can keep learning interesting for them. Little victories en route are so very important. Illuminate and celebrate the moments and segments of time when output works. Teach the ADHDer that frustrations are temporary. Believing that things can work and will get better is a good default mode for our mind and body. Even when the worst gets worse, why not believe the best is yet to come.

When a kid's output is deemed inadequate by others, it's easy to look for something from the outside to make the inside feel better. Whether it's food, drugs, alcohol, shopping, video games, whatever, feeling pacified, even if for a short duration, is desirable. Who wouldn't want to feel better immediately? Voluntary and involuntary enslavement to behaviors that distract us from our inner world, affect all forms of output. Incessant subcortical firing in the limbic system drenches the prefrontal cortex with limbic lava, gumming up and disabling the accommodating and nurturing properties of the prefrontal cortex that supports output. When we can't access the prefrontal cortex's nurturing and supportive properties, output becomes derailed, sending us lurching down the low road into toxic emotional ravines. Immediate towing is necessary.

Waiting on someone to produce quality output is not one of society's more generous offerings to ADHD individuals. So, it's up to us to be patient while the ADHDer is trying to catch up.

CHAPTER 20

Estimating, Allocating, and Utilizing Time

> *"The two most powerful warriors are patience and time."*
>
> ~ Leo Tolstoy

I'll never forget this interaction with my son. That day I needed to leave the house at a specific time to be at a particularly important session. And I needed to drop the boys off at school a little earlier than usual.

My ADHDer, Jordan, was sitting on the floor fully dressed except for his shoes and socks. He was in the midst of bringing to life one of his Ghostbuster figures, orchestrating a highly theatrical dialogue. I said to my sweet and loving ADHD descendant, "Let's go, buddy. We've got to get out of here. Put on your shoes and socks, and let's roll."

A few minutes later I returned to find him shoeless. I nicely repeated, "Jordan, we've got to go. I can't be late for this meeting. Get your socks and shoes on *now*, please. We gotta fly."

A moment later I returned to find Jordan again paralyzed in thought, one foot adorned with a sock, the other bare.

"Jordan, we have to go, put on your other sock, and where are your shoes?" He looked at me blankly and shrugged his shoulders. I rushed upstairs to his room, found the shoes, flew back down, and placed them in front of him. "Here you go. Let's move. We need to leave, NOW, or I'm going to be late. I can't be late to this meeting, honey, let's roll."

Returning a minute later I found him with one shoe on and one shoe off. He seemed to be examining his toes through his socks. Finally, I lost it. "What the hell are you doing?" I yelled. "We've got to go now; I've asked you over and over. Please put on your other shoe right now!"

He looked up at me a bit befuddled, slightly irritated, and asked, "Why are you yelling?" Eventually, I put his shoe on him in the car and rushed him to school and me to my office, only to find that my patients were running late.

For the ADHDer, learning to experience time as a precious and welcoming benefactor offers cognitive and behavioral guardrails. Rather than time being a badgering boss looming over them, they learn to experience time as an opportunity to enjoy their own company. Sadly, children and adults with ADHD have horrendous clashes with time. Squandered and mismanaged chunks of time are pervasive and a central frustration for ADHDers and those close to them. It's important they learn to meet and greet this challenge early on in order to contend with and overcome it. This impairment has a wide, rippling effect reaching well beyond just the people closest to them. Well-meaning people suggest, "Maybe a class in time management might be helpful." It's not "time" they have difficulty managing; it's managing themselves "<u>within time.</u>"

There are numerous ways ADHDers mismanage time. Allocating enough time for them to become organized is futile if they don't know how to "organize." We need to show them over and over how to organize their room, backpack, or desks. Modeling for them *"how to"* become organized nurtures their ability to sense time. But you know what, they always like the feeling that's generated from a clean and organized locker, desk, room, closet, or backpack. And yes, even a made bed. When we learn to be organized, we are much more aware if we're ahead or behind schedule. It's difficult for the ADHDer to see any long-term benefits in the effort and energy it takes to become organized at the moment, especially if it's not fun. One kid told me, "I'm forever being rushed." If it's not fun and you're being rushed, everything feels tedious. I mean why make a bed when it's just going to get messed up again that night?

Teaching the ADHD child how to manage themselves within time draws directly on *executive functioning skills*. The daily demand to shift and transition both physically and intellectually, while remembering what had previously worked, then implementing and replicating that specific action, then following through and finishing what you started, is expected many times throughout the day. The previous sentence may seem like a laborious evolution of thought, but that process comes naturally for non-ADHDers.

However, for ADHD kids, there never seems to be enough time to figure out how to get things right, especially when they're holding up the group. Being fast-forwarded into stages of emotional, behavioral, and academic development that your mind isn't ready for is both emotionally and physiologically painful. Whether it be completing a thought, a fruitful interaction or silently trying to observe and understand a process or sequence, ADHDers often feel hurried, angry, confused, and eventually stall out. When you're not ready life sweeps your mind and body into the next moment and things feel very incomplete.

The wiring that supports planning, plotting, and impulse control within the prefrontal cortex, is the last part of the brain to mature. Unfortunately, when it comes to time, *planning* and *plotting* play a major role in getting anything done. Such capabilities do not come standard in the ADHD brain, nor can they be whimsically ordered through Amazon. Impairments with time need to be specifically identified and explained to the ADHDer. Together we as caregivers can help the ADHDer implement strategies which escort their attention to comprehensible places within a reasonable length of time.

We can help the ADHD child by making a schedule visible on paper, a marking board, phone, or iPad, that breaks time into small manageable chunks. In some cases, hour by hour, or even minute by minute. You can use alarms on the phone to give them a heads-up, as to what's next, and when. Being able to <u>see</u> on a list "what to do next" raises the likelihood that exact action will be taken, and deadlines met. Visible schedules help keep the mind's wheels on the road. Being able to literally see what's expected next, helps them latch on to the immediate priority, moving them along the timeline toward task completion.

I also recommend that your child wear a watch with a sweeping second hand and arms that slowly move. No digital. This way they can see and experience for themselves the passage of time, segment by segment. I used to love looking at the clock in grade school and the smooth consistent movement of the red second hand. I would shut my eyes when the second hand passed twelve, then count 60 seconds in my head, then open my eyes to see how close I had come to twelve. I guess I was trying to sense time. Looking back, I suppose the teacher might have been saying something important, who knows.

Here are a few things we can do to help a child increase their capacity to manage themselves "within time" in order to make life work:

- Decide on specific and consistent times. Flexibility is important, but when it comes to "mind work" a specific nonnegotiable time should be set. Prepare them to anticipate the brain sit-ups necessary to complete the task. Let them know it might be a little frustrating and uncomfortable, but everybody has to do it. You can jovially refer to them as "mental gymnastics" or "a brain workout." Presenting it like this helps them understand that there's a benefit, a strengthening to what might otherwise be considered torture. Let them know the strength and determination it takes to regulate themselves is not a virtue that you either do or don't have. Explain to them that it's a strength that can be built. Prepare the ADHDer to understand that they're going to need to extend themselves outside of their comfort zone. They need to be told to "buckle up because we're going to venture into new areas of learning that won't be easy at first but will become easier with effort and time." And most importantly, "there's a beginning and an ending to this endeavor." Tell them it won't last forever. But let them know that once they've agreed to the time and setting, it's nonnegotiable though that might seem unfair. But be sure to point out that many of life's responsibilities are fixed in that way, and again, everybody has to do it. Reassure them that the sustained intentional action of focusing attention and managing themselves within time, will make them stronger, right now and move them toward completion. Be sure to reiterate the immediate benefit of self-discipline and praise their follow-through. Assure them that

the older they get, the easier it will become. And everything is hard before it becomes easier.
- Even if there is no specific homework, utilize this same time for something entertaining, fun, and enriching. This time is allotted for growth and learning even when there's no homework pending. Let them choose the topics and even teach you what they know. That specific time should still be used to enrich.
- Help your child get started. (See chapter on Jump Starting Jordan.) For some ADHD kids getting started is the hardest part. They believe that once they've begun, they won't see daylight or come up for air for quite some time. Completing a task is very satisfying, but we need to teach them how to sense progress along the way. Getting on a roll and plowing through a large amount of work can give a child a sense of inner mastery of the outside world. Taking breaks are important, but they need to be timed; a break starts, then it's over. The first break needs to be experienced well into the body of work, where it's experienced as a welcomed reprieve. Whether it's a little nudge of encouragement, a jump start, or a theoretical swift kick in the butt, they need to be paced and accompanied at least to the halfway point by someone willing to think out loud in order to help them keep the ball rolling. This can make all the difference between starting and finishing. When the ADHDer senses your patience, commitment, and compassion, they do not want to disappoint you, or themselves in front of you.
- Be available to help research or answer questions. Being available is quite different than spoonfeeding. Model for them the diligence that leads to resourcefulness. Model for them how to look up something, then have them do it. Many kids today

have never opened a dictionary. Show them how to find information, words and meaning in sources other than the Internet.
- There is nothing wrong with assisting your child in organizing their desk, work area, notebook, and backpack over and over. But make sure they watch you as well as help you do it. If they see it done often enough, they'll sense how the process works, rather than just the results. They will also begin to like it that way because being organized feels good. They'll start to demand it from themselves for their own comfort and sense of predictability. But don't expect them to readily admit it.

<u>Steps you and your child can collaborate on to help them utilize time</u>

1. Help the ADHDer identify specifically what's being asked. Have them clearly verbalize to you the assignment or project.

2. Set a time that they think they might be finished, then shoot for somewhere close.

3. Guesstimate how long it will take to get to certain points. Know if it's going to be minutes, hours, or days to complete.

4. Have them occasionally look backward and see what they've traversed. Also, have them look ahead and crystalize how they want this to look when they're finished.

5. Anticipate and organize a list of tasks that moves them closer to their goal.

6. Arrange the steps or tasks in the best order.

7. Assess how long each task is going to take.

8. Plan for recesses and breaks that allow them to stretch out and decompress.

9. Monitor progress: Draw a line through completed steps and record how long each took.

10. Check to see if they are on schedule.

11. When completed, check to see where they were flowing and where they might have felt clogged up.

These steps will help in assessing efficiency and increasing sensitivity to future obstacles.

Help the individual learn to create a plan of action based on priority. ADHD kids want to do the easy or fun parts first, with zeal and energy, then get bogged down in academic paralysis when the more tedious work is required. It's essential for them to understand the order and sequence of actions. No understanding, no action; no action, no growth; no growth, no sense of self-satisfaction; no satisfaction, no motivation; no motivation, no accountability; no accountability then no fun or privileges that come with being responsible.

Help them divide the material into small manageable segments. Some people when reading a book like short chapters. It gives them the impression that they are flying through the pages. Same with managing a workload. For the ADHD individual, manageability motivates.

Praise and acknowledge the effort and discipline required rather than results. When I ran races, it was always good to have people along the course or track encouraging me to keep going, to stick with it, cheering and acknowledging my effort. I didn't need someone at the end to evaluate my effort. I could do that myself. The same goes for learning. I needed people along the way to help me understand things and push me along. I might not have run a great race, but the support of others kept me moving.

Do not let your child bail out when the going gets tough, because it will. Bailing out is not a break. Get to a clearing in the forest instead of stopping in the swampy muck. Get to a spot that's above water and then take a break. No one wants to go back into the woods to start again with something they bailed on. They can find relief, catch their breath, reboot their brain and body when they've reached an intellectual and emotional clearing. The ADHDer needs to feel they're not alone in the forest. They need to experience your willingness to hunker down with them. Even calling a short timeout and stepping away from the experience for a moment, gives both of you time to breathe, brush off and resume without ever leaving the playing field. ADHD individuals respond more readily to graphic directions than to words thrown at them. Coupling verbal instruction with actions that can be seen and felt, increases the likelihood of movement toward the goal.

Squandering time is a result of several different impairments. The cause of the deficiency and its origin must be determined so aid can be delivered where it's most needed. For some reason, I tend to believe that I'm 20 minutes away from everything. My inability to accurately estimate and allocate time has been challenging. It certainly hurt my ability to self-supervise and self-regulate "within" time. But with age and the repetitive practice of learning to be aware of my awareness, or lack of, I've become quite proficient in managing myself "within" time. My daily routine, a private practice, is constructed hour by hour. Pretty clear cut. Explain to the ADHDer that managing themselves within time requires a lot of practice. With a heightened awareness and a willingness to tolerate discomfort, they too will begin to believe they can manage moment-to-moment events.

Demonstrate for the ADHDer that repetitive efforts help change fleeting states of frustration and doubt into stable traits of determination and confidence. It's about activating good redeeming experiences of mastery and then installing them into easily accessible storage. This action literally changes the neural structure of the brain. New neural pathways lead to a more basic faith in themselves. This rewiring or repaving is called neuroplasticity which says our brains are malleable.

When you're distracted, there is no awareness of time passing. Lack of awareness thwarts the intentional channeling of mental energy toward sequential organizing and planning. These deficits impede the automatic thoughts necessary to ignite actions mandatory to managing yourself within specific time constraints. It's hard to appreciate anything if you don't notice it.

Inefficient retrieval of specific information wastes a lot of time. The inability to shift from observation to understanding and then to action must occur concurrently. Often there's a lot of avoidant and escape behaviors that prevent the actions which lead to understanding. Not being able to convert thought and observation into language and action, depletes time rapidly. I've seen many ADHD individuals get stuck within time not because they don't care, but because of over-the-top obsessive-compulsive perfectionism. With ADHDers, there are many game-stopping frustrations when it comes to self-regulation within time.

When preparing to study, help the ADHDer avoid getting stuck by having their notes, reference materials, and a watch handy where they can see the passage of time.

When I find my brain's attention control system gaining no traction, sort of spinning its tires, I will turn on my telephone's stopwatch and set it next to the keyboard. I can see the seconds ticking away and compete within myself to try and set new attention span records. Externalizing time helps me become aware of when I'm piddling, and time is being squandered. This awareness also helps me begin to install some limits on the stages of a task. When my mind starts to wander, I stop the watch. Sometimes I will only go two minutes and 20 seconds before getting distracted. There are other times I can go for 50 minutes to an hour and a half without a brain blurp.

When an ADHD child doesn't experience a progressive sense of mastery when attempting to develop an awareness of time, their skills become sluggish at best. Pointing out segments in which they progressed helps them document in their mind, the sensation of upgrading and recalibrating their skills. That right there is enough of an intrinsic reward, a brain blast of dopamine and endorphins if I may, to want to continue to increase the flow of mental energy to those areas. This flow is the fuel that moves them closer to completion where the sensation of proficiency resides. The actual felt sense of knowing they've done well is a feeling that wants and needs to be replicated over and over. If they're not accustomed to the experience of doing well, they'll sometimes feel a bit sheepish or embarrassed when praised.

Society tends to pound on the fast-forward button of ADHD children, demanding rapidity while in turn pumping them full of medication intended to slow them down. There are other ways to help the ADHDer learn to engage their mind. Having them ingest a pill, then be left on their own to make sense of their now narcotized inner self in relation to the demands of the outside world is not helpful or inspiring. Nor does it take any heavy lifting on the part of the parents or teacher. Heavy lifting makes everybody stronger.

Being able to ascertain what's worked and what hasn't, needs to be talked about out loud quite a bit. Taking <u>time</u> to mentally digest and problem solve an experience within time, provides the opportunity and capacity for a child to self-correct.

The ADHD individual truly begins to feel and perform better as they become more comfortable in their body, and time feels more manageable in their minds. Transforming awareness into action is self-regulation. Both the slow and fast swirling thoughts that inhabit their minds need more than just medication, but also a language of comfort in that moment, at that specific time.

Sadly, when the ADHDer is continually shoved along the educational "time" continuum, they experience distress and develop a harrowing social, emotional, and academic limp. Unfortunately, everybody notices. Of course, we can't give them "all the time they need", because a lot of them would never complete a thing. What we can do is provide patient instruction and structure both in and out of school. When it comes to managing themselves within time, the ADHDer's greatest lessons will be learned outside of school. But know that's the last thing the ADHD individual wants to invest their time in, a brain-bleeding, gut-wrenching academic pursuit outside of school. Being allotted extra time might feel like an extended sentence for some ADHDers, but it's often what's needed in order for them to catch up. Making sure they put in the time to get the job done requires skillful negotiating and cutting a few deals. Just make sure they hold up their end of the bargain.

Small cumulative victories in self-regulation and the successful utilization of time builds confidence which directly fuels motivation. Confidence and motivation help the ADHDer more comfortably direct and set their sights on the future. Unfortunately, for some ADHDers confidence has a short shelf life and wears off quickly. Since time management never stops, the ADHDer can feel like life is a barrage of tests, tribulations, and deadlines. Well, it is. We need to help the ADHDer learn to hold the sensation of mastery in the forefront of their minds longer. Intentionally extending its stay in their window of awareness longer than normal promotes neurogenesis, the growing of new cells in the hippocampus. Over time, new neural structures get built and that sense of competency becomes internalized as a stable neural trait.

Most of this work needs to take place at home rather than expecting the school to handle it all. <u>Home experiences transfer more easily to school than school experiences to home.</u> Remember that it's experience that sculpts our brain and lays down new circuitry. The more positive the experience, the more efficient the circuitry. Know we can develop our brain like we can a muscle—with intentional repetitive action.

When ADHD kids believe they can never please the adult world when it comes to managing themselves within time, why try? Hope and motivation evaporate into a nothingness vacuum of time. Hopelessness produces apathy, and apathy discourages effort. Why take the "time" to drive toward anything if you believe you'll never arrive? And even if you do, big whoop.

It's important that the ADHDer comprehends what's not possible time-wise. "There's no way we can do ____ and be on time." Or "It's going to take a lot more than a half an hour to get this done." They'd rather hear an estimation as to how long an intellectual or physical pursuit might take, rather than not know, and run out of brain fuel, halfway there. But a "what's possible" inquisitive growth mindset is important. Large doses of hope and fortitude need to be infused into the child's struggling mind and body with a narrative that can override the brain's natural negative bias. With no pun intended, learning to manage time takes time, and repetitive adjustments. Hope aids in regulating the quality, direction, and cadence of their thinking. Again, I'll repeat the cherished words of Emily Dickinson's interpretation of hope. "A thing with feathers that perches in the soul and sings the tune without the words and never stops at all." Isn't "never stops at all" the way hope is supposed to work? With or without ADHD, sustaining hope takes faith and practice. And it takes <u>time</u> to unfold. There it is again, that word time.

So, if you're not organized within time, efficiency doesn't develop. Showing the ADHD child how to manage the workload by organizing themselves within time, keeps them from continually doing things the hard way. By externalizing time (making it visible) and its passage, helps the ADHDer know when they should shift into managerial and organizational mode. Knowing what to do first, second or third, while engaging the intentional behaviors that action requires for completion, is what prioritizing is. The result is productivity. Temporal consideration and its mastery are crucial in every aspect of school and adult endeavors.

The Talmud, a huge collection of Jewish doctrines and laws compiled and written before the eighth century, offers a beautiful quote depicting hope and encouragement, "Every blade of grass has its own angel that bends over it and whispers "grow, grow."

Being able to consistently call upon a strategy that can be applied to a problem or task leads the ADHDer toward an organized understanding. Completion brings about the experience of achievement, and achievement feels good. Especially if it's on time.

CHAPTER 21

Thoughts Are Not Facts: Is It True? Is It Good? Is It Useful?

"Don't believe everything your mind tells you."

~ Me

For most ADHD kids, what seems like one darn thing after another is usually the same darn thing over and over, but at a different time, in a different place, and with a different person. One of my priorities is helping ADHDers hear the tones, taste the flavor, and note the intention of their personal narratives coming from their mental recordings. Once noted, they can reflect on the content of these dialogues and note the automatic habitual responses that lead them to despair and immobility.

We can teach the ADHDer to again ask themselves more questions. "Do the themes of my internal dialogue keep repeating themselves?" "Do these refrains help me or hurt me?" "Whose voices that I've internalized are carping at me?" "What do I need to do to stop this tape from looping around in my head?" "Do I need to do something immediately, or only when it gets really bad?" Questions like these help the ADHDer crystalize exactly what's been hammering them. They can begin to see what has clearly been blocking their self-awareness. They can begin to know exactly what's limited their beliefs in themselves and stunted their potential. They get to see precisely what's kept them from believing in and experiencing their better parts. When the ADHDer learns to slow down their mind, they begin to better understand and sense the motive behind messages they've internalized from others. Here is where they begin to add, subtract, and consolidate whatever is needed to oil their thinking. They can loosen, then dislodge themselves from a prescripted narrative that has nothing to do with who they really are. Challenging the accounts of yourself helps you begin to change the distasteful ingredients that go into a self-destructive porridge. Severe thoughts don't help a thing. Harshness doesn't usher in peaceful persistent patience. Loving determination does. When the ADHDer learns to pump the breaks of their mind and slow down their thinking rather than rush to judgment, a space is created where active awareness happens. In this space, they learn to detach themselves from their story and simply deal with their sadness, anger, despair, and anxiety. In this space, they learn patient understanding while cultivating self-compassion leading to self-acceptance. This is where they practice offering themselves a type of warmheartedness that begins to complete the past, repair the moments, and build resilience in order to handle the next internal order of business.

Three important questions, we should ask ourselves when in doubt. These questions add clarity that tilts our thoughts, feelings, and decisions in our favor.

1.) Q: <u>Is it true?</u> Is it true that I'm not good enough, since I have a poor command of fractional equations? A: No. Math isn't my strong suit, but I'm good at many other things.

2.) Q: <u>Is it good</u>? Q: Is it good for me to believe that I'm a complete dolt due to my inability to compute fractions? A: Fractions play no role in my life today. I could probably learn fractions more easily now, but there is no need to. To this date, no one has ever accosted me with an equation to solve.

3.) Q: <u>Is it useful</u>? A: Feeling bad about myself is never useful. I'm so much more than my deficiencies. When I was young, I learned to believe bad things about myself. Not only are they not true, but they were never true.

These three questions help us rewrite and rewire what we've come to believe as true. The ADHDer actually gets to choose and replace the negative litany with something good and useful. They get to be the chooser, intentionally influencing the outcome of a given moment with a deliberate choice. They become the hammer rather than the nail. This everyday human right "to make your own choices" is news to a lot of ADHDers. It goes directly against the old dialogue they've subconsciously tattooed and internalized into their psyche. They can choose the ingredients of their thoughts, spicing things up from dismal and defeating to uplifting and motivating. Yes, it's a choice we get. Putting a space between our thoughts and reactions is empowering.

ADHD individuals are extremely interested and appreciative when they learn about their minds and how their brains work. They not only find it fascinating but a welcome relief when they discover they aren't to blame for all the crap they've come to believe about themselves. Proper instruction illuminates understanding. ADHDers use this newfound knowledge and freedom to gain perspective and build moment-to-moment resilience. They can learn to circumvent some of their mind's distortions that have created glitches that they had sadly mistaken for defectiveness.

Cell phones today do much more than make calls. And so, it is with our brains; they do much more than just think. By simply asking themselves the right questions, the ADHD individual can begin a process leading to the construction of a reliable self-monitoring system. Again, this system creates the space where strategies can be generated, and new brain circuitry fashioned. This leads to new neural constructions. By developing strategies, the ADHDer starts to notice, then avoid familiar exit ramps reading, "Misery Ville 1 mile." Or the warning sign that reads, "Road Out." This way they can begin to avoid their first impulse. They can bypass the mental exits that have led them down the emotional and behavioral "low roads." Staying on the "high roads" and adhering to this deliberate pause, helps them reflect and redirect.

We all have experienced the unsavory destination and shoddy accommodations that the low road leads us to. That route is never "true," "good," or "useful."

CHAPTER 22

Learning How to Learn

> *"Sometimes you win and sometimes you learn."*
>
> ~ Anonymous

I have shared with many people that when I first got to college, I had to learn how to learn. I truly don't remember studying more than 25 cumulative hours my entire high school experience, though I'm sure I must have. When I got to college I had to learn how to remember and remember how to learn.

I was a bit taken aback when I realized that the professors really expected me to read the assigned chapters. This whole study thing plowed deep inroads into my lounging around time. I had to put off getting high, playing table tennis, shooting baskets, or listening to music. Was studying really expected to come first? It seemed like it was supposed to. I mean hypothetically that sounded correct. Wasn't that why I was there? Study first, then play. It seemed I had the energy for all activities except studying. For me, the quickest way to catch a nap or fall asleep at night was to begin studying. Nothing like reading a few chapters of geology, philosophy, or English to escort me right into sleepy time. As a distance runner, infused with that special ADHD carbonation, I would expend more energy in a couple of days than some people could generate in a month. Unfortunately, I had to learn to channel it toward my studies. It really took a lot of energy to simply hunker down, start, endure the middle slog, then finish my assignments strongly.

As mentioned throughout this book, time is one of the most frustrating and elusive sequences ADHDers have to contend with. I had difficulty allocating, estimating, and utilizing time. It was difficult distributing the exact amount of mental energy to maintain a consistent effort. It was hard keeping pace in just one class, much less five. Trying to steer my attention toward intellectual pursuits and sequential processes, with the hope of some semblances of measurable productivity, was more exhausting than running ten miles in 100 percent humidity on a 99-degree Kansas afternoon.

First, I had to learn what and when to study. Just getting myself in the right place, at the right time, focusing on the right material for the proper amount of time, considerably taxed my ADHD mind.

I learned quickly that I couldn't study in the dorm because it was too <u>loud</u> and offered many more enjoyable options than any intrigue Plato, plankton and Pythagoras could offer. My sophomore year I got my first apartment. I quickly learned that I couldn't study there either because it was <u>too quiet</u>. I overheard everything. I wasn't attention deficit at those moments, it was attention overload. I couldn't filter out the faintest of sounds. If a twig snapped or a cricket belched, I would jump up and peer out the window to see if I could locate the origin of the sound. So, it was not that I couldn't pay attention or listen, it was that I paid attention and listened to everything other than what I was supposed to be focusing on.

CHAPTER 22

During this time, I was running 75-90 miles a week, so I was in a constant state of depletion and hunger, while genetically revved up. It was when I would sit down to study, I'd all of a sudden become aware of how famished I was. I'd get up, abandoning the books, and ravenously rummage through the refrigerator. I'd then notice that the floor needed sweeping and I'd oblige. With janitorial experience in my repertoire, I knew that a clean floor is only clean after a good hot mopping. And isn't it said that "cleanliness" in a cat box is next to Godliness? I'd scoop. Then a magazine cover would catch my attention and suck me in, and I'd settle down and read an article or three. I would become completely dissociated from my studies, willing to do anything constructive or interesting to avoid the brain work. Eventually, I'd end up back in the chair to complete my studies. It would take me three hours to do what most others could have done in one.

I soon discovered that I could get things accomplished in two distinctly opposite settings. I found that I could focus much more easily by putting myself in a busy food court at the mall. With my back to the masses, I could block out large amounts of indistinguishable noise, rather than scuffle to block out a few faint sounds. For instance, the house creaking or the furnace going on and off would derail my concentration. If I placed myself in a busy location, I could immerse myself and concentrate for long periods of time. I also discovered that if the music was playing, it had to be instrumental because I was unable to keep myself from listening to the lyrics. I'd get caught up in the lyrics and I'd become the storyline itself. I've been known to get a little misty internalizing the angst of betrayals the cowboy felt out on the lone prairie, horse below 'em, holding on to the sorrow of ruptured dreams. Then all of a sudden, I'd get all charged up listening to other instructions, "Two steps to the right, two steps to the left, jump, now back it up ..." and so on. I'd do it in my chair.

Conversely, but equally effective, I discovered that I could really get a lot done studying in the university library, but only under certain conditions. The library is a place where people go to concentrate. Sounds great; the problem for me was getting there, which involved a bit of gamesmanship and self-trickery. If I knew I needed to study for at least three hours, I would often lollygag around until 8:30 or 9:00 p.m. By that time, I was tired from running, sufficiently buzzed from pot, and satiated with an abnormal amount of food. Studying would put me to sleep in less than 30 minutes, not completing my assignment or remembering a single thing I read or wrote down. After getting slapped with a couple of poor marks on homework, quizzes, and tests, I realized something had to change immediately, or this college experience would forcibly have to be taken up at a future date.

I had to tighten the parameters around my thinking and doing. I needed to be precise. I had to think ahead, projecting my thoughts and assessments into the future. It's amazing that we are the only species that can bring the future into the present. Animals don't think about this upcoming Tuesday or what's happening after dinner. We have prefrontal lobes that allow us to create language, symbols, and time travel. So, I had to project my mind out into the future and pick a precise time that I needed to be at the library, sitting in my chair, with the books open, my mind focused on doing my work. If I told myself I needed to be there sometime around 8:00, I would often wander in closer to 9:00. With such loose time constraints, I would find myself flipping through magazines or newspapers, rapidly becoming weary from the workout, THC, and food. I learned I had to be exact, specific, and then punctual to just get started. So, I would tell myself that I __had__ to be sitting down at precisely 7:04, 6:41, or 7:57. An odd time, but it had to be precise. I would find myself having to dash from the parking lot across campus, bound upstairs, and scurry to the desk sequestered back in the stacks to meet the designated time and "NOT" be late. Being late gave me a sense of disappointment in myself, even if it was just for a few seconds. And Lord knows I didn't need any more of that. I felt I was letting down the part of me that I knew was begging to be disciplined. It was a simple self-challenge that I did not want to lose. It sure got me in the chair. It wasn't that I needed to manage time, but I had to learn how to manage myself within time. There is a big difference.

I quickly learned that there was no way I could sit at one of the open tables on the ground floor of the library. When anyone would walk in or out, I would raise my head and notice. Again, I needed to sequester myself away on the top floor, among the stacks, at a lone desk facing the wall. No sounds and scarce traffic made it much easier to stay on task. I would sometimes have to plug my ears if someone encroached upon "my" territory or was having a conversation with a librarian. The magazine and newspaper racks were strictly forbidden until all work was completed.

I knew I needed to put in more time than the average bear to pass, much less excel. More brain sit-ups were required, and as you know, crunches aren't fun. I learned that if it wasn't fun, exciting, or riveting, my ADHD mind had a difficult time engaging itself. I incorporated what is referred to as "step wisdom." I would break my work down into small manageable chunks so it would feel as if I were accomplishing something. Instead of having one finish line three hours away, I had numerous little way stations where I would stop the clock, stretch a bit, hit the can, and gobble some peanut M&Ms.

Running was the carrot. So, to be able to run and compete for the university, I had to be eligible. To be eligible, I had to produce. To produce I had to learn how to remember and remember how to learn. That meant studying.

CHAPTER 23

Being Okay with Being Okay: What the Mind Simulates

"I'm okay."

~ Me

Over the past two million years our brain has tripled in mass. It has not only gotten bigger but has developed new structures. One of the assemblages that evolution has provided only the human brain and no other species, is the prefrontal cortex. Among the fringe benefits, the prefrontal cortex affords humans the unique ability to form a complex language and create and simulate experiences in our minds. Which is good if you're not hamstrung by the anxiety that gets ratcheted up with uncertainty. The brain has the amazing capacity to symbolize both our inner and outer world experiences. Most of what is perceived in the outer world is manufactured in the inner world. In fact, only a fraction of the inputs your occipital lobe receives comes straight from the external world. The rest comes from your internal memory storeroom and perceptual-processing modules. Your brain simulates a virtual reality that's close enough to the real thing to be believed. Simulations of previous events and experiences allow us to learn from the past and avoid certain consequences. Simulation of future events grants us the opportunity to identify, select and compare possible outcomes, so we can direct our behavior toward the best possible results.

Sadly, with most ADHD individuals their simulator distracts them from being present in the moment, skewing their comparative projective thinking about future choices. It's difficult to learn from the past if you don't exactly know how you arrived in the present. The simulator in the ADHD individual's brain is constantly rewinding itself, replaying mini-movies and their sequels, both real and imagined. Sadly, these perpetual looping thoughts, beliefs, and experiences don't stir up the most uplifting and inspiring memories. Remember the brain has a natural negative bias. Velcro for the bad and Teflon for the good. These mental snippets can range from mild upsets to traumatic paralysis. The more we play the clips of negativity, anxiety, and doom, the deeper these themes get entrenched in our story, then reinforced throughout the neural structures.

The key to limiting our suffering is to first, become aware of the themes, patterns, and triggers of our negative narrative. Once aware, we commit to just sitting with what we noticed our mind is producing, in an observatory fashion. By doing this we create an intentional pause where we can reflect as opposed to impulsively reacting. By not responding defensively, or recoiling in shame, we can, in this space, begin to rewrite our old warmed over, leftover story using a language of patience and self-compassion that's comforting and reassuring.

Completely off the subject, my first experience with a real live simulator was in driver's education class, back in the early '70s. We sat in the driver's seat of these automobile simulators and watched films intended to mimic true-to-life driving experiences. I was always amazed how within the course of a few blocks, someone would run a stop sign, a huge can would fall off a garbage truck, a child would chase a wayward ball into the street and, of course, the proverbial dog would dash out from nowhere. This was readying us for real life. Though the events were manufactured, so goes our mind's simulator; we, too. manufacture events. But please, don't believe everything your mind tells you. One of my favorite Mark Twain quotes states, "My life has been filled with terrible misfortunes, most of which have never happened." The simulator prepares us for things that might not ever happen, but by God, I was ready.

My late and cherished friend, Alan, sat next to me in driver's ed. He was removed from his simulator, told to take his chair, and sit in the hall for traveling upwards of 120 mph down a neighborhood side street. This set off all sorts of alarms in the simulator and uproarious pandemonium in the class. A small group of comrades and I anointed Alan superstar status after that stunt.

Like these machines, our brain provides us with the capability to simulate experiences before they happen. It's called imagining. We can imagine an event or behavior and then move it from our mind, onto the future. We simulate these events on our mind's stage. For example, we can simulate taste in our mind by imagining the flavor and consistency of an entrée described as a soufflé of tuna yogurt, seasoned with paprika and fresh dill, sprinkled with chocolate shavings, floating in sardine oil, drizzled in barbeque sauce, and topped with fresh mint. Most anyone who can simulate the flavor of such a delicacy in their mind would probably never order it. Why? Because we can imagine its assault on our taste buds and the havoc it would wreak on the old colon. We can simulate the results without ever taking a bite.

The good news is we have a simulator; the bad news is that the ADHDer's simulator tends to work poorly. The simulator has what Dan Gilbert, a Harvard psychology professor, refers to as "Impact Bias." The simulator leads you to believe that most outcomes are inevitably disappointing and at times torturous. He says that losing an election, a broken relationship, uncontrollable weight gain, a startling medical diagnosis, or flunking a test, affects us less traumatically and for a shorter amount of time than we anticipated during the moment it's happening.

Gilbert believes that most of life's smaller traumas which occurred over three months ago have very little effect on overall happiness. That's because happiness can be synthesized by the overused refrain, "Turn lemons into lemonade." We humans can synthesize despair into hope, poverty into resources, and adversity into opportunity. The upshot is that a properly manned simulator strengthens our resilience and fortifies hope.

Realistic and clear cognitive restructuring, coupled with relaxed mindful awareness, jump-start our mind's natural perceptive processes. A healthy simulator helps us sort out, rationalize, and regulate our assessments. Awareness instructs us to hit the brakes when we know our mind is beginning to jump the guardrail and descend down its dark embankment. Sometimes the simulator needlessly prepares us to endure and tolerate imagined interactions and anticipated events. For instance, I can drive by a police officer with a radar gun pointed at me and become anxious immediately. Fortunately, I'm driving the speed limit and no chase ensues. But down the road, I can simulate (imagine) in my mind exactly what I would say if that son-of-a-bitch tried to slap me with a ticket. Sometimes I'll even say it out loud.

Most ADHDers are not born with a competent simulator. Clarity does not come naturally for ADHD individuals. But with thoughtful and consistent effort, the simulator can be programmed, tuned, tweaked, and reprogrammed and programmed and reprogrammed in such a way that we make now better so that later is easier. The effect of consistent reprogramming is quite welcomed, though the time and effort it takes isn't. I've found that when explained generically, the ADHD individual is excited about learning how to enjoy the benefits of <u>a compassionately based cerebral system</u>. They can learn to immunize and safeguard themselves from activating, then cueing up old toxic footage, reels of despairing dialogues the amygdala offers. The ADHDer can learn to immediately recognize the negative bias. They can ask themselves, "Is this flick good for me and worth watching in its entirety or shall I switch the channel?" "Is this mental and emotional direction which my mind is traveling right now the neural pathway I want to take, or is there a better way to go?" The answer is often a resounding "NO, this isn't good for me, and there is a better direction." These questions provide the ADHDer with a little mental space, where they can undergo a brief momentary mental rehab. Here they can evaluate the moment and sanitize their thinking. This physical and mental pause provides the space for the ADHDer to generate answers and adjust their feeling tone. Such renovation equips them to manage the next immediate moment with balance and resilience.

ADHD kids have a tough time guarding their mental health, which is critical in order to maintain solid mental footing and a hopeful demeanor. Teach the ADHDer to shoot for "okay-ness" rather than complete happiness and joy. Okay-ness is really a good place to be. Okay-ness should never be regarded as a "ho-hum" mental state. Teach them that okay-ness is a fertile soil where happiness can grow. But throughout life we have to remix the soil quite often, adding nutrients. But that's okay also. For ADHDers okay-ness can feel elusive. Remember our minds are wired to react with a negative bias to life's pressures, exaggerated expectations, and baffling conundrums. Happiness is not something to be found, but a trait and temperament to be developed.

When the ADHDer learns to intentionally and compassionately reassure themselves that they're going to be okay in what feels like an irreparable moment, they begin to believe that they truly have some say in the matter. At first, it can feel frustrating, futile, and ineffective because nothing magically shifts. Chances are they'll doubt the validity and the legitimate strength behind their own kindness, especially if emotional restoration isn't delivered as swiftly as Google or Amazon. Some ADHDers feel they don't deserve sensitive nurturing compassion. Compassion is very informing and supportive. It's an antidote to the shame our inner critic continually foments. It balances out the brain and body's ecosystems. Compassion is the first step in shifting our outlook and building a foundation of resilience that will steer our minds and alter outcomes. Cultivating the beliefs that insist, "I'm going to be okay," "I can figure this out," "This too shall pass," and "I can make it through anything," creates durable mental hardware. Such words are very nourishing for our forever-changing brain to absorb. These simple but nutritionally packed words are like a preventative virus app worth installing. They literally shorten the depth of the emotional dive and the duration of the spinout that the ADHDer's mind takes.

The earlier an ADHD kid can create a soothing and stabilizing mantra, and then begin practicing it, the more proficient they'll become at circumventing frustrations. They can bring things to a screeching halt by challenging their toxic self-to-self narrative. When left unchallenged these toxic mental loops can last a lifetime.

Humans tend to believe that it's easy to be happy when you get what you want. I've seen many individuals who thought they had what they wanted and were still miserable.

Dr. Gilbert says, "Natural happiness is what we get when we get what we wanted. Synthetic happiness is what we make when we don't get what we wanted."

Synthetic happiness is just as real, quenching, and enduring as natural happiness. Learning to adjust to what you have, even if you didn't want it, is an arrangement you make with yourself. A sincere and durable arrangement creates resilience, flexibility, and stability. When an ADHD individual learns to accept things they cannot change and then adjusts, their psychological immune system automatically strengthens.

When an ADHD individual discovers a way to be okay, even if where they find themselves is not where they want to be, they've manufactured synthetic happiness. If you want to multiply your okay-ness, then infuse it with gratitude. Realistically, no one can be constantly happy. But learning to be "gratefully okay" sounds darn good to me.

CHAPTER 24

Santayana

> *"A child educated only at school is an uneducated child."*
>
> ~ Santayana

When the ADHDer becomes hopeful about what lies ahead, I believe their optimism becomes, as George Santayana wrote, "A great renovator and disinfectant in the world." Optimism as a renovator. And Lord knows we all require renovation throughout the stretch of our journey. I like that—a constant cleansing, a makeover of our inner world. Santayana was a Harvard-trained philosopher, essayist, poet, and novelist who taught the likes of T.S. Eliot, Robert Frost, Gertrude Stein, Walter Lippmann, and W.E.B. Du Bois. He wrote the *Phases of Human Progress* and several works chock-full of timeless and familiar quotes such as:

"Those who don't remember the past are bound to repeat it."

ADHD kids need to remember what it was that they did that worked. Especially if it was just five minutes ago. Their minds can be so porous. And since our brains have an evolutionary built-in negative bias, it's no wonder the ADHDer's mind and body are ensconced by memories that create physical and emotional upheaval. They are constantly reminded by the exasperated expressions they garner based on what they didn't do or did poorly. Learning to recognize the bias, then repeatedly applying the correct interpretation, thought, or action onto the moment, helps the ADHDer rewire their brain, avoid their first impulse, and not continually repeat the misinterpretation. When sequences of thoughts and events get broken down into interpretable segments, they can see where things fractured. Through awareness, the ADHDer can learn "not" to repeat things.

"The family is one of nature's masterpieces."

ADHD individuals crave a sense of belonging, connection, and family. I once read on a friend's sweatshirt, "A family is a close circle of friends who care." It's a real plus when you can honestly say that your brother, sister, mom, or dad are good friends and your biggest supporters. Sadly, ADHDers for many different reasons can splinter their families and foment contempt. An understanding of the disorder makes it easier to forgive. ADHD is not an excuse, but an explanation for behaviors and thoughts that don't seem to work. The good news is with quality therapy, patience, and support, emotions, thoughts, and behaviors can be modified. The bad news is the adjustments probably won't happen on your or society's schedule. Self-compassion chock-full of forgiveness allows us to begin completing the past. Competition among family members is somewhat natural, but so unnecessary. Sometimes parents set up rivalries. When a family is a growth unit, no one needs to compete. Understanding and support can go a long way when offered consistently. Breath in Santayana's quote.

"To be interested in the changing of the season is a happier state of mind than to be hopelessly in love with the spring."

I love this quote so much, especially when dealing with seasonal affective disorders. It's natural for a child to be curious and to anticipate what's next. For ADHD kids, that curiosity is more a requisite for security. Just having an inkling of what's going to follow "now", makes it easier to plan ahead. Through no fault of their own, they find it difficult to immerse themselves in the present moment. Nature is healing. Sure, we have our preferences as to what season we prefer, but I've heard ADHD kids say, "I like all of them." Their keen sense of unique seasonal changes connects them to the natural order of things in a profound way.

"<u>Nonsense is good because common sense is so limited.</u>"

I've never seen a study that boasts the benefits of being, "way too serious." It's good to laugh and be silly. Nonsensical moments of humor can decompress our mind and body. Though ADHD kids may have difficulty comprehending a given situation as funny, they have the uncanny perspicacity to sense people and themes, below the surface of the moment. This doesn't necessarily mean they know what to do, but their astute sensory acuity can often pick up and see through a person's persona. Among other things, this insight informs them whether or not there's potential fun in that person. ADHDers seek to avoid the no-nonsense type of person.

"<u>Never build your emotional life on the weaknesses of others.</u>"

There is a distinct portion of the population that feels better about themselves when they make someone else feel worse. ADHD children are frequently the target of another's contempt and personal disdain. You will find that ADHD children will subconsciously volunteer for that role and take the bait. Even if it's not comfortable or uplifting such acquiescence allows them to feel they belong or are at least part of something.

Cool stuff. This small sample of Santayana's wisdom is quite applicable to the conditions that the ADHD individual experiences. Teaching such early insights needs to be woven into the ADHDer's self-to-self dialogue and philosophy. This will ensure that they can begin to make now better so that later will be easier.

CHAPTER 25

Committing to Improvement

> *"Luck is the residue of design."*
>
> – John Milton

Research shows that committing to change, the resolution to renovate, yields immediate results in immune system functioning. Now we know that how you feel inside matters much more than what you think. In fact, I implore you not to believe everything your mind tells you. When we make a pledge to improving our wellness, measures of real hope, resilience, and confidence begin to spike. We become more self-confident rather than self-conscious. But there's also a bit of a kickback; the false hope syndrome. This is when the initial brain parade of neurotransmitters and the pageantry of fervor begin to wear off. They then realize that the difficult and continual work it takes to consistently feel okay is just beginning. It's like when you buy a car and then drive it off the lot with glee and a sense of cosmic renewal. Then a week or so later you receive in the mail a payment book, thick as your thumb, depicting your obligation for the next 48 months. The actions it takes the ADHDer to change don't provide the emotional boost of the initial resolution to change. It's then they realize it's a process, not an event.

Technology is a huge distraction and can literally install distractibility into people who are not innately distractible. The discoveries in artificial intelligence are vast, but so too are the discoveries in neurosciences that encompass the body, brain, and spirit. A broad range of modern truths and ancient wisdom help us attune to the inner workings of our mind and the regulation of our attention. In fact, some helpful suggestions have been around for centuries.

A Buddhist Zen master, being interviewed at the end of his life, was asked about his enlightenment and his tremendously positive effect on thousands. He was asked, "How did you achieve such a complete realm of peace, tranquility, and acceptance?" It was reported that he dropped his head and said, "Mistake after mistake after mistake." We cannot upgrade experiences in our outer lives or the quality of the atmosphere of our inner world without making mistakes. Unfortunately, many ADHD individuals have come to believe that they "are a mistake." ADHD kids need to learn, then believe that every misstep isn't necessarily a mistake. I read a quote somewhere that stated, "Sometimes we win and sometimes we learn." When the ADHDer learns from their mistakes, it's an impressionably valuable moment. George Bernard Shaw stated, "A life spent making mistakes, is not only more honorable but more useful, than a life spent doing nothing."

Mistakes are plentiful for ADHDers. For some, mistakes motivate, making bravery easier when undertaking a second effort. For others, ADHDers "trying again" is wrought with anxiety, shame, and the fear of more bumbling exposure, recoiling into feelings of incompetency. Teach the ADHD child that when they consciously avoid making mistakes, they'll lose the opportunity to practice being brave. Simply believing this reduces anxiety. Internalizing this makes mistakes acceptable and manageable. When we surrender to the okayness of mistake-making, we can then commit to understanding and improvement.

A commitment, a pledge you make to yourself, develops beneficial habits which help you construct your ideal self. Invest in yourself from that perspective, not the downtrodden self who might still be trying to motivate with pain and shame. A true commitment fertilizes a growth mindset where you believe that effort and support will move you forward to meaningful changes. Consistent habits are what keep us moving the ball up the field. ADHDers need to be open to simple thought restructuring, especially when it serves the better part of them, the part that wants to change. Changing your thinking can lead to better habits, and experiencing better habits recalibrates your thinking, which in turn helps the body relax. But, for a commitment to become a way of life, the ADHDer needs something strong, something decisive inside their head, powered by their heart to prioritize and trigger new moment-to-moment thoughts and behaviors. Something needs to immediately trigger this new awareness. Something that says, "It's time to do this now" or, "It's time to get up and go, right now!" A trigger alerts you to jump into action. For instance, waking up in the morning might trigger, "Okay, time to work out, now." Or the trigger might be when dinner's over, the proclamation, "It's time to start homework now." Committing to a specific time can trigger habitual actions. Notice the word "now" at the end of each example. Exact times can be triggers, let's say 10:00 a.m. This designated time triggers the awareness of your commitment to check on your mother. Or 11:45 a.m. reminds you that you have a support group meeting at 12:00. Sunday evening before bed and the beginning of the workweek can trigger the need to have the trash on the curb Monday morning.

Weave into your commitment a reward. A benefit that incentivizes you to act. There's a difference between pursuing happiness and seeking rewards. Rewards are things we desire after doing well. Like a new pair of shoes if we've been working out hard. Or a bucket of chicken if we've been resolute in our dieting. But the most meaningful returns are not always material things. Material rewards seem to have a short shelf life and don't necessarily add meaning to our lives in a way that supports basic okayness. But approval and acknowledgment sink into our soul, bringing us a sense of satisfaction and pride. Mark Twain said, "I can live on a good compliment for months." Keeping a pledge, we've made to ourselves is "happy-making." But don't use that brief moment of reprieve as the sole reason for changing. Our brain recognizes rewards that loom in the immediate future. And it's dopamine, the "feel good" chemical messenger that gives us a little bump or an assist toward our desired end. Hold within your window of awareness, a bit longer than usual, the good feeling that is produced by your own self-satisfaction.

To get into a good habit, the ADHDer needs satisfying rewards, and as I have said, the best rewards are intrinsic. A good feeling that healthy pride elicits lasts much longer than a candy bar, though a candy bar might provide a more immediate gratifying punch. (In no way am I diminishing the vital and seductive nature of a Butterfinger or Mounds bar.) Unfortunately, the ADHDer will get lost in the flavor and will need to be reminded how they earned "said" delicacy.

Demonstrate for the ADHDer how to verbalize a direct and explicit acknowledgment of praise, from themselves to themselves when they've made a sustained quality effort. So, you tell yourself, "Good job!" "Way to go!" "I'm proud of myself!" "Well done." Develop your own end zone dance and let out a whoop. This verbalization produces a hit of the neurotransmitter, dopamine, motivating the ADHDer to want to replicate the behavior so they can feel good again and again. Sure, candy bars are great, but feeling proud is a sensation the ADHDer longs to be repeated. You can only eat so many candy bars before they start to turn on you, like on Halloween around 11:30 on a school night.

ADHD individuals expand more fervently and contract more drastically than their comrades. They succeed and bumble, then bumble, then succeed. But life goes on. Albert Einstein believed, "Life is like riding a bicycle. To keep your balance, you must keep moving." Committing to the belief that, "Much good lies ahead if I keep doing _____," requires a fine, delicate, and agile letting go while holding on at the same time. People who sit and wait for their "ship to arrive," might be surprised when they discover there is nothing on it. We must commit to noticing the good that's already present while creating more of the same in order to have good memories. Seek out the good and gravitate toward it.

Bill Vaughn, a syndicated columnist for the Kansas City Star was an exceptional writer and wit. He was a colleague of my father, gracing the paper's pages from 1946-1977. He wrote folksy little aphorisms titled "Star Beams." He once wrote, "In the game of life it's a good idea to have a few early losses, which relieves you of the pressure of trying to maintain an undefeated season." Losses can fortify your commitment to do better.

Neither we nor our kids will ever attain the promise of perfection as alluring as it may seem. No one can. Anyway, who would want to hang around with someone who believed or professed flawlessness? If internalized properly, failure can ramp up our commitment to continue moving toward our ideal self.

Again, mistakes are how we learn. If you seek to appear immortal by attaining everlasting fame and praise, you've made some gigantic error in judgment. We're going to make mistakes, damn it, but those mistakes are inconsequential. But if you really screw up, trust me, very few people will forget. A respected individual who makes a ghastly error in behavior or judgment will be vilified harder and fall deeper than some scoundrel will ever be lifted for doing a good deed. When we make a mistake and refuse to acknowledge it, we're committing to more mistakes.

William D. Brown, who was said to have founded Omaha, Nebraska, was quoted as saying, "Failure is an event, never a person." That's certainly important for the ADHD person to know since they personalize so much. We can always reboot our commitment by depersonalizing mistakes.

Winston Churchill, who would have certainly been diagnosed with ADHD (read his history) said, "Success is going from failure to failure without losing enthusiasm." Nothing is a waste of time if you learned something from it. So, help the ADHDer commit to learning.

Commitments help the ADHDer set up their days in a way that ensures they'll get done what needs to get done. Some obstacles are predictable, some unexpected, and complications need to be dealt with sooner rather than later. So, create a plan, and even when frustrations surface, commit to implementing it. Theodore Isaac Rubin, M.D. said, "All doing takes is doing, it doesn't take a lot of thinking."

CHAPTER 26

I Wonder if Anybody Ever Told These People, "You'll Never Amount to Anything?"

> *"Well then.*
> *Will the naysayers*
> *please leave the universe?"*
>
> ~ Charles Stross

When my high school counselor, Florence Leisure, told me, "You better learn to run a cash register because you're not college material," I refused to believe her. I knew deep down inside (thanks to quality therapy with Dr. Scott Morrison) that I had value and could be effective somewhere at some time. These were not self-beliefs nurtured by my biological family.

Though I got canned from my first job as a dishwasher, I learned early on that I was a better boss of myself, than an employee for someone else. Nobody wants to feel incompetent or unreliable. When you're consistently inconsistent, your mind doesn't sponsor a confident reliable self-image. But when I could do things my way, things usually turned out really well, or at least, okay.

Being consistent takes a commitment. None of this "middle of the road" stuff. Jim Hightower, a syndicated progressive columnist was the commissioner of the Texas Department of Agriculture from 1983-1991. In his book, *If God Had Meant Us to Vote He Would Have Given Us Candidates*, he wrote, "The middle of the road is for yellow lines and dead armadillos." So, the middle might be good for having a balance, but not so much for commitment.

Though many successful creative people have been labeled inconsistent, they were never middle-of-the-road types. They didn't necessarily "go with the flow," but created their own. Hightower wrote, "Even a dead fish can go with the flow." The man's a genius.

Swimming upstream is diagnosed as "oppositional defiant." But too much conformity is stifling, and certainly uneventful. It drains creativity and vigor from the ADHDer's personality. ADHDers are seldom accused of being conformists. But it's essential they learn to channel their overflow of energy and curiosity in definable, experiential, and productive ways. ADHDers take great risks, and some risks are not all bad. But the only way you can accomplish great feats or create awe-inspiring masterpieces is to roll the dice. The more consistently "staid" or "grave" type of folk, label the ADHDer wayward, odd, unfocused, or simply not living up to their potential. I remember in high school when I got in trouble for drugs (a bad acid trip) and was placed on probation for six months, my probation officer described me in a report as a "wayward youth." I'll never forget my father laughing, telling me, "Wayward, don't believe it."

Many wayward, disenfranchised, and distractible youths have gone on to become quite influential. Today, they would have been tagged with a scathing diagnosis and pumped full of medication: Andrew Carnegie, Albert

Einstein, Thomas Edison, Henry Ford, Walt Disney, Galileo, John Lennon, Abe Lincoln, Pablo Picasso, Louis Pasteur, Orville and Wilbur Wright, Alexander Bell, Dwight D. Eisenhower, Leonardo da Vinci, Ben Franklin, Frank Lloyd Wright, Eleanor Roosevelt, Agatha Christie, Beethoven, Michael Jordan, Magic Johnson, Dustin Hoffman, Stevie Wonder, Carl Lewis, Steven Spielberg, Robin Williams, Nolan Ryan, Mozart, Caitlyn (Bruce) Jenner, Pete Rose, Paul Orfalea (founder of Kinko's), James Carville, Terry Bradshaw, Howie Mandel, Michael Phelps, Ty Pennington, Jim Carrey, Justin Timberlake, and Ted Turner, have all done alright. In fact, I'll bet many parents would have cast scorn upon their child if they had started dating one of these characters in their formative years before fame and big bucks kicked in.

Audra McDonald, a seven-time Tony Award-winning singer, and actress publicly thanked her mother at an award ceremony, for not putting her on medication to treat her ADHD. She said that doing so would have muted her creativity and would have changed the whole trajectory of her life. She was bombarded with letters from moms who were offended, saying "Medication <u>saved</u> my child's life." And that's great! I have no doubt, there are many cases in which medication has been helpful, but I'm also aware of many cases where a kid was medicated in order to <u>save</u> the parent's sanity.

I'm sure neither Audra nor I intend to offend anyone. But if you can discover, feed, and cultivate a child's interests, passions, and proclivities, you'll find that rather than medication there are other arrangements and accommodations that can be made. Measures that nourish the child's soul and emotional well-being are wonderful, as opposed to acts or treatments that stunt their appetite, pizzazz, and innate instinctual data.

Winston Churchill, the former Prime Minister of the United Kingdom, made quite a name for himself. Due to his clear display of insolent ADHD-ness, many forecasted for him nothing but a life of failure and debauchery. Winston struggled mightily in school. Learning was very difficult for him. Years later he said, "Personally I'm always ready to learn, although I do not always like being taught." Boy, if that doesn't hit the nail on the head for many undiscovered geniuses.

CHAPTER 27

What Is It We're Paying Attention To?

> "*We either learn to steer our mind, or our mind steers us.*"
>
> ~ Me

Rick Hanson is one of my respected mentors and the author of many important books, including *Buddha's Brain* and *Hardwiring Happiness*. He wrote, "Our minds are like both a spotlight and a vacuum cleaner. Whatever your mind is focusing on gets illuminated by the spotlight, then gets vacuumed up into our very being." Great analogy. We must then ask ourselves, "Is what I'm focusing on good for me?" "Is it helping me feel better about myself?" "Is it motivating?" If it's not, we better learn to pull ourselves away from whatever it is we're illuminating and direct the spotlight to an area, thought or belief that is good. If we keep the spotlight on a thought or memory that doesn't help, anxiety seeps in flooding our mind and body. Continual exposure to this discomfort can morph into dread. Dread can snowball into panic, finalizing a total coup d'état over the ADHDer's mind, body, and awareness. Behaviors and thoughts that were once viable defensive strategies can feel weakened and overtaken by traitorous obsessive-compulsive remedies. I've seen children develop obsessive compulsions and ritualistic behaviors and thoughts when placed on certain medications. Sadly, more medication is often prescribed to counteract the side effects of the first pill.

So, it's important to know where the ADHD individual is shining their attention, and what's being illuminated. Is it for the better, traveling down new fresh, floodlit, beautiful, peaceful, and promising terrain with their prefrontal cortex as their tour guide, or for the worse, banging and bouncing off-road through rocky, uneven, murky, and disheartened territory with Mr. Amygdala at the wheel? Whatever it is that's holding their attention has the special power to change, actually sculpting the mindscape of their brain. Our state of being is experience-dependent, based on how we emotionally and physiologically process it. Whether your mind is focusing on flowers or manure, your intentional attention will direct you to its scent.

Early on we learn to adapt to both goodness and distress. The ways we've learned to adapt have helped us survive, even when life takes a bit of tread off our hearts. These patterns of adaptation become deeply ingrained on a neurological level. And this is good, because having a pattern of thought or behavior that works, gets deeply entrenched also, which means we don't have to learn something over and over.

But what if the form of emotional and behavioral strategies we've been utilizing isn't a healthy adaptation? What if avoidance or submission that first helped us dodge some pain and suffering doesn't work anymore? Then bummer, we'd thought we had found a fix only to find we had just duct taped it. But when we discover the repair was temporary, we now have to find an adaptive action that sticks. But what if avoidance or submission became habitual after continual activation and we never believed there was another solution? What if this form of adapting became automatic and our default mindset is maladaptive? The good news is that these behaviors did work at first because they gave us time to gather ourselves and adjust in ways that manage the discomfort. Unfortunately, what was meant to provide us a momentary reprieve becomes a chronic way of life. It's important to learn what to do when you don't know what to do. So, it's not just the resistance to getting better and trying new things, it's the old, ingrained brain circuitry running on automatic which pulls us down pathways that aren't good for us. We can teach ADHDers how to install new wiring. They can learn to create new circuitry, rendering the old motherboard obsolete.

Trying to suppress and resist powerful irrational fears is difficult and can be frightening. Irrationality can produce images that encircle then permeate the ADHDer's mind, trapping them in a cyclic loop which can become thought disorders. Distorted beliefs can prompt detailed rituals of thoughts and behaviors, convincing the ADHDer that if they stick to this maladaptive program (believing and adhering to fears and doubts) then implement the plan (of avoidance or submission), they'll feel safe. These formalities become cemented in their repertoire and are hard to break out of, especially if they worked in the beginning. A rhythmic verse, incessant counting, a repetitive physical routine, a calculated mantra, or organized rituals are believed to stave off catastrophe. This is what's referred to as OCD, obsessive-compulsive disorder. Sometimes these beliefs and seemingly essential sacraments can also apply to someone else's well-being. So, in order to keep others safe from harm, these ritualistic responsibilities cannot be ignored, or something could go seriously wrong. These behaviors and thoughts invite well-intentioned medications.

Many physicians are quick to offer anti-anxiety medication as a cure-all for OCD. But simply sedating the beast is temporary, it will eventually wake up, more pissed. A small amount of medication can alleviate distress and create an opening where therapy can be effective. You can't just medicate the symptoms and offer little else. That would be like throwing a drowning person a buoy, but not helping them back up into the boat; they're afloat, but they just aren't gathered in. We must help the ADHDer understand how they fell out of the boat and into the water in the first place.

When the "fear" and "worry" circuits are being constantly triggered over a long period of time, they become automatic, firing at will. The more they fire, the more they buddy up, wiring together, creating huge cables that transmit their disparaging accounts and predictions throughout the body. An ADHDer's thoughts can be like a tire spinning in the mud. They can feel stuck in a circular narrative, a loop that deeply entrenches them in a quagmire of doubt and distortion. Once beliefs are ingrained, seared into their neural network, a greater effort is required over a longer period of time to convince them of their worth and capabilities. When they eventually believe there's a better part of themselves that "can learn" to manage moment-to-moment weirdness, this newly experienced freedom of perspective is a big relief. This is also where they begin to notice and take into consideration their fatigue points. The good news is when they begin to consistently believe in themselves from a new and deeper perspective, they'll want to continue to replicate that sensation. It can be done with patience, time, patience, repetition, and more patience. They'll get it, but probably not the first several times.

Again, it's the irascible little tyrant from the land of limbic, the amygdala, that stokes fear and anxiety. The spontaneous activation of these survival circuits is meant to keep us safe. They work better when danger is truly imminent. Unfortunately, the "on button" gets stuck, and the electrical circuitry fires at will, even when there's no apparent threat. Just imagining danger can throw the ADHDer's entire mind, body, and spirit into overload, shutting down and imploding.

The amygdala believes itself to be an honorable superintendent of both the ADHDer's mind and body. Though it has kept us safe on many occasions the amygdala has taken its responsibilities way too seriously, well past the point of necessity. This creates a real credibility issue regarding its over-concern about its duties in the present moment. The amygdala has been quite helpful when it instructed us to stick close to the ladder when we were learning to swim. Or when it insisted that we hasten our pace while crossing a busy intersection. In fact, it offered great advice when strongly demanding that we check our rearview mirror twice, keeping us from hitting a trash can. We all have this superintendent or controller in our minds, and that's good. The problem arises when it becomes over-reactive and hypervigilant, attempting to control and direct every waking thought and action. Eventually, the ADHDer stops listening to their true self and begins to rely solely on the superintendent's voice, which can be controlling, punitive and paranoid. You've heard the old saying, "Prepare for the worst, but hope for the best." Spending a lifetime preparing for the worst is not tranquil, nor is it a cheerful way to creep through life.

Some medication chemically incites the amygdala, putting it on high alert and triggering the mind and body's nervous system whether or not there's any impending danger. Conversely, other medications disable the amygdala, completely shutting down apprehension controls, making the ADHDer less aware of psychic danger. Too much concern or too little concern are both problems. ADHDers need to be taught the middle ground. There's a balance point between being wired and oblivious. The superintendent (amygdala) appears devoted to our safety, claiming it only wants to shield us from painful humiliation, exposure, and threat. Regrettably, such constriction leaves the ADHDer doubting their own perceptions and instinctual data, thwarting their ability to strengthen two of the most important traits for success: observation and realistic interpretation. Unfortunately, unbridled anticipation of an activity the ADHDer looks forward to participating in can be vetoed by the superintendent. The powerful amygdala can render the activity unsafe, risking too much vulnerability. The legitimacy of the superintendent's convincingly rash assertions can override and overwhelm the prefrontal cortex's soft, wise, and thoughtful suggestions.

Our overactive and reactive superintendent is exhausted, secretly wanting time off. But it won't listen unless we assert ourselves, challenging and literally interrupting its endless stream of anxious reminders. Imagine telling the superintendent, "Hey, cool it, relax. I know you mean well but give me a damn break. I know you're just a bundle of overactive brain circuitry and you are accustomed to me adhering to every disastrous ominous prognosis you posit, but I must stop you. It sucks when you are always like this. It isn't good for either of us. Your incessant clamoring keeps me from having fun and believing in myself."

Learning a healthy, believable internal self-to-self dialogue gives the ADHDer permission to "stand their ground" while developing strategies and learning a language of comfort that provides clarity and assurance. The mind can then shift into problem-solving mode; a process that strengthens encourages, and creates new healthier brain circuitry, stabilizing the self-regulatory system.

Make this problem-solving mode a game, a fun requirement, an adventure into awareness. Learning to catch, restrain and prevent the superintendent from going off on some demeaning, controlling rant is both relieving and amusing. Promote the importance of heightening your awareness by holding on longer than usual to the feelings of protection and deep comfort you've created for yourself. Let the good feeling become a neural trait rather than a fleeting state. Supportive assertiveness creates an inner allegiance, from self-to-self as you wrestle back control. ADHDers can learn to sit with their observations and refuse to be sucked down into the swirl of drama and indignity the amygdala so desperately needs to stir up.

Once the ADHDer begins to solidify a compassionate, natural well-deserved dialogue that exalts a basic faith in themselves, they can choose whether to respond to the superintendent at all. Having choices creates a pause, where better selections can be made. Options create a feeling of control and relief in and of themselves. Relish the feeling of being the chooser, where you are actually influencing your experience in the immediate moment. Remember to practice letting "Life go through you, not to you." I interpret this to mean, we should not let our mind and body become a landing strip for our amygdala, a perpetual frequent flier. Imagine closing that landing strip so no cargo full of apprehension and doubt can be delivered. We need to learn to schedule our own intentional and productive flights. The motive behind our superintendent's themes can become quite clear by asking ourselves, "What is the story behind the emotional state the amygdala is pitching?" "Is this helpful to me or hurtful?"

Once you've created a space between fear, worry, and yourself, you can begin to evaluate and challenge the pros and cons of ritualistic thoughts and behaviors. By learning to check, then reject the amygdala's pressure to respond to habitual patterns of thought which impound self-determination, you become distinctly aware pinpointing the exact moment the superintendent sends you into a state of "high alert." By directly confronting and exposing its mirage of power, you can stop the amygdala dead in its tracks. This is the first step in moment-to-moment repair and renovation, how new, more friendly brain circuitry and neural pathways get laid. Again, by naming and exposing the amygdala's intention we can tame the moment and begin to still and soothe the limbic firings. Naming and taming teach the ADHD individual to move their mind forward, by learning to describe what's happening without becoming entangled in the explanation and trapped in the story. Labeling feelings activate a specific region in the prefrontal cortex which MRIs reveal is less active in depressed people. Naming and taming reduces activity in the amygdala, which is more active in unhappy, and anxiety-ridden individuals. Labeling can interrupt fear and calm down the amygdala so the prefrontal cortex can work its magic, moving the mind and body back to a state of equilibrium. We need to teach the ADHDer to practice noticing and holding on to the sensation of the shift from amygdala reactivity to the prefrontal cortex's comfortable nurturing knowing. Inform the ADHDer that when they actually feel the shift, in that exact moment, there's a rewiring of the brain's circuitry taking place.

The ability to name and tame kicks into operation the knowledgeable and experientially textured right-side of the brain. The right side deals with emotions, using metaphors and images which help reduce stress. It can alter historical recollections and insert them into a healthier narrative that gets filed in memory. The right side sees opportunities to change the dialogue that can then feed off a series of interconnected experiences. The right side is inclusive and welcoming, thinking of the whole package and less about the parts. The right side thinks globally as opposed to regionally.

The superintendent resides on the left side and is the gatekeeper to the brain. The left side of the brain directs a firm, rational and commonsensical dialogue. The left side loves to label things as "good or bad" or "right or wrong." The left side sees the world divided and separate a friend or foe mentality. The left believes there's only one legitimate point of view; its own. Right side ideas and beliefs which don't embrace the superintendent's left-sided brain beliefs are deemed misguided and just plain wrong.

It's interesting that in the world of politics the "right" is usually the uptight conservative, with a take-no-prisoners mentality. The "left" is open, flexible to diversity, and respects others' differences without throwing a hissy fit. The inner workings of the brain function in the reverse.

When children are raised in self-righteous, inflexible left-brain environments, only one side of their brain is being fueled, and that side becomes excessively dominant. When a child's brain is dominated and forced to the left for extended periods of time during their formative years, oftentimes confusion and severe resentment can result. Defense mechanisms are set up to protect the brain's left side from becoming ensconced by the right side's mushy, gooey, touchy-feely sincerity and sentiment. Sadly, this is exactly what the left side needs to soften up. Medication can keep you stuck on the left side.

When the ADHDer's needs aren't being met, and their emotions discounted by a caregiver's lack of compassion and patience, or worse yet, the ADHDer experiences or witnesses abuse, the right hemisphere of their brain goes into hiding, like a puppy in a storm. The brain's natural inclination is to default into a left dominant, negative bias, defensive posture, adapting strategies that guard its vulnerability. This is not the time for the right brain to display weaknesses or be indecisive. It's time for the ADHDer's right brain to learn how to stand its ground.

We can help the ADHD child build new neural pathways, creating new synaptic connections by harvesting new integrative neurons that feel hopeful. Dr. Siegel has a wonderful acronym in his insightful book, *Mindsight*, that talks about stimulating the "right" neural circuits so they become more involved and influential. Hence the science of neuroplasticity advocates just that. The acronym SNAG stands for Stimulate Neuronal Activation and Growth. I believe that the ADHD kid can learn to SNAG their brain and reroute their thoughts, creating new neural highways with smoother roads leading to better places. Explain to them that by doing this they are synaptogenesis-ing or creating new pathways. By heightening awareness, the ADHDer is changing neuronal firing patterns. Convince them that by constructing these new neural highways in their brain (crafting new synaptic relationships) they will feel better. Tell them they are synaptogenesis-ing right now by even considering the possibility of better moments and decisions. Teach them that they are using the power and influence of their minds. By heightening their awareness, they're literally changing physical firing patterns in their brain. This is like cutting or bulldozing through the brain's rocks, laying down new circuitry as you go. By helping develop a new direction for their mind to travel, they will come to realize they don't have to respond the same way every time, especially when it doesn't seem to be working. There are many ways we can get to better places.

Convincing the ADHD individual that these changes are within their control, empowers them, providing a sensation of influence and ownership over their reactivity. Assure them that there are thousands and thousands of miles of undeveloped real estate in their brain, and they can construct whatever they want on their property. These new highways create different routes and options, making life measurably easier. But it takes a commitment to never give up because the construction is lifelong.

Again, tell the ADHD child that they're engaging in the act of neurogenesis at that very moment. Share with them that they are generating neurons, right now, from neural stem cells and progenitor cells that are important for learning and memory. Painting pictures with words is much easier for the ADHD mind to comprehend than some flavorless explanation. In fact, the intentional act of synaptogenesis-ing is more beneficial, and longer-lasting than sticking a pill in a child's face and saying, "Take this." The purpose of good therapy is to expand, not constrict the brain. Mindfulness and relaxation heighten awareness, giving the ADHD kid, some say in their biochemical reactions.

It should be emphasized that in no way are we attempting to change who the kid is; we're just helping them become who they want to be. Teaching the ADHD individual how to build wide shoulders on their new neural highways, gives them a place and the space to pull over, refocus and redirect their attention. It doesn't necessarily keep them from careening off into the ditch of distraction, rather it helps them return to the route much more quickly. Helping the ADHDer learn how to self-regulate, prevents them from taking an unsavory exit, where troubles and difficulties abound.

The overflow of energy that ADHDers experience can be forceful and heated. This dysregulation of the right side of their brain could use a little left side linkage, counsel, and rational redirection. Let them know that a little left-brain linkage and guidance is advisable and helps them stay in control, maintaining the right direction. Though the left brain doesn't offer the language of comfort that's soothing and pacifying, its abrupt influence can stop a full-blown ADHD freak-out right in its tracks. By identifying and naming the distressing influences in that very precise moment, the ADHDer can learn to calm the limbic system's excessive left-brain firing. Siegel said it ever so well, "The key is to link the left and right, not replace one imbalance with another." Aristotle referred to balance as the "golden mean." When you're able to look directly into the areas you've strategically avoided, you become consciously aware of how you can shift and break some of your useless habitual responses. This has a positive effect not just on the ADHDer, but those closest to them as well.

When the ADHD individual becomes convinced that their sensory and learning mechanisms are defective, they can spend a lifetime wasting energy that could've been used for self-compassionate rewiring, discovery, and the installation of clarity. Through enhanced self-awareness, patient understanding, and relentless self-compassion, the ADHDer can experience moment-to-moment healing. Learning to grow new linkage between the equally important right and left sides of the brain, allows the ADHDer to feel less intimidated and more authentically present. The more the ADHDer becomes aware of exactly what's draining their attentional energy away, the greater the likelihood they'll do something about it.

ADHD kids are constantly seeking reassurance. They continually search for faces that shine approval and acceptance. They ascertain by observing others' reactions to them whether or not they're "doing it right." The feeling of getting things right is sometimes a rare luxury for the ADHDer. Doing things right helps them feel as if they matter, and their contributions are vital. Remember we value ourselves to the degree we feel valued.

For the ADHDer learning to relax their mind helps their body and relaxing their body helps their mind. Some ADHDers may never have known a space like that could exist within them. When trying to make sense of things the best direction to travel is inward. When the ADHDer begins to trust themselves, their emotional dimensions expand. When they begin to truly feel safe within, that feeling of safety begs to be replicated. They'll no longer allow someone's external point of view to become their internal makeup. They come to instinctually "know" they can and will eventually figure out how to do things right.

You've possibly heard or read about "original sin." What I like to believe and have found worthy to explore with my ADHD "sinners" is the idea of "original goodness." Imagine that. The superintendent (the amygdala) might not agree with your new beliefs and discoveries, but that's okay. It's accustomed to being on guard and ready to spin into an uproar upon immediate notice. The superintendent will try to convince you that its intention is to keep you safe (and it was, at first), but even more importantly, prevent you from sliding into worst-ness. We must help the ADHDer generate the gumption and confidence to reassign, then teach, the superintendent to adapt to a whole new job description. We can train our amygdala to detach from its rigid mindset and reflectively notice what's pleasant and enjoyable, harsh, and disruptive, tedious, and boring, and fascinating and invigorating without overreacting and becoming defensive. This is the beginning of the amygdala learning to calm itself down and not get swept away by its own old warmed-over story. Such attentiveness is a gallant step, that literally constructs and lays new neural pathways leading to much better places. This new circuitry creates factual structural changes in the brain.

ADHD individuals mentally metabolize stress with an intense urgency to fix something. They are easily triggered by external stimuli that snags something in the archives of their implicit memory. Implicit indicates they're unaware of the origin of their discomfort, but it just continually shows up. Just as importantly, their attention can also be derailed by internal distractions that are explicit, meaning they know exactly where the hurt and anguish originate. The ADHDer is desperate to neutralize their distress. Even a troubling thought can trigger bodily sensations that disable attention and focus. A crick in the neck, a tightening of the shoulders, shortness of breath, a nauseating sensation in the stomach are all physical phenomena that need to be noticed and understood. Often times it doesn't take a physician or medication to handle such bodily grievances. When working with young ADHDers, one of my goals is to help them get back in touch with their bodies. I teach them that their body presents its bill for thoughts and feelings they stuff away. Ignoring their pain doesn't help. By encouraging the ADHD child to heighten their self-awareness, they'll want to uproot any old mindset, beliefs, and behaviors that have not served them well. Once they learn to weed their mind's garden they can choose to seed, cultivate, and grow new foliage that preserves a sense of hope and protects their crop from the inevitability of life's acid rain. We talk about anger management, behavior management and mood management. What about hope-management? Hope management convinces the ADHDer that much good still lies ahead and that everyone survives. When they begin to believe something better is coming and they recognize that all things are temporary, they'll then believe that they can make now better, so that later is easier. When we lose hope, much repair work is needed. Hope is putting faith to work when doubt has become a pervasive belief. Nothing is gained by jabbering about how wonderful things are when they're not. If we don't convince the ADHD child of the importance of hope, then they've lost that moment, but only temporarily. Hope is a doggedly determined remedy that can elevate an individual as well as an entire population. Resilient ADHD individuals must learn to pay close attention to what's going on, both inside and out in order to side-step adversity.

    We grow when things are challenging. We can befriend our stresses and fears when we believe we have what it takes to get to the other side. What hurts us the most can and will instruct us the most if we're willing to pay attention. Hardships need to be turned into learning experiences. That's what resilience is.

People who are resilient have more activation in the right prefrontal cortex than in the left. Remember, the left side delivers a "Get up off your ass right now," message, where the right is more emotional and reactive. The right is more likely to say, "What can I do to help you get up?" The left intimidates, while the right assists. When an individual lacks resilience the degree of anxious activation in the left prefrontal area is greater than in the right. Though the left's approach is less diplomatic, it might just stop the amygdala's freak-outs right in its tracks. By paying attention to both sides of the brain the ADHDer can learn more ways to respond to life's conundrums. It's the right brain that is responsible for making sense of what "just" went on and comforting both the mind and body.

Axons, the white matter that connects the neurons to one another, helps build highways to the prefrontal cortex and the amygdala. MRI studies show that when there are more axons between the comforting grandmotherly prefrontal cortex and the cantankerous, apprehensive amygdala the more resilient the individual is. The narrower and fewer highways leading from the soothing and constructive prefrontal cortex to the irascible amygdala, the less resilient the person is. It's up to us to teach the ADHDer how to construct these highways. The good news is we can assist our brain by building wider connections between these two very influential areas which increases the baseline activity in the prefrontal region.

ADHDers need to learn that by feeling compassion and empathy, a molecule, or chemical messenger, oxytocin, is released into their brain reducing the anxiety the amygdala produces. Oxytocin is associated with the emotional state that comes from maternal nurturing behavior as well as romantic attachments. When you're relaxed, and you feel treasured and adored, you can bet oxytocin is circulating around in your brain. Minnie Ripperton's wonderful song from the 70s, "Loving You," is not a song the amygdala wants to hear. (YouTube it.)

So, what is it that the ADHDer is paying the most attention to? The most fundamental influence on our physical well-being is our emotional life and thoughts. Both positive and negative spirits that originate in our brains leak into our bodies. When you're angry, nervous, worried, apprehensive, or fearful your body presents its bill in sundry forms: high blood pressure, an accelerated pulse, headaches, heart, and respiratory difficulties, etc. When we're feeling content, secure and resilient, we're strengthening our immune system. By studying and understanding their most consistent personality states and traits, the ADHDer can begin to foresee problems before they occur. There is a huge preventative aspect that needs to be taught while treating ADHDers, especially when they find their minds involved in a chronic and continual ruckus.

Patience, patience, patience, and more patience. In gym class, during the mile run, you wouldn't berate a youngster for "not trying," especially if they're wearing a permanent leg brace and a corrective shoe built up six inches. You wouldn't harangue them saying, "You have a bad attitude." Nor would you say, "You're not living up to your potential." "Push it." For God's sake, the poor kid has visible disabilities. But what if you're ADHD, and you have an invisible brace on your brain? Other's well-intentioned encouragement intended to support the ADHDer can backfire due to historical distrust and fear of exposure. Such apprehension imprisons hope and thwarts resilience. Kids who have brain braces don't trust their own instinctual data and become very frustrated when trying to move with dexterity from thought to action. But again, <u>the good news,</u> self-knowledge can be acquired, self-compassion cultivated, skills upgraded, and impairments outgrown.

There is nothing so wrong with the ADHD person that can't be made better by utilizing what is so right about them. You can improve upon the impairments by focusing on their strengths. I have found most all ADHDers are interested in the inner workings of their brain and the different roles each area plays. Curiosity can free them up to believe they can and will get better with time. Teach them to give in, when necessary, but to never give up.

Assure the ADHD kid, that with patient self-compassion, and the desire to learn about the inner workings of their mind, they can develop strategies, while still paying close attention and filtering out endless streams of stimuli. They can plug the leaks in their thinking. Believing they can overcome frustration is empowering and provides the so-very-necessary relief. But attaining this relief takes work and can feel exhausting because it requires rerouting their mental energy in a direction that feels uphill. It takes some real heavy lifting for the ADHD child to deliberately steer their attention in a direction that recalibrates their mind. Learning to pry themselves away from entertaining but otherwise non-productive stuff is fatiguing and feels like an unwanted surrender.

Most ADHD kids' thoughts are glorious, colorful, and have creative themes. We need to preserve their ingenuity, imagination, and originality, which are highly valuable and eventually marketable. For instance, one time I was driving my young sons through a neighborhood when my seven-year-old son Jordan turned to his 10-year-old brother TJ and said, "Hey T, let's pretend we're ninjas and we're riding through the jungle and there are bad guys on the roofs of the houses, and they can't see us, but we can see them, and that we have these super-secret laser ionizers and submachine guns that will make them disappear and transport them to a super-secret prison camp. We automatically get their weapons and powers, and we can stockpile all their ammo. When they reappear in the secret prison camp, we can then learn all their secrets and discover where all the other platoons and soldiers are located. We can then take over the world and become heroes. Sound cool T? What do you think T, sound cool?" TJ responded, "Nah." Which one do you think is ADHD?

I watched Jordan's proud face in the mirror as he spun an irresistible scenario to impress and engage his big brother in his imaginary world. His face quickly transformed from excitement to baffled bewilderment. Just listening to him describing this virtual adventure in his mind, then having the best he could offer rejected, reminded me of some of my innocent attempts at connecting. It helped me realize the fine line and deep gulf between acknowledgment and indifference, acceptance, and rejection.

CHAPTER 28

To Flow or Not to Flow, That is the Dilemma

> "*Sometimes my mind flows,
> sometimes it runs dry.
> Often it overflows,
> and other times it just splatters.*"
>
> ~ Me

You often hear people talk about "being in the flow." I believe we experience "flow" when our actions and intentions meet at a point of performance. It is when we glide, then soar unencumbered toward a definable goal. It's as if we were on cruise control, automatic. Things just seem to work.

Navigating through life with ADHD often felt more like a spill or splatter than "flow." I think I mentioned somewhere that James Hightower, a very insightful syndicated columnist, progressive political activist, and author states, "Even a dead fish can go with the flow."

Just the word "flow" feels good to say. Try saying it as you make gestures with your arms, like a conductor inspiring a symphony. Exhale and let the word "flow" effortlessly drift across your lips. Exhilarating, is it not? Now stick your middle three fingers in your mouth and repeat the previous instruction. No flow. This is often what flow or lack of, feels like for the ADHDer. ADHD clogs up not just the ADHDer's flow but can impede the flow of others and at times entire groups. For instance, on a field trip, all it takes is one kid freaking out to ruin it for everybody. When the ADHDer learns about their glitches and how to navigate around obstacles in a non-shaming, blaming, or self-brutalizing manner, they can then notice the fingers in their mouth and intentionally remove them. The goal is to help the ADHD kid remain curious and hopeful despite some of their frustrating proclivities. We can help them learn to tolerate the process and endure the time it takes to start, continue, and complete what's expected. There are so many other things to enjoy that don't include isosceles triangles, conjugating verbs, or understanding the ever-so-mystical properties of plankton.

We all pretty much want the same things: peace, joy, health, security, and friendships. A meaningful belief system provides hope and stability, even in the most anxiety-ridden moments. Learning to flow is all part of the journey. It's not instant or automatic. You just don't add water to your dehydrated parts.

Our mind and body inform us when our thoughts, behaviors, and outlook are restricting flow. ADHD individuals have difficulty shifting toward an emotional and behavioral balancing point. For example, it's difficult to be in the flow and move on to the next subject in class, when the previous lesson made no sense. Nothing feels complete.

Science has just recently begun to recognize the role of emotions when discussing flow. Emotions not only attach the body to the brain but also connect us to one another. Dan Siegel eloquently describes in his very important book, *Mindsight,* the role integration plays in our definition of the mind as an "embodied and relational process." When there is no emotional integration, there is no flow. I've had the privilege of being his student on many occasions.

If we're not careful at different junctures of our life, it's easy to get stuck, vacillating between the following states, unable to complete the motion of the emotions: fear, sadness, anger, and depression. As a psychotherapist, I've met many kind-hearted, loving, and gentle ADHD souls who, through no fault of their own, found themselves jammed into traumatic mindsets. Like a frozen information loop, with no remote to dampen down, then mute the incessant verbiage, the ADHDer becomes stuck in a negative internal dialogue. It is difficult for the ADHDer to privatize their thoughts and feelings when they are hurting. Sadly, the thin brake lining of their brain prompts them to share their feelings and perceptions at inappropriate and inopportune times. ADHD individuals need to learn how to get their mind and tongue on their side, as a trusted companion, not as a traitor. When we defect from ourselves, there ain't no flow.

Integration is indeed a function of stable mental health. It seems to me that when we are not integrating, we are disintegrating. When our minds lose a sense of balance and harmony, then we are prone to live on the polarities of chaos and rigidity.

Dan Siegel and his students came up with an acronym describing a coherent self-narrative. The acronym helps the ADHDer make sense of their life, freeing them from the past. Such coherency is an important predictor of relational health. Siegel chose FACES as the acronym that specifies the qualities necessary for an integrated flow. Again, Dr. Siegel has so eloquently been able to put into both words and pictures what needs to happen in our brain and body. I will add my own take in regard to the ADHDer.

F-Flexible

A-Adaptive

C-Coherent

E-Energized

S-Stable

Flexible: Flexibility helps us adapt to life in a manner that makes sense. It energizes the ADHDer to venture into the world confident and curious, comfortably cultivating a stable emotional and behavioral repertoire that directs their flow.

I used to share with the ADHD kids in my running group the importance of all of us flowing in the same direction at the exact same time, for instance, crossing a street. I emphasized the value of helping one another, not policing. We are individuals, but we need to move as a collective whole when transitioning. However, most of our congestive moments, or lack of flow, surfaced when each member of the group attempted to get their minds and bodies transitioning to the next physical space and activity at the same time.

I've always found the old analogy of a river to be very effective when explaining flow to ADHD children. Awareness is vital when ascertaining where you are in the river. The center is the most direct pathway the water travels as it unfurls toward its many destinations. First, I point out that none of us can flow all the time, but it is essential that we try to stay in the middle of the river. When we get close to the banks, we will find the water moves much slower. ADHD children have a difficult time staying in the middle.

When we talk about polarities or extremes, we can view the banks of the river as we do the brain, the left, and right hemispheres. The left is rigid, inflexible, and non-negotiable, a constricted approach to living. That's the river's left bank.

The right side of the brain (or river's right bank) can be a bit excessive and out of balance. It can be too permissive and malleable. It's the "I don't give a damn" side. Too much permissiveness creates little restraint and/or no boundaries.

Though the ADHDer's mind can move quickly, the river's flow of information moves at a pace more rapidly than the ADHDer's mind is wired to travel. What the ADHD child consciously and subconsciously hears from parents and teachers is, "You need to adjust immediately and return to the middle of the river "RIGHT NOW." Such a demand for rapid compliance is usually an unrealistic expectation in that given moment, especially if they don't know how to swim. In no way does this indicate that self-correction isn't possible but when the current is tossing the ADHDer up and down, over, and sideways, it's hard for them to comply when they feel they're drowning. Rapid compliance is unrealistic, but it can be expedited with a heightening sense of self-awareness. When a moment-to-moment mindful approach to managing and accepting oneself is cultivated, then self-regulation begins to be experienced. Remember, self-regulation is what's missing in the ADHD child, and experiences of self-control are like revelations. Self-regulation is a process requiring constant tweaking and refinement. We flow, adjust, and reflow over a course of minutes, mornings, days, years, and a lifetime.

<u>Adaptive</u>: Like the river, time waits for no one. The river keeps moving and the clock keeps ticking. Unfortunately, learning is expected to continue. Due to

learning frustrations and neurodevelopmental impairments, ADHD kids often fall behind, losing contact with the pack. ADHDers are expected to adapt then continue to adjust with few instructions. Adaptation is where the ADHD individual learns to regulate themselves in specific moments in order to make life work. Learning to adapt takes a lot of rehearsing and explanation. Time, patience, and repetition are the most vital ingredients for such learning. All three are mandatory for the ADHDer to become aware so they can adapt. Sadly, our society is in short supply of the first two, time and patience. ADHD kids can bounce between the river banks of rigidity and chaos all within stretches of a few minutes. They don't need help getting out of the water, but rather being taught how to stay close to the middle. Unfortunately, all they know is to flail and flop around. We need to teach them to comfortably dog paddle to stay afloat. Once learned, these skills help them gradually stay in the middle without the fear of drowning. It's important that they stay in the water because bad things tend to happen when they climb up onto the banks.

<u>Coherence</u>: We're all right where we need to be, partly because there are still things, we haven't learned yet. Most of my stupendous blunders have taken place when I've climbed out of the river and onto the bank, but at least I could pretend I wasn't being swept away by the river. Things seemed to be easier when I was out of the river because I expected little of myself. Unfortunately, my self-to-self narrative was anything but coherent.

Now don't get me wrong, I've had wonderful flowing moments, where I experienced enormous pride, pleasure, and success. In those moments, things seemed to make perfect sense. If I worked hard and did the right thing, I produced the right results. Imagine that (think of baffled emoji face). I also did a lot of wrong things, but for what seemed like the right reasons. Running and music helped me flow. Running helped my mind and body come together, in a cohesive and coherent manner. Running gave me a sense of okay-ness as did music. It's hard to unify yourself and adapt when your mind is bouncing around like a ball in a pinball machine. Running cleared space in my mind, sort of like moving all of the furniture against the walls. In this space, I learned to reflect now and react later, where before I reacted with no real aim. ADHDers tend to react more and reflect less. Learning to pause helps thicken the brake lining of their brains. Learning to build a pause in your mind creates the space where coherence takes place.

Movement and cardio activity continue to reboot my brain. When I lacked coherence, my mind felt like a blender without a lid, turned to high speed. Running helped me put a lid on the blender, bringing me back to what was pure and important, both physically and emotionally. It sanitized my spirit. When things were coherent, and my mind and body were in sync, I was "in the flow."

Energized: Most ADHDers don't have to worry about feeling energized. It's the channeling of that energy to a definable productive endeavor or state of mind and heart that's the challenge for most. With running, I was energized by the training much more than I was by the competition. The training was very balancing for me. Sometimes before a race, a video reel would run in my head, posting scenes of past failures and frustrations, narrated by some of my most fervent detractors, de-energizing me with self-doubt well before the starter's gun went off. My body felt energized when I was training, but my mind felt diminished and depleted when it came time to race. Unfortunately, I didn't realize that the other competitors felt the same angst that I did before races. The difference was that they weren't afraid to fail. They believed in themselves and were curious about learning what their energy could produce. I was more afraid of learning what I couldn't do. Sadly, again, I thought it was just me. But the one thing I was sure of was, if I didn't give 100 percent, then I wouldn't have to take my performance seriously. I could tell myself, "I really didn't try that hard," or "I really don't care." But in reality, I cared a lot. I ran just hard enough to look like I was trying, moving from sixth or seventh place to second or third which didn't look "too bad." Very seldom did I ever really try to win. Regrettably, knowing privately that I hadn't given 100 percent multiplied the shame that was already in place. People would say, "Good job, great finish, you almost had him." A lot of times I wasn't even tired. Unfortunately, they don't have "do-overs" for those who weren't quite properly mentally energized a few minutes before. I always felt that if I had the chance to race again, right then and there, my disappointment would be enough fuel to carry me to a win. Just think of using disappointment as fuel. It's a great idea, and it works, but not something you want to rely on. My body was ready, but my mind was besieged with doubt. But I really did care. I so badly wanted to trust my own instincts and run my hardest, but my instincts weren't flowing. I didn't want to have to accept the results of a full-throttle effort and end up being just average. I wanted to "race pretty," which is hard to do if you're giving it your all. Tremendous sacrifice and preparation can go to waste if you're energized with doubt. This fed right into the theme of, "Not being good enough." Anxiety and fear of exposure outweighed the attractiveness of the goal.

But the times when I was energized and, in the flow, I could blast off a turn and run-down people in the stretch. Now that was gratifying. When I would get out of my head and allow my body to do what it was trained to do, I would usually win or at least finish in the top two or three. I would feel satisfied because I got out of my own way and competed within myself while racing others.

Stability: I still exercise, sweat, breathe deeply, and stretch daily because my ADHD brain and body require it. Exercise helps me rake away the neurological underbrush of self-doubt and frustrations.

Music, as I mentioned, has also been stabilizing. I flow with certain songs, words, and beats. Playing a few tasteful licks on my harmonica to a Muddy Waters or an Eric Clapton CD, and getting it right, damn I'm flowing. Spending hours in the yard cleaning, planting, clipping, and watering, then standing back to consider the effort and absorb the beauty is stabilizing. Spending time at Unity Temple hearing beautiful music and insightful spiritual messages stabilizes me so I can flow later. Any time spent with my best friend, Betty, my children, and my grandkids is very stabilizing. Love stabilizes our system and aids in directing the flow of energy to all the right areas. Cleaning and straightening in order to make my surroundings aesthetically pleasing grounds me in the space and place I want to be. Conversing with my adoring but obligatory audience, my cats, helps me feel flexible, grounded in a different dimension, animal flow. We, humans, are the only species that brings the future into the present. Baba Ram Das's mantra, "Be here now," works well for my pets. And since they don't possess the advanced prefrontal lobes that we do, "Being here now", is their only choice.

Sadly, a lot of ADHD children don't consider their true self as a stable refuge, a place where they can refuel. It's hard to feel stabilized when different parts of ourselves battle one another. We can teach the ADHDer how to construct an inner space designed for comfort, clarity, and replenishing. We all need a port of humor where we can dock our mind and body and laugh at the absurdities of life and our own distorted perspectives. Learning to still our mind and body is stabilizing and energizing and promotes present and future flow.

Medication can add clarity, but kids have told me when medicated they don't rest comfortably in flow. I've heard people say it's like having a hand in the middle of your back pushing you along until the dose wears off. Unfortunately, many ADHDers experience developmental and emotional stuckness because of the yin and yang of the medicine. And in some cases, the rebound effect can be destabilizing to the ADHDer's own instinctual data. Many parents have reported to me that when their child gets in the car following a day at school, and the medication is wearing off, they rip apart at the seams. I've had kids tell me that they get awakened every day for school by a parent standing over them with a pill and a glass of water. So, before they can even put their feet on the floor their flow is being choreographed by a chemical. So much for learning how to adapt and adjust through your own volition. Pent-up anger and frustrations can be volcanic when flow has been restricted by a substance. When the medication begins to wear off and the ADHDer's brain and body go into withdrawal, they are still expected to behave and express themselves in a pleasant manner. That's hard to do if your brain and body feel as if it's flipping around like a fish out of water. Medication works as long as the chemical's inside you, but it wears off. Regrettably, this physiological and emotional backlash is reported to the psychiatrist or physician as "intolerable behavior that's affecting the mood of the whole family." Unfortunately, this is often remedied by another big blast of compressed powder in the form of a mood stabilizer. Maybe if parents and schools would commit to meeting the child on their map of development instead of trying to bend and mend a child's brain that isn't broken in the first place, they'd get better results. Again, meds are certainly appropriate in some situations, but not without quality emotional and cognitive therapy. Medication should be the last option for some and be viewed as temporary. I'm happy to say there are many parents, doctors, and teachers who work very hard to understand and accommodate the ADHD population.

A NO-FLOW STORY

Let me share with you a time when I experienced no flow whatsoever. A time when my inflamed amygdala was wreaking havoc in the land of limbic, screaming danger, inciting panic, and dread. Some 35 years ago I was working at a mental health center when a regional community college called and asked if someone at the clinic would address a class on self-esteem. I accepted the assignment on a Monday to address the class that following Friday at noon. Around ten o'clock on that Friday morning, the day of the talk, I scribbled down a few scattered notes to work from. Self-esteem: It's derived from your family of origin. It has to do with liking yourself. It's based on approval and is maintained and cultivated by a sense of competency and task mastery. Self-esteem is important to have in order to navigate through life and maintain a realistic self-image. Along with a few other shallow notes, I was ready to portray the role of an expert.

That morning I was all pressed and smelling good, sporting what my father would refer to as a "major tie." A major tie is one that leaves a lasting impression. Feeling quite smug and virtuous I wandered into the classroom ten minutes early just to scope out the setting. I didn't realize that it was a class for "administrative assistants," which in those days were all women. Most were my age or slightly younger. The teacher greeted me, thanked me for coming, and informed me that the class had ten minutes left on their assignment, so I took a seat in the back. As I sat down, numerous heads turned to scope out who would be helping them enhance their self-esteem.

This was one of my first public presentations ever. As I perused my scarce and feeble notes, I realized that I had no more than minutes worth of material. All sorts of mental and physical alarms went off, and I began to privately freak out. What the hell was I going to talk about for the remaining 50 minutes? Will I lead them in a discussion? How in the hell do I do that? What if they ask a bunch of questions? What if I don't know the answers? Let me get this straight, I'm supposed to be teaching and modeling self-assurance, composure, and confidence. It soon became clear to me that this wasn't going to happen. I started to panic. My self-esteem cupboard was empty, and no self-soothing words helped me build wings to fly above the fray. As the students finished their assignments, more heads turned as I pretended to be thumbing through my notes, which didn't take much thumbing because it was a single sheet of paper. My heart started to race, sawdust swiftly filled my mouth, and my stomach became knotted like a five-year-old's shoelace. I felt a bead of sweat slowly roll down my back.

The limbic system which plays a central regulatory role by way of the hypothalamus was spewing limbic lava. My amygdala was goading the adrenals to release the toxic hormone cortisol, so it could circulate throughout my brain and body. Whether real or imagined, my system was on high alert, anticipating a humiliating public slaughter while wearing a major tie. This execution was to be staged in front of a gallery of administrative assistants, which admittedly, before my demise, I viewed as a potential dating pool.

My amygdala prompted an instantaneous survival response of flight, fight, freeze or faint. Since I had no ammunition to fight, and freezing was not an option, I had to flee, before I fainted. My mind and body were preparing for a Jihad on my DWD (department of worth and dignity). My brain was misfiring like a fireworks display gone sorely wrong. The implicit memories (subconscious recollections) of shame and humiliation boiled over the rim of my mind's limbic kettle, completely gumming up and disabling my prefrontal cortex's self-soothing capacities. When the amygdala overrides the comforting properties of the prefrontal cortex, we're unable to regulate the energy that's being stirred up. My hippocampus operated like a "search engine," scouring my memory's files, retrieving, and providing my amygdala with evidence of past fears, blunders, and miseries, creating a compelling case as to why I should truly be afraid. Anxiety disabled my brain's mental dexterity, amplifying an emotional tone of fear and impending doom. With my hippocampus now restricted, I couldn't ask myself, "Tom, what can I do that would help?" "How can we handle this constructively?" Implicit memories create a painful "subterranean" autobiographical story. These unsolicited implicit memories that were both real and imagined, both conscious and subconscious, felt and sounded like glass in a blender. These jagged shards of implicit memories provided me no clue of their origin as they sliced into my awareness. Like the mob kicking down my mind's door, it sprayed my brain with bullets of anxiety and doubt. When the images and sensations of my experiences remain in "implicit form only," they can't be assembled properly in my awareness by my hippocampus, which is considered a master puzzle piece assembler. When sensations of fear and shame aren't identified as being from the past, it's hard to put things in perspective.

Things remained in neural disarray. Sitting there freaking out, my prefrontal cortex no longer had the ability to perceive, pretend, plan, and correct. The only directive I heard was my amygdala telling me, "Get the hell out of here and fast."

As I mentioned, implicit memories "prime" our minds, preparing our brain to react in a previously encoded fashion, again, fight, flight, freeze, or faint. All four impede our flow.

Three distinct facets of implicit memory are:

- You don't have to intentionally direct your attention to something specific, for these memories to become activated. No construction or the uploading of implicit memory is necessary to feel the thump. It just happens.
- When implicit memories emerge from the brain's storage, you do not have the sensation that tells you, "Hey, this is something from the past."
- Implicit memories are not assisted by the hippocampus, the puzzle master. It does not assemble the sharp shards of experiences from memory into an explainable narrative.

Nothing alerted me by saying, "Tom, I know you don't realize this, but the fear you're having right now regarding this talk is well-founded. It's based on your lousy preparation, years of other people's mean and shaming doubt, as well a self-collecting catalog of previous bumbling experiences. This is nothing new, just a new setting."

I sat there panicking, but surprisingly I still possessed the wherewithal to not spring out of my chair and make a frantic break for the door. In a sort of James Bond fashion, I reached down and set off my beeper, (shows you how long ago.) The shrill sound of the gadget turned all heads, and I pretended that I was scanning a message. With a furrowed brow and a pensive look, I approached the teacher, still peering down at the "no" message. If there had been one, it would have implored me to, "Stay calm, don't blow it, and get out now while you still can." I told the instructor there was an emergency at the clinic, and I needed to return promptly. With a countenance of compassion, she placed her hands on her cheeks, "By all means, hurry up." She whisked me out the door hoping I could convince some tortured soul to come in off the ledge. Little did she know it was me on the ledge. Bless her heart. Clutching my one page of feeble notes, with a moist forehead and sweat racing down my back I lurched out the door, feeling like a spineless imposter.

The following week I worked diligently on the presentation and returned delivering an informative and enlightening talk on the importance of self-esteem. I flowed and even received a dinner date offer. I was prepared. By talking about my own doubts and fears with the class I didn't pretend to be something I wasn't. It was a tremendous relief.

A TOTAL FLOW STORY

In contrast to my classroom debacle, let us fast-forward 25 years to a lecture I gave to The Association of Family Physicians, titled "Finding a Balance." It was humorous, informative, and poignant. The message was how both real and imagined tragedies create absurd irrational fears that tear down our resilience and throw us off balance. By this time, I had taught college classes, presented numerous workshops and seminars, been on panels, consulted with hospitals, schools, corporations, and had presented in Germany, Italy, and Ethiopia. On this particular day, I was confident, clear, spontaneous, funny, and informative. I was flowing.

Following the talk, I soaked in warm applause. While walking to the car I glanced at my watch and saw that I had 45 minutes before I needed to be back at my office. I planned my movement: Go by the cleaners, stop by the house, let the dogs out, make a deposit, stop by the post office, get some stamps, grab something to eat, and arrive at my office a few minutes early.

The reason I'm pointing this out is to reveal that between the end of my talk and my walk to the car, I had completely moved on from a very successful presentation. I didn't hold the "good feeling" in my window of awareness long at all. It was more of a fleeting state of okay-ness, rather than becoming a stable neural trait. I didn't install it in my neural network. Now on the contrary, if I would have stuttered, drooled, lost my focus, chopped my pace, bored the masses, and stammered to a close, I'd still be beating myself up privately to this day. The goal is to notice and celebrate the successful experiences and befriend and comfort the parts of ourselves that have felt diminished. By using reassuring words we've longed to hear, we create flow. Kindness and self-compassion are the gatekeepers to our flow and need to become a permanent part of the story we tell ourselves.

CHAPTER 29

Memories and the Brain's Natural Negative Bias

> *"We can complain because roses have thorns or rejoice because thorns have roses."*
>
> ~ Alphonso Karr

The moment-to-moment flow of thoughts, feelings, emotions, and desires, both conscious and subconscious, sculpt and shape our nervous system. Our mindscape is graded, plowed daily by the experiences we encounter. The thoughts that ruminate, the feeling tones that resonate, can be like a peaceful predictable wind chime or screeching brakes and crashing metal. Memories and our conclusions from these experiences course through our minds. Like water-carrying archived experiences down the side of a dirt mound, a pathway is created depositing both implicit and explicit memories at the base of the mound. This is where the ADHDer brews and blends the flavor of their thoughts that guide and shape their feelings and behaviors.

Most of these memories are <u>explicit,</u> clearly resting on the surface of our awareness. For example, I can explicitly recall how I learned to throw a ball and who taught me.

However, the actions of throwing a ball, the way my mind and body react when doing so, remain below the surface of my awareness. I just do it. These unconscious memories beneath my awareness are called <u>implicit</u> memories. I implicitly pick up the ball and throw it, without having to reference the original lesson. The mindscapes of both our implicit and explicit memories shape who we are. For the ADHD individual, difficult learning, embarrassing experiences, and bumbled interactions suffered throughout the day pile up. And that sense of distress is cataloged unconsciously into implicit memory. We are largely unaware of both the explicit and implicit memories that drive our thoughts, feelings, and actions. They just happen, greatly influencing our perceptions and choices as we mosey along or careen throughout the day.

In the book, *Buddha's Brain*, Dr. Rick Hanson states that you can sort experiences into two piles: those that help you and those that hurt you. But here's the snag: Our brains have a negative bias, automatically scanning for, recalling, and reacting to negative experiences and memories, both real and imagined. Our minds are like Velcro for the negative experiences and Teflon for the positive. Following a successful presentation to a group of physicians, my sense of satisfaction and mastery didn't last five minutes. Whereas, if I had blown the presentation, my mind would have pickled and preserved the distress in both my explicit and implicit memory. It would then seep into my present-day subconscious dialogue implicitly tainting my awareness; that is until I learned to notice which thoughts are helpful and which are not.

When children are needy and vulnerable, they unconsciously internalize and install memories of life and parents at their worst, not their best. They file terror and shame much deeper and more efficiently than they do pleasure or pride. These painful experiences create a feeling tone, a theme that reverberates inside. Sadly, certain tunes can become expected. The ADHDer experiences these toxically tainted melodies in the form of fear, anxiety, doubt, and in many cases, trauma. The angst that comes from implicit memories is reproduced, consolidated then magnified, and returned to our implicit vault. Though we didn't voluntarily record these songs we can learn to pull the plug on this unauthorized jukebox. Untitled (implicit) sonnets of apprehension, ballads of foreboding, and jingles of anxiety are just waiting to be triggered in order to strike up the band. Unfortunately, the playlist is not the happiest batch of uplifting tunes. The negative melody is meant to keep us alert, on guard, wary of impending doom. The music incites the brain and body to lean toward its natural negative bias. We don't just receive the sheet music, but rather the whole production gets downloaded unbeknownst to us. Consequently, when the ADHDer does shine and excel, they minimize their own successes, thinking, "Maybe I tricked them or maybe my doing well was just a fluke."

Other people's assumptions and opinions about me were quite impactful and carried more weight than did my own. ADHD individuals can be very codependent, accepting other people's assessments of their self-worth as facts. The ADHDer might think, "You're fine, how am I?" That's a lot of power to give away. If others were always right, then that made me always wrong. Looking back with my adult eyes, I know now, I wasn't always wrong.

My intrinsic worth and projected value always seemed to be in the hands of someone else. Possibly some who should never have been trusted. I remember reading somewhere that "Parents are the last people who should raise kids." That always gave me a chuckle.

I believed that others had an astonishingly paranormal understanding of me. When I was young, I seemed to have lost access to my own instinctual data relying completely on someone else's assessments. There were times I felt data-less, like a blank spreadsheet, waiting for others to fill in the numbers. This type of suffering became embodied, which simply means I carried it in my body. And our body eventually presents its bills for the pain, sadness, anger, anxiety, and disappointments we lug around in both our conscious and subconscious awareness. Think of all the files archived in implicit and explicit memory that in no way aid our well-being. We can teach the ADHDer how to delete these files when they surface.

It's sad when what you're anticipating are discomfort and confrontation. It's sad when you feel you must constantly defend your worth. Living life in a defensive ninja-like posture is hard on the knees. We need to ask ourselves, "Why do I feel the need to constantly be on guard, ready to counter?" "Who are the people that have been so offensive I need to consciously be on watch?" Some ADHD kids are so hypervigilant they impulsively contemplate tactical maneuvers even if nothing is impending.

I still to this day, naively assume that if I don't hurt anybody, no one will hurt me. But following some pretty severe emotional concussions, my natural ADHD inclination is to always be a bit leery. Even as an adult I sometimes find myself ready to defend the competency, mastery, and dignity that I've earned and enjoyed from good life experiences. However, I've never been good at letting other people's mistreatment of me or someone else, roll off my back. For the ADHDer everything seems to penetrate deeply. The ADHDer can really affiliate with the underdog. I would ask myself, "What did I, or someone else do to deserve that?" Often times it wasn't clear, and I'd demand an explanation, discovering that some people were simply insensitive jerks.

To understand the compulsive need ADHDers have to defend themselves, it's important to understand how our nervous system has evolved. In the beginning, there was a trade-off between quickness and speed, and the ability to just adjust and adapt. Being flexible and vigilant meant survival. Our ancestors didn't contemplate the intentions of a saber-toothed tiger as it charged. They didn't think, "I wonder what it's feeling?" Or "Why is he limping?" You automatically chose speed (getting the hell out of there) over adaptability (how do I take into consideration the tiger's needs?) You run first and ask questions later. Automatic responses were necessary back then. But today when these automatic rigid, inflexible, and maladaptive reactions are acted out, they take a toll on relationships.

The good news is ADHDers can learn new ways to respond and adapt. The bad news is it may take them longer than others to learn. Maybe upwards of 10-15 seconds, which may seem like an eternity when the ADHDer is trying to suppress impulsivity. But more good news: By avoiding their first impulse, they provide time for the prefrontal cortex to come online, in a judicious and nurturing way. The prefrontal cortex helps the ADHDer make sense and enjoy the complexity of life's montage that exists both inside and outside of themselves. Consequently, the brain's natural negative bias tends to focus on the snippets of film that were distressing or traumatic, transferring them onto the present moment, even if the context is different.

I've learned to saturate frustrating experiences and internal assaults with positive notions and loving philosophies that echo evidence of my decency and good character. Sautéed with gratitude, I have found that life can be pretty damn good at times. When I fail to notice the good that already exists around me, I descend down the low road, washed away by torrential subcortical storms that momentarily sink my mental survival raft.

What sinks most people's rafts are what the Buddha's referred to as the *Three Poisons*, greed, anger, and disgust. Certainly not the ingredients found in a soothing porridge, but more in chemical warfare. In fact, these three poisons create a mental kettle full of gruel that nourishes inflexibility, rigidity, and revulsion. When I ingest the "Three Poisons", it's not only bitter and disgusting but also agitating. It creates apprehension and uncertainty, and my perspectives can become delusional. Next thing I know, I've adopted the belief that "I'm a victim of others' maltreatment and disdain." What a bunch of crap. I needed to learn that I was the one, who by believing it, allowed it to happen. The old saying in recovery circles goes, "We either get better or bitter." The three poisons are bitter.

Anger, disgust, and greed discolor our mindsight lenses and slam our body's nervous system. This negative bias affects our entire central nervous system, described later in this chapter, throwing other systems out of whack. First off, these three poisons activate the amygdala (implicitly), well before you're aware of it, setting off numerous domino responses throughout our brain and body. The thalamus, our brain's relay station, gets the amygdala's neurons all up in a wad, screaming at us, "Beware!" In turn, our brainstem releases action provoking norepinephrine. The sympathetic nervous system readies the rest of your body for the famous "fight, flight, freeze or faint response." You either fight the tiger (bad idea), run from the tiger (you'll never win), freeze (that just might freak it out), or faint (I can't predict what would happen then). The hypothalamus supervises the endocrine system, instructing the pituitary gland to alert the adrenal glands so they can discharge the "stress hormones" epinephrine (adrenaline) and cortisol. Elevated cortisol causes neurons to accept too much calcium through their membrane causing the cells to fire too frequently, killing them off.

These three poisons can be provoked by both low-level as well as hyper-aroused negative brain biases. The hippocampus and the prefrontal cortex are particularly vulnerable to cortisol. Cortisol kills neurons in the hippocampus and disrupts the creation of new ones. Short-term memory is weakened, and new memories are distorted. Cortisol thwarts the hippocampus's capacity to corral the irascible amygdala. With the hippocampus restrained, the amygdala tends to walk around like an agitated mob boss shooting at will. This in turn sends yet more potent surges of cortisol throughout our system. Cortisol also kills off the neurons in the prefrontal cortex, thwarting the ADHDer's ability to use their best judgment to plan for the future which happens to be here, right now. And since our brains are hardwired to converge on negative experiences (the bias) the prefrontal cortex (the seat of well-being) becomes disabled, as if our mind is being drained of all its steering fluid.

By overreacting a switch gets flipped on in the sympathetic nervous system, pushing us into the danger zone. Too much cortisol will decrease serotonin, the hormone that has been said to make us happy. This decrease in serotonin will magnify the bias prompting us to defend ourselves even more. Though our system evolved this way, most of our reactions are learned, then solidified through experiences. There is another saying in the field of recovery that's good to remember, "Pain is inevitable, but suffering is optional." The sooner the ADHDer accepts life's predictable pain, emanating from life's inevitable dilemmas, they can then learn to limit their suffering, and not be blown about by every wind.

You don't have to be explosive, ripping the tread off your heart, to find yourself living in a habitually defensive posture. In fact, you can be mildly but chronically peeved with your "on button" stuck on simmer, slowly melting away your heart's tread. This directly affects your thyroid functioning, weakening the immune system, reducing the number of natural killer cells which stave off illness and disease. It's exhausting, and your overall peace and well-being are affected when you're both consciously and subconsciously trying to keep small fires from spreading. Eventually our body truly presents us with a bill

Negative biases can stimulate primal reactions that are completely disproportionate to the threat. One of my more miserable adverse triggers is discussing money. Simply talking about money makes me move closer to the ledge. I know the origin of this torment—my mother. It is said that the hand that rocks the cradle will indeed rock the world. Amen. When I was young, I remember watching mom turn her head to the sky, place the back of her hand theatrically upon her forehead, as if she was about ready to faint. She'd announce to all, "We're going to the poor house." I'm sure that made dad feel really proud of the effort he was putting in 52 weeks out of the year. The "poor house," what could that possibly look like? I was scared to death. I remember raking a neighbor's yard, thinking I could help the family by bringing in a little extra money. I believed we were destined to live in our station wagon, under a bridge, eating cold beans from a can. I wonder if it ever occurred to my mom that maybe she could get a job and thwart our descent into poverty and rot. Though this never transpired, I've been ready my whole life for a devastating financial collapse. It never occurred to me that my father's job, editor of The Kansas City Star newspaper was a good-paying job, or that both of my grandfathers were physicians and there was probably some level of security somewhere. It never occurred to me there were people who would have helped us avoid homelessness, malnutrition and eventually a life of crime and debauchery. I mean really, I'm sure my relatives had a couple of canned goods they could have tossed our way.

Unconsciously listening only to my brain's negative biases, my frantic and frightened amygdala drips with implicit residue from mother's lamenting. Cortisol obliterates the magical restorative synaptic connections in the hippocampus, thus thwarting the formation of new healthier connections. Bad things happen when the amygdala is over-sensitized, and the hippocampus is restricted.

Now more about the central nervous system. When we freak out, we need to get back on the "high road," or at least flat land, as quickly as possible to minimize the damage our mind and body incurs when careening off into cortisol-filled culverts. Once back on the road we can steer our mind toward, then into the confines of our loving and soothing prefrontal cortex. The PFC's nurturing nature and sage-like wisdom enable us to regulate our body, balancing the two branches of the autonomic nervous system. First, the <u>sympathetic nervous system</u>, is like an accelerator on a car, moving us forward, toward flames that could singe our well-being. The second branch is the <u>parasympathetic nervous system</u>. It's like the brake which slows our system down when a flashing light might indicate, "Fire Ahead-Detour Now." The sympathetic and parasympathetic branches work together. But like a teeter-totter, both sides cannot be up at the same time. Our goal is to keep these two systems in balance.

The parasympathetic system and the prefrontal cortex are the firemen, that when during a freak-out are called upon to hose down the limbic infernos (the mind and body) which have been set ablaze by the brain's negative biases, fueled by implicit memories. The firemen douse these subcortical flames with the neurotransmitter gamma-aminobutyric acid. This cools down the limbic lava balancing the nervous system's two branches.

So, the brain is the starting point of the negative bias but is also the ending point. We can't completely keep a negative tune from entering our awareness, but once we recognize the tune, we can surely pull the plug on our mind's turntable. This is the beginning of self-regulation, composure, and balance. We don't eliminate the negative bias, but we greet it at the door, invite it in, dance with it a bit, then usher it out the back. We can say to it, "Here you are again Mr. Negativity, no need to set off all my bodily alarms, you're not going to be here that long, nor am I going to buy into your pessimism and distrust. I can handle this. What is it you want me to know or become aware of? Is it going to help me or hurt me?" When we're aware of the thoughts or memories that flavor our mindset and steer our attention, then we can begin to reduce and defend ourselves from the natural evolutionary biases. Response flexibility that the prefrontal cortex wants us to begin practicing helps us realize that we have many options. We can climb out of our entrenched neural pathways by intentionally raising our awareness and deliberately rewiring our inner workings. When we create space between our thoughts, feelings, and actions we can reflect rather than react. We then can choose our mental, physical, and emotional stance, rather than being swept away like a piece of tumbleweed in an old western flick. This is how we develop discernment, and this perspicacity widens the playing field.

With our newfound awareness, and a lifetime to practice refining it, we can become capable of shifting from a bad or forlorn place to a better more connected place. This self-to-self attunement helps us resonate with life and others. Empathy and compassion are some of the more nurturing qualities of the prefrontal cortex. It so badly wants to help us understand our natural negative bias so we can minimize the struggle and reunite our divided selves. Siding with oneself is both unfamiliar and liberating to the ADHDer. They learn to neutralize the negative bias when they access loving and intuitive awareness that the prefrontal cortex is waiting to share. Compassion and empathy from oneself to your other self, allows you to "feel felt." When we feel felt, we know we've been listened to and understood from our perspective.

I've always loved Douglas Adams, an English playwright, author, and humorist who wrote *The Hitchhiker's Guide to the Galaxy*. One of my favorite lines from the book is, "I may not have gone where I intended to go, but I think I've ended up where I needed to be." That is so applicable to me. By continually uprooting and challenging my negative biases, my mind continues to produce a beautiful garden.

CHAPTER 30

"Dad, ADHD Is Not a Disease"

> *"If we all did the things, we were capable of doing, we would astound ourselves."*
>
> ~ Thomas Edison

I remember sitting with a boy and his parents when the father blurted out, "Troy's disease is controlling the whole family." When his son heard the word disease, his head dropped. I could feel him starting to percolate. He jumped up, pointed his finger directly in his dad's face and said, "I don't have a disease. You do and it's called, 'You don't 'understand deficit.' Do you think I choose to struggle? Do you think I choose to be on your shit list day and night? Do you think I decide every day to feel like an idiot in class unable to keep pace with the other students? Do you think I want to be sitting here so you can pretend in front of Mr. Scott that you give a damn? Well, you don't. Why don't you tell him how you really treat mom and the rest of our family? You don't want to help us, but just hurt us with your never-ending complaining about, 'How hard I work, and no one appreciates it.' Well, I work pretty damn hard also, so does mom and so does sis. I've learned from you how not to raise my kids. And if one of them is struggling I will do everything I can to be patient and loving so they will never feel the way I have felt growing up with your disapproval and emotional grime." Troy then got up and stormed out. His mother started to follow, but I said let him go, he'll be back.

My office was on the first floor near the front door. I opened the shade so we could see if he went to the parking lot. He didn't so I suspected he was in the waiting room, hall, or bathroom. I asked his dad, "Did you know Troy had been coming to a therapist who also has 'the disease'?" He was obviously shocked by Troy's words and my question. "Do you have ADHD?" he asked. "Yes, I do, and with a capital H (hyperactive), " I replied.

I explained to him the pivotal role he could play in helping Troy navigate through this very difficult time, and how he could help Troy feel loved in a way that would foster optimism and a hopeful growth mindset. I told his father, "A child's self-esteem is based on whether or not they are the type of kid their parents approve of." I told his dad that he had this magic tonic inside his heart that could really help Troy if he chose to find it, develop it and learn to use it. I explained, Troy doesn't wake up every morning, pop out of bed and say, "Okay, today I'm going to look stupid, piss off my dad, bumble through my classes, encourage people to laugh at me, all the while deepening a total disregard for my worth and well-being." It just happens. Troy feels horrible about himself, and you make it much worse when he knows you're constantly disappointed. It's very hard being a disappointment. Troy will get better whether or not you are in his corner because his mother is committed to his growth and well-being. I can teach you how to be in his corner and earn back his trust despite his developmental frustrations and dependency needs. He's dependent on you two to get these needs met. He will get better when he feels safe."

The best treatment for ADHD is time, patience, and direct but gentle feedback. Most of us get better with time. "Aren't you better off now, than you were ten years ago?" I asked. I shared with the father that I can help him, and Troy learn to turn vision back on themselves, to see and hear how you both sound, so a positive shift can take place. You'll both learn how to regulate your mind, choosing, then changing, your responses at that very moment. Learning a language of comfort, modeled by you, dad, instead of Troy anticipating belittlement and defeat, will prepare him for the types of trials that lie ahead for all of us. That includes in the next five minutes." I told him that I too was bothered by his misguided belief about Troy's condition being a disease. I even have a hard time with the word "disorder." If we can refer to his struggles as frustrations, annoyances, disturbances, and aggravations, then he won't believe all his symptoms to be permanent. Frustrations can be alleviated, annoyances remedied, disturbances quelled, and aggravations calmed. But, for a kid, there's no sense of temporariness in the word "disease."

I explained that if you want to change a child's behavior and belief in themselves, then you have to start with the parents. But parents don't want to hear that. They want you to stick the kid in the microwave of life, set it for two minutes, then pop them out refined and refreshed, taking charge of their own learning and responsibilities.

His father did come around, and Troy did get better. He was beginning to do really well until he died in a car accident at the age of 16.

Acknowledgments

I'd like to thank Dr. Scott Morrison, my therapist from the age of 15 to 35 for believing in me in my best and worst moments and not pumping me full of medication. Scott, you were the one who inspired me to go into this field. I'd also like to acknowledge my best friend, Bob Eye, an ACLU attorney, and activist who's received many awards and national acknowledgment for always being on the right side of common sense and human dignity. Bob, the lessons I've learned from you during our well over 8,000 miles of running are more than special to me. I'd like to acknowledge my father who for many years was editor of the Kansas City Star. Dad, you modeled for me the importance of the content of one's character and the capacity to reinvent oneself at any stage of life. You so emphasized the importance of equality and compassion. Mom, you demonstrated the importance of art, creativity, and imagination. You also modeled for me the capacity to make it through many physical and emotional tragedies in life and still be able to laugh at life's absurdities.

My mentors, professors, and colleagues whose exhaustive work and illuminating insights have helped me continue to develop, expand, and cultivate new ways of understanding myself, the world, and the human condition.

My wonderful children, Queen Addie, Sgt. TJ and Jordan bug, you guys have always been the best part of my life. You have been patient with me as I've attempted to grow up. I'm very proud of each of you, but most of all I'm so proud of the huge hearts you so lovingly display.

I'd also like to express my love, respect, and my forever indebtedness to Phyllis Stevens. Your kindness and compassion toward me and the world have touched the very depth of every part of me. Your patience and belief in this project and the many hours we spent chopping it up can never be repaid, though Lord knows I try. You helped me feel valued, loved, and cared for. You taught me the importance of the "long game." What a true treasure you are to me and many, many others. I love you, Phyllis. You made me feel like a writer.

And I'm saving the best for last (sniffle), my true soul mate and companion, who has kept me and our family afloat for 32 years. When life's waters became quite turbulent, you, Betty Grace, have been there for me like no one else has ever been. Your love and consistency are nothing I had ever experienced. We raised children and animals, laughed, and cried. I have seen you battle immunological diseases, and I've never seen anyone work so hard to try to feel better. I've never known anyone so smart and so talented across a wide spectrum of endeavors. I've never ever heard you blame anyone for anything, and I've never seen you hold a grudge. You've shown me that it's just a waste of time and energy. And yes, 32 years later you're still the prettiest woman I've ever seen.

Also, I want to acknowledge Dr. Jan Roosa, Adam, Pat and Char, Jim and Joanne, Dan and Kathy Burdette, Cindy Schendel, Terry and Marcus, John and Dena, Kerry and Margaret, Raul and family, Jim and Ned, Briggs, Desi, and Trey, and Janet ... Rest in peace, Janet. Also, I'd like to thank Young Melton, a friend who has worked harder on herself in a week than most people invest in a lifetime. And last but surely not least, Dan, Katie, Ethan, Luke, Traci, and Bella. Thank you all.

CPSIA information can be obtained
at www.ICGtesting.com
Printed in the USA
LVHW011228170522
718963LV00015B/340